D0075761

WITHDRAWAL

LITERACY AND GENDER: RESEARCHING TEXTS, CONTEXTS AND READERS

'In the context of continuing debates about how to teach reading, and about boys' underachievement, Gemma Moss brings us right up close to what children are actually doing with books in classrooms. Her ethnographic research is meticulous and fine-grained, and she presents some striking findings about how the dynamics between literacy, gender and attainment are configured within particular schools and classrooms. This accessible, subtle book raises important questions for current policy makers and is recommended reading for anyone who cares about children, literacy and education.'

Janet Maybin, *The Open University*, UK

Why are girls outperforming boys in literacy skills in the Western education system today? To date, there have been few attempts to answer this question. *Literacy and Gender* sets out to redress this state of affairs by re-examining the social organisation of literacy in primary schools.

In studying schooling as a social process, this book focuses on the links between literacy, gender and attainment, the role school plays in producing social differences and the changing pattern of interest in this topic both within the feminist community and beyond. Gemma Moss argues that the reason for girls' relative success in literacy lies in the structure of schooling and, in particular, the role the reading curriculum plays in constructing a hierarchy of learners in class. Using fine-grained ethnographic analysis of reading in context, this book outlines methods for researching literacy as a social practice and understanding how different versions of what counts as literacy can be created in the same site.

Literacy and Gender makes a valuable contribution to current debates about literacy pedagogy and outlines a principled basis upon which to review the literacy curriculum in action.

Gemma Moss is Reader in Education at the Institute of Education, University of London.

LITERACIES

Series Editor: David Barton
Lancaster University

Literacy practices are changing rapidly in contemporary society in response to broad social, economic and technological changes: in education, the workplace, the media and in everyday life. This series reflects the burgeoning research and scholarship in the field of literacy studies and its increasingly interdisciplinary nature. The series aims to provide a home for books on reading and writing which consider literacy as a social practice and which situate it within broader institutional contexts. The books develop and draw together work in the field; they aim to be accessible, interdisciplinary and international in scope, and to cover a wide range of social and institutional contexts.

HIPHOP LITERACIES
Elaine Richardson

CITY LITERACIES
Learning to Read Across Generations and Cultures
Eve Gregory and Ann Williams

LITERACY AND DEVELOPMENT
Ethnographic Perspectives
Edited by Brian V. Street

SITUATED LITERACIES
Theorising Reading and Writing in Context
Edited by David Barton, Mary Hamilton and Roz Ivanic

MULTILITERACIES
Literacy Learning and the Design of Social Futures
Edited by Bill Cope and Mary Kalantzis

GLOBAL LITERACIES AND THE WORLD-WIDE WEB
Edited by Gail E. Hawisher and Cynthia L. Selfe

STUDENT WRITING
Access, Regulation, Desire
Theresa M. Lillis

SILICON LITERACIES
Communication, Innovation and Education in the Electronic Age
Edited by Ilana Snyder

AFRICAN AMERICAN LITERACIES
Elaine Richardson

LITERACY IN THE NEW MEDIA AGE
Gunther Kress

Editorial Board:

Elsa Auerbach *Boston University*
Mike Baynham *University of Leeds*
David Bloome *Vanderbilt University*
Norman Fairclough *Lancaster University*
James Gee *University of Wisconsin*
Nigel Hall *Manchester Metropolitan University*
Mary Hamilton *Lancaster University*
Peter Hannon *Sheffield University*
Shirley Brice Heath *Stanford University*

Roz Ivanic *Lancaster University*
Gunther Kress *University of London*
Jane Mace *Southbank University*
Janet Maybin *The Open University*
Greg Myers *Lancaster University*
Mastin Prinsloo *University of Cape Town*
Brian Street *University of London*
Michael Stubbs *University of Trier*
Denny Taylor *Hofstra University*
Daniel Wagner *University of Pennsylvania*

HARVARD UNIVERSITY
GRADUATE SCHOOL OF EDUCATION
MONROE C. GUTMAN LIBRARY

LITERACY AND GENDER

Researching texts, contexts and readers

Gemma Moss

Routledge
Taylor & Francis Group

LONDON AND NEW YORK

LC
149
.M62
2007

HARVARD UNIVERSITY
GRADUATE SCHOOL OF EDUCATION
MONROE C. GUTMAN LIBRARY

#11408630-1

First published 2007
by Routledge
2 Park Square, Milton Park, Abingdon, Oxon OX14 4RN

Simultaneously published in the USA and Canada
by Routledge
270 Madison Ave, New York, NY 10016

*Routledge is an imprint of the Taylor & Francis Group,
an informa business*

© 2007 Gemma Moss

Typeset in Baskerville by
GreenGate Publishing Services, Tonbridge, Kent
Printed and bound in Great Britain by
T J International Ltd, Padstow, Cornwall

All rights reserved. No part of this book may be reprinted or
reproduced or utilised in any form or by any electronic, mechanical,
or other means, now known or hereafter invented, including
photocopying and recording, or in any information storage or
retrieval system, without permission in writing from the publishers.

British Library Cataloguing in Publication Data
A catalogue record for this book is available from the British Library

Library of Congress Cataloging in Publication Data
Moss, Gemma, 1954-
  Literacy and gender: researching texts, contexts, and readers/
Gemma Moss.
  p. cm.
Includes bibliographical references.
1. Literacy–Social aspects. 2. Sex differences in education. 3.
Girls–Education (Elementary) 4. Educational attainment. I. Title.
LC149.M62 2007
371.822–dc22

                                    2007008401

ISBN-10: 0–415–23456–5 (hbk)
ISBN-10: 0–415–23457–3 (pbk)
ISBN-10: 0–203–46427–3 (ebk)

ISBN-13: 978–0–415–23456–6 (hbk)
ISBN-13: 978–0–415–23457–3 (pbk)
ISBN-13: 978–0–203–46427–4 (ebk)

April 15, 2008

TO TOM AND ELLEN, DEDICATED READERS BOTH

AND

IN MEMORY OF MY PARENTS, RACHEL AND BASIL MOSS
1920– AND 1918–2006

The last two people I knew to sit in companionable silence in the evening, each reading their way through their own book, occasionally breaking off to read a particularly interesting passage aloud to anyone who might listen before taking up where they had left off.

CONTENTS

ACKNOWLEDGEMENTS

The Economic and Social Research Council funded the series of research projects which underpin this book. The book itself has benefited enormously from on-going conversations about the data held over a number of years with many different individuals, including: Dena Attar, who worked as a researcher on the initial project; Myra Barrs, who gave the work one of its first outings in a public forum; Basil Bernstein, who took an interest in the original bid; Valerie Hey and Carey Jewitt, who have helpfully commented on the manuscript in various stages of its evolution; Laura Huxford and Elaine Millard, who encouraged me to write up some of the findings early on; and Brian Street, who first got me to think about literacy practices. David Barton has patiently waited for the book to turn up. Whilst particular thanks go to Eileen Carnell for helping me struggle through to the final draft.

Portions of Chapter 3 and Chapter 4 have been adapted from material which has previously appeared in: Moss, G. (2003a) 'Analysing literacy events: mapping gendered configurations of readers, texts and contexts' in S. Goodman *et al.* (eds) *The Open University Reader Language, Literacy and Education*, Stoke on Trent: Trentham Books; in Moss, G. (1999) 'Texts in context: mapping out the gender differentiation of the reading curriculum' in *Pedagogy, Culture and Society*, 7(3), 507–522; and in Moss, G. (2001b) 'To work or play? Junior age non-fiction as objects of design' in *Reading: Literacy and language*, 35(3), 106–110. Some of the data quoted in Chapter 6 appeared first in Moss, G. (2004) 'Changing practice: the National Literacy Strategy (NLS) and the politics of literacy policy' in *Literacy*, 38(3), 126–133.

I am indebted to the schools which hosted the research and gave so generously of their time, and to the pupils, parents and teachers who participated in the research in various ways.

This has been a very slow book to write. Thanks to all those who have suffered so patiently whilst it's been brewing, especially my family: Mike, Tom and Ellen Chisholm.

INTRODUCTION

Literacy, gender and research

This book is about literacy, gender and attainment, how they have been linked and defined as a social problem, and the changing pattern of interest in this topic both within the feminist community and beyond. It acts as a response to the increasing visibility of boys' underachievement in literacy within the education systems of countries such as the UK, USA, Canada and Australia, where this issue is increasingly treated as a particular kind of literacy problem that schools are expected to solve. Yet to date any explanations for boys' comparative weakness in reading and writing remain poorly theorised and often lack empirical evidence to support them. The book sets out to redress this state of affairs by re-examining the social organisation of literacy in the primary school. It argues that the ground rules for what counts as literacy in school are diverse. This provides the basis upon which literacy itself becomes gender-differentiated as boys and girls react to their designation in classrooms as more or less able readers. The social construction of gender and ability interact to produce the pattern of gender differences in performance outcomes. The book explores these themes through a focus on the reading curriculum.

The book uses a range of ethnographic research tools to identify the social processes that shape both boys' and girls' development as readers and the choices they make about their reading. In so doing, it reconsiders the respective roles that the social context, the reader and the text have in shaping reading as a social practice. By analysing how different groups of readers are formed and then take different paths through the reading curriculum in schools, the book outlines a set of qualitative research tools that can be used to investigate literacy more generally in a variety of different social contexts, taking account of the array of resources which help shape reading (and writing) under different conditions.

Setting a feminist agenda for new times

There has been considerable concern within the feminist community about the new prominence that has been given to the topic of boys'

1

underachievement within education, as well as some uncertainty about whether this is really warranted, or is simply a distraction from the broader issues (Epstein *et al.*, 1998). This book accepts that boys' under-achievement in reading and writing is of long standing and can be traced back some considerable way within the examination system and in standard-ised reading tests (Millard, 1997). Such a pattern predates the more recent concerns about boys' underperformance in education, a discourse which seems to have been triggered by the closing gap between girls' and boys' edu-cational achievements elsewhere on the curriculum (Arnot *et al.*, 1999).

One of the most prevalent explanations for boys' underperformance in reading and writing suggests that it results from a feminised literacy cur-riculum which one way or another fails to adequately incorporate their interests. This is to apply to boys analysis of the relative educational failure of other marginalised social groups (working class children; girls; ethnic minorities) which explains their underachievement in terms of a mismatch between that group's own cultural experience and the culture and values of the school. How to bridge the divide between school and home cultures, or the official culture of the curriculum and the informal cultures of the child, is a recurring theme in discussions of social equity. The solution is often imagined to lie in finding more space within the school curriculum for whatever has to date remained excluded.

By contrast, this book argues that the literacy curriculum itself pro-duces points of tension that all children have to grapple with. In particular, the high social value put on doing well at literacy creates the conditions in classrooms where children's relative progress in mastering reading and writing becomes all too apparent to children themselves, to teachers and to parents, through where children are asked to sit, who they are asked to work with, and what they are asked to read. The literacy curriculum creates social distinctions which children cannot easily avoid. This book explores how the tensions within the literacy curriculum impact on boys' and girls' development as readers within the primary school setting. It investigates what is at stake in becoming a reader within the reading curriculum and how teachers, parents and children manage the potential conflicts this social process creates. Neither boys nor girls are treated as a unitary category. Rather, this book focuses on the differ-ences within as well as between each group.

Feminism, education and attainment

There are intriguing parallels and absences in the ways in which gender has surfaced in relation to the theme of education and attainment, first in respect of girls and more recently in respect of boys. Historically, feminists have analysed the relationship between gender and literacy in different ways, drawing on different kinds of research traditions to do so. In the seventies and eighties, feminist debate centred largely on the role the content of the literacy curriculum played in the formation of gendered identities, locking girls into patterns of social disadvantage (Barrs and Pidgeon, 1993). The link between literacy and educational achievement was rarely broached. Girls' relative success and boys' relative failure in reading and writing went unremarked. Instead, feminists homed in on those areas of the school curriculum where girls' performance lagged behind boys'. When feminists expressed an interest in literacy attainment, they focused on those contexts where girls and women did less well, often in particular communities which were already seen as economically excluded and where women's role could therefore be represented as doubly marginalised in their relationship to the broader society, through ethnicity, class or their position in the fragile economies of the developing world (Cameron, 1985; Mace, 1998; Rockhill, 1993; Horsman, 1991). As boys' literacy attainment has surfaced as a topic of concern, many commentators have reached back to feminist work on girls' underachievement in education as a resource for making sense of the data on boys. Part of what this book considers is whether such borrowings are either appropriate or helpful.

Policy, attainment and education reform

Recent shifts in government education policy both in the UK and elsewhere have set a new kind of agenda for reviewing educational attainment. Governments increasingly expect higher outcomes for more students passing through the education system, and consequently have established more visible means of adjudicating on those outcomes, as well as entering into new kinds of relationship with the professionals charged with delivering on these goals. This kind of educational reform is driven by a social logic in which flexibility and mobility are seen as key attributes in developing the necessary skills base for higher economic growth. Literacy has become a crucial signifier of the new kind of flexibility which is sought. In this guise it is treated as a relatively finite set of skills which can yet be infinitely deployed in many different contexts. To achieve these new educational priorities, the reformed English curriculum emphasises not so much the need to produce the right kind of personal sensibilities but rather to teach the necessary means to develop accuracy and fluency in constructing an infinite number of texts in a multitude of settings. Boys' underachievement in the literacy curriculum, made visible in this current context, takes on a new meaning under these conditions. Inevitably, the gender politics of the literacy curriculum shift too. Any proffered explanation for the patterns observed will be heard in a political context which seems increasingly unsettled, and where old alliances are breaking down. The kind of feminist politics which might best match these times are neither immediately clear nor straightforward. This book steers its way through these debates with the following points in mind:

- How to account for (some) boys' failures in terms which don't act to the detriment of girls.
- How to remedy (some) boys' failures in terms which don't act to the detriment of girls.
- How to interpret the role of school and community in both producing, reinforcing and altering what it means to read and to be a reader.
- How to identify ways of researching and thinking about the literacy curriculum in an educational climate which itself is rapidly altering.

The kind of curriculum reform programmes now in favour measure the quality of education through the outputs generated by children's performance in tests or examinations. They look for homogeneity in results and seek to achieve this by standardising teacher input. In this kind of context it is easy to reduce thinking about teaching and learning to the specification of what teachers should tell children to do. Arguments about reading pedagogy narrow into arguments about teacher input rather than fuller consideration of what and how children learn.

Yet children learn more than teachers tell them. Schooling involves them in making choices too. In part, this book considers the choices children make in classrooms as they participate in the literacy curriculum. What kinds of choices do they make about what and how to read? How are those choices shaped by the social regulation of literacy in school? And what consequences do the choices they make have for the progress they make as readers? These questions will be pursued over the length of the book.

An overview of the book's structure

This book enters into the debates over literacy, gender and education reform by examining: the changing nature of school literacy and the demands it makes upon pupils; how literacy and gender interact within school settings; and what this means for tackling patterns of underachievement in literacy.

Chapter 1 begins by reviewing how feminist concerns about girls' educational attainment have changed and developed over time and how feminist thinking has adapted in the light of new questions about boys' literacy attainment generated by the new round of educational reform. It considers the relevance of the earlier work on girls' underachievement for understanding the patterns of boys' performance in literacy and concludes that the conditions which create gendered outcomes from the literacy curriculum stem from the social organisation of literacy in school and the tension points it creates for literacy learners.

Chapter 2 considers the range of research tools which have developed within *literacy as social practice* perspectives and their usefulness in exploring how the same range of literacy practices adopted within the same community can produce gender-differentiated outcomes.

Literacy as social practice perspectives have developed within a broadly ethnographic research frame and document how literacy evolves as a socially and culturally specific practice in different social settings. Whilst sensitive to variation between communities, this tradition has put much less emphasis on looking at differences within communities. Gender is rarely centre stage. One of the aims of this book is to redress this absence and encourage a more active dialogue between literacy as social practice and feminist perspectives.

Chapter 3 turns to empirical data collected in a series of studies of reading in the primary school and examines how the range of literacy events which make up the school curriculum offer competing logics for what it means to read and to be a reader. It identifies a series of tensions and dilemmas that the literacy curriculum poses children, in particular through the stratification of the reading curriculum which happens round the use of fiction texts. Chapter 4 considers the place of non-fiction on the school curriculum, and the characteristic design of the kind of picture-led non-fiction texts which proved most popular amongst a sub-sample of boys during quiet reading time. Chapter 5 looks at the choices children make about their own reading and how this links both to the design characteristics of different texts and the contexts in which they will be read. Chapter 6 ends with consideration of the implications of the research findings presented here for teachers and their classrooms and how they fit with current policy contexts which put a high premium on fixing results.

The empirical data

The book draws on a succession of research projects funded by the Economic and Social Research Council and based variously at Southampton University and the Institute of Education, University of London. These took place between 1996 and 2003, and involved a number of schools. Some schools participated in more than one phase of the research.

An ethnographic study
of boys' development as readers

The initial research, called 'The Fact and Fiction Project', focused quite explicitly on boys' development as readers and ran between 1996 and 1998.[1] Originally conceived as a means of exploring the potential link between genre preferences and literacy attainment, this was an ethnographic study which considered children's reading both inside and outside school (for previously published accounts of this research see: Moss and Attar, 1999; Moss, 1999; Moss, 2000a; Moss, 2001a; Moss, 2003a). The study placed a particular emphasis on the social construction of literacy as a gender-differentiated practice. If genre preferences were gendered, then it looked for evidence of where and how such preferences might arise.

Data I collected on previous projects looking at children's informal literacy practices,[2] had suggested that girls and boys adopted a different kind of stance towards reading. This observation was made through documenting informal literacy events in which children talked about the range of texts they circulated amongst themselves, outside the context of formal schooling. There seemed to be a distinction between the ways in which girls talked about their favourite texts such as the television soap, *Neighbours*, or the *Sweet Valley High* books, and how boys talked about their favourite texts such as computer magazines, or WWF wrestling (Moss, 1993b; Moss, 1996; Moss, 2000b). Girls seemed to be staking out their 'familiarity' with particular texts, whilst boys established their 'expertise'. In effect, their claims to know the texts were often articulated quite differently. Some, though not all, of the boys' claims to know revolved around non-fiction texts. These texts often related to activities which the boys pursued elsewhere. Football would be an obvious example here. The few girl readers who talked about non-fiction texts placed this kind of reading material firmly in the context of educational pursuits and doing well at school.

The premium boys put on knowing the most and being able to display that knowledge began to suggest a reason for their interest in non-fiction. I had read an article on gender and the IT classroom which argued that boys handicapped themselves by taking up the role of experts and hosts in relation to the technology, regardless of their actual level of competence; whilst girls actually benefited by behaving as guests in the IT classroom, thereby getting more support and task-orientated attention from the teacher (Elkjaer, 1992. See Chapter 1). This somehow came together with a memory from my teaching days of a class of fourteen-year-olds being asked to indicate their preferred choices for study at GCSE. A forest of hands shot up from the boys when the class were asked who wanted to do physics, though many were already in sets for maths and science which put this well beyond their grasp. Perhaps boys' preference for non-fiction led them towards texts which were actually more difficult to read on account of the more specialised forms of textual organisation and indeed complex sentence structure which they encompassed (Kress, 1994). In this sense, boys' preference for non-fiction might in some way be linked to their underachievement in reading if they put themselves in the position of dealing with the most difficult material without the means to ask for help. (Despite the plausibility of this line of argument, the research found no supporting evidence for the implied sequence from a preference for non-fiction to difficulties with reading. Quite the reverse, as the chapters which follow demonstrate.)

As the interest in boys' comparative underachievement in literacy came to the fore as a policy issue, it seemed both timely and useful to explore what the potential links might be between genre preferences and underachievement at reading in school (QCA, 1998). But the research was also designed to establish more broadly where and how boys' engagement with the reading curriculum began to diverge from girls'. If boys did indeed have a preference for non-fiction then how and why did this preference emerge? There seemed to be no clear answers to these questions within the existing research literature.

The kinds of issues outlined above led to the decision to focus data collection on the 7–9 age group, precisely because this is when children really begin to take off into independent reading which they can steer for themselves. Studying children's reading within this age group would provide an ideal opportunity to explore what was happening round non-fiction texts, both within the school reading curriculum and more generally, and indeed how both adults and children discriminated between fiction and non-fiction texts. The 7–9 age group seemed particularly apt because it is at Key Stage 2 that the gap between boys' and girls' achievements at reading significantly widens – a trend which continues further up the school system.

Designing the research

The aims of the initial study were to look at the reading curriculum within school and also to examine how reading was undertaken in the less formal settings of the home and peer interaction. This was done by tracking how fiction and non-fiction texts were used in both these settings. The project aims were broadly:

- to identify the range of practices in use with fiction and non-fiction texts by the 7–9 age group in school and home;
- to examine how such practices are gender-differentiated for children, and how they gender-differentiate them for themselves.

The research tools were shaped by traditions which see literacy as primarily a social practice, forged in relationship to others, and intimately shaped by the many different social contexts in which it takes place. Literacy in this respect varies in relation to who is doing what, where, with whom and for what purpose. Accordingly, the emphasis in the research design fell on documenting the range of social encounters in which texts find a place. The assumption was that such encounters would be varied and lead to literacy being done differently. Gender differentiation was sought at this level.

The research design was by case-study. The case-studies were based in four different schools, two in London, two in smaller conurbations in the south of England. Each pair of schools was chosen to provide broad contrasts in social catchment area so that the project could take into account potentially different levels of resourcing for reading in both home and community (Moss, 2001a). Farthing and Bluebird Schools served largely middle-class communities, whilst Kingfisher and Shepherd Schools were positioned in areas of much greater social disadvantage. Data were collected in Year 3 and Year 5 classes in the first two project schools (Bluebird and Kingfisher), and in Year 4 classes in the second two project schools (Shepherd and Farthing).

Classroom observation of the texts in use and the range of literacy events in which they were embedded formed the central part of data collection. The research identified and documented a sequence of key literacy events which represented typical encounters involving both fiction and non-fiction texts in the context of each of these schools. Alongside this, a sequence of interviews with both teachers and pupils were conducted to elicit participants' views of reading in school and reading in the home. To gain a further perspective on literacy within the home, up to six children in each school were invited to take cameras home and record literacy resources and events within a given time frame (see Moss, 2001a for a detailed account of this activity). The photographs were subsequently used in interview with both parents and children. Parents in each year group were also asked to complete a detailed questionnaire about reading in the home. Finally, on the basis of observation, a selection of salient texts, encompassing fiction and non-fiction genres, were used in interview with selected groups of children, their teachers and parents (see Chapters 3–6 for fuller details of the research tools employed). An ethnographic perspective was adopted throughout in so far as the research team set out to understand what they were observing from the position of the participants, and to capture the logic of events from their viewpoint. The book as a whole reflects upon the data collected in this way in the light of broader arguments within the feminist community about children's genre preferences, about unequal outcomes from the literacy curriculum and about how these are both formed and sustained.

A mixed methods study of children's library borrowing

A follow-up to the initial study, called 'Mixed Methods in the Study of Pattern and Variation in Children's Reading Habits',[3] analysed the school library-borrowing records of a cohort of roughly ninety Year 6 children in Bluebird School collected over the course of a year. Two-thirds of this cohort were boys. One of the three classes had participated in the original study. The mix of methods included generating coding categories for the texts borrowed from the library using design characteristics that had been identified as salient to their readers from the earlier ethnographic research. Of the actual 739 texts that these children had borrowed over the year, 672 were retrieved from the school library and coded in this way. The resulting data were analysed alongside answers to a questionnaire administered to the group when they were in Year 6 and which focused on their friendship networks (who they socialised with); their reading networks (who they lent books to or borrowed from); and their reading habits. The study also had access to the standardised reading test scores for this cohort stretching back over the previous three years; their SATs results at Key Stages 1 and 2; information on free school meals take-up; and which children had been designated as having Special Educational Needs and at what level over that time period. This study took place between 2000 and 2001 after the children concerned had left the school. After the analysis was complete, follow-up interviews were conducted with the teachers who had taught this cohort and with the school librarian. (For previously published accounts of this work, see Moss and McDonald, 2004. Further information on this project can be found on the ESRC website: http://www.esrcsocietytoday.ac.uk)

An ethnographic study of the impact of educational reform on literacy practices in the primary school

Finally, following the introduction of the National Literacy Strategy to English primary schools, an ethnographic study using some of the same methods of observation and interview used in the Fact and Fiction Project was conducted. Called 'Building a New Literacy Practice through the Adoption of the National Literacy Strategy'[4] and funded by the ESRC between 2001 and 2003, this project was based at the Institute of Education, University of London. The research took place in one of the same schools which had participated in the original study and in one other school in a different authority (Merchant School). This study tested the robustness of the research tools devised in the Fact and Fiction Project for tracking change in the shape and structure of the literacy events which made up the literacy curriculum. It also pursued new questions about the impact of a top-down system of educational reform on literacy practices, including the salience of the policy documents which introduced the reform package and the events in which they were enacted. (For previously published accounts of this work, see Moss, 2002b and Moss, 2004.)

The focus of the research

This book draws selectively on the wealth of data collected in these three studies. It does not set out to give a comprehensive account of everything that was done. In particular, it is comparatively silent on literacy outside school and the kind of informal literacy practices which children develop for themselves in relation to a range of different media. This is quite deliberate. The Fact and Fiction Project certainly collected data in these areas. But for the age cohort concerned it found no evidence in parental interview or in questionnaires for a pre-existing preference for non-fiction texts amongst young boy readers. Non-fiction might well be where some of this age group were heading, with some parents nominating non-fiction texts as the kinds of things they would now be interested in giving to their sons, but it was not where this group had been. This underlined other findings from the research which led to the conclusion that the decisive influence on young children's development as readers lay with their encounter with schooled literacy and what it comes to stand for within their peer networks and communities. This really is the central preoccupation and theme of this book.

Standing behind that and operating at a more abstract level is the view of the literacy event as always encompassing three elements: texts, contexts and readers. The research recorded here has in different ways sought to bring these three into a dynamic relationship. It holds that none will inevitably hold more sway than the others. A lot depends on the individual literacy event and the way in which it plays out. Any one of these elements can be foregrounded or backgrounded depending on the circumstances. Gender identities have to find their own space within literacy events in school as children take up their position as readers. They may be more or less strongly articulated, but in this context are also always intercut by the child's perceived proficiency at reading. This holds the dominant position in classroom settings which are geared to monitoring and tracking children's progress in developing competence in reading using many different measures. Whilst the emphasis on developing competence can be demonstrated in many different ways, it is never far from mind.

Boys as readers: a moment in time

To take this discussion forward, this book focuses on the patterns of children's reading as they evolve in relation to the primary school English curriculum and the range of resources which find a place within that setting. This introduction closes with an example of the kind of data that will underpin this book: a brief snatch of conversation in a Year 3 classroom, taped as three boys sitting at the same table during quiet reading time individually and collectively tackled the range of texts they had chosen with that setting in mind. Josh was reading *Tattercoats* (Greaves, 1990), a picture book which he read aloud to himself as he worked his way through the pages. Miles was browsing through *Eyewitness Guides: Desert* (Macquitty, 1994), a large-format non-fiction text with plentiful colour illustrations. Alan was reading Dr Seuss's *I can read with my eyes shut!* (1979). The interweaving of texts and talk represented here was very typical of these kinds of literacy events, just as the kinds of texts this group of boys had chosen demonstrate some of the different reading experiences on offer to pupils in classrooms.

MILES: Look at that, it's very sick, isn't it? {Pausing over picture, probably of a mummified corpse. See below}

JOSH:	Miles, what does that say?
MILES:	*Tattercoats* {reading text}
JOSH:	*Tattercoats* does that say?
MILES:	Right
JOSH:	*To be caref*
MILES:	careful
JOSH:	it ought to have two es in
MILES:	cheerful
JOSH:	*cheerful* {he carries on reading aloud to himself}
MILES:	Hey, Desert, Deserts
INTERVIEWER:	What was it you were just drawing my attention to, Miles?
MILES:	That/ It's a lady or man, died in a desert in about cos you can see there's all sand {pointing to a picture of a mummified corpse, p. 12}
INTERVIEWER:	Yeah, all dried up, yeah
MILES:	(She) dried, Blip! Aghh {makes choking sound} Look poisonous, poisonous, Aghh {acts choking and dying – probably in response to a picture of a cobra on p. 15}
JOSH:	Look (...) Miles, Miles, Miles, shall I tell you something, tell you what, I'm looking, they look like {possibly looking at a picture of tadpole shrimps on p. 14}
MILES:	What?
JOSH:	like egg burgers,
MILES:	Egg burgers?
JOSH:	Yes, yes you could make a sausage chip (mountain) {laughter}
ALAN:	Look, look, read this, *you can read about (anchors?) and all about cows, you can read about (anchors) and crocodiles* (...)
MILES:	Oh, what I've read that one before
ALAN:	yeah it's brilliant
JOSH:	{reading to self} *She had a wide b* {hesitates} *a boy*
MILES:	Read that, look I'll show you a really good one, over there look you can see it's dead {pointing to picture}
ALAN:	Yeah, you know what that is?
JOSH:	I need a new book now
ALAN:	That is odd isn't it
MILES:	Oh wow look, dur, dur, dur dur, camel dead {Turning over the pages}
MILES:	Ah there's (....), tur, chck, chk, ckh, please, you've got to lend it to me, look
ALAN:	OK, well, *How to make doughnuts or kangaroo collars, learn to read music and play hutzuts.* (sic) What's hutzuts?
MILES:	*If you play with your eyes open but not with them shut*

ALAN:	*you're likely to, if you read with your eyes shut, you're likely to find that the place where you're going far far away.* Tokyo {sings oriental soundtrack} Ma Hah, shu {making kung fu noises}
ALAN AND: MILES	*So that's why I tell you to keep your eyes wide, keep them wide open at least on one side* {reading aloud together}
ALAN:	What a book, what a book
MILES:	Let me read that now. *I can read with my eyes closed.*

(Bluebird, Year 3)

This fragment of classroom discourse brings with it a glimpse of boys as readers and the different kinds of relationships they stake out using the texts available to them in school. In the chapters that lie ahead this book will explore the contradictory impulses that help structure their engagement with the range of texts they encounter in school settings. It will examine how both girls and boys make use of the opportunities that schools provide for pupils to read, under what conditions.

1

LITERACY, GENDER AND THE POLITICS OF SCHOOL ACHIEVEMENT
Explaining educational failure and success

Introduction

This chapter explores the conditions under which boys' comparative failure in literacy has become visible over the last decade, and considers feminist reactions to this turn of events in the broader context of the feminist struggle for gender equality in education. It asks how far a gender politics predicated on girls' relative failure within the education system can be used to understand boys' underachievement in literacy and whether the time has come to reflect more broadly on the role the social organisation of literacy in school plays in creating distinctions between readers and writers. At a time when homogeneity in measurable outcomes from the education system is increasingly seen as a desirable political goal, what is at stake for both girls and boys as they navigate their way through the literacy curriculum?

It has become increasingly hard to remember a time when the phrase 'literacy and gender' did not evoke a discourse about boys' failings within the education system in general, and within the core subject of English in particular. Yet until recently, boys' comparative underachievement in literacy went largely unremarked. Not so long ago the topic of gender and literacy would instead have elicited questions about inequalities in girls' access to schooling, or literacy's ideological role in sustaining women's subordinate position as part of the unequal distribution of power within the wider society (Cameron, 1985; Horsman, 1991; Rockhill, 1993). Such a feminist agenda has increasingly been replaced by more technocratic questions about uneven educational performance demonstrated in the measurable outcomes of the system: exam passes and test scores. These demonstrate that boys are doing less well at literacy than girls, with many more clustered in the lowest quartile. This appears to be a consistent finding in comparable contexts internationally (OECD, 2004). The all too apparent inequalities of boys' attainment within English seem to demand a technical quick fix which will iron out the discrepancy. Inevitably, from such a starting point, the politics of gender and literacy have been transformed.

Whilst the change in the discourse has been only too striking, deciding what an appropriate feminist response might be has proved more difficult. After all, many of the conditions which seemed to have produced girls' educational underachievement persist, whilst factors that were assumed to work in boys' favour still hold too (Epstein *et al.*, 1998). How can these points be squared with tales of male underachievement in the literacy classroom? Myra Barrs explores this paradox the other way round:

> Among the paradoxes that characterise this area, then, is the fact that despite some of the apparent obstacles that they face in primary classrooms – the propensity of boys to seek more of the teacher's attention, and be given it; the continuing tendency of children's books to deal in stereotypes, and to show boys as more active and lively agents of their own destiny; the fact that boys have access to more powerful role models, and that men teachers tend to carry more weight and occupy more responsibility posts within school than women teachers do – girls continue to achieve more highly than boys in reading.
>
> (Barrs, 1993)

Is the anomaly that of girls' success in a system weighted against them, or of boys' failure in a system which should work in their favour?

Accounting for educational inequality from a feminist perspective

Feminists have long regarded education both as a mechanism for reproducing gender inequalities and as a possible institutional site for challenge and redress. This has meant arguing for a better place for women within the education system and using the system itself to foster further change. Quite how the argument has been pursued has altered over time, as has the particular target for reform. In the closing years of the nineteenth century women fought to gain access to education on a par with male students. This included access to the same kind of educational institutions; the same curricular content; and to educational futures which were not simply tied to the domestic roles of wife, servant or mother (Attar, 1990; Miller, 1996). Yet despite some early gains, institutionalised inequalities have continued to resonate through successive phases of educational reform in many countries.

In post-war Britain, the educational settlement which established grammar and secondary modern schools as a way of opening up education to more of the population for longer, also carried within it a significant act of discrimination against women. The 11+ examinations used to determine entrance to grammar schools routinely adjusted boys' scores in reading and writing upwards whilst marking girls' scores down, so as to balance out the numbers going forward (Millard, 1997). Justification for this act of positive discrimination rested on the notion of differing rates of biological maturity. Boys were seen as late developers, particularly in the areas of language skills. From this point of view, to treat boys and girls equally at the age of eleven would penalise the former unfairly. At the time it was perfectly possible to view the end results of the grammar school system, and boys' success within it, as a vindication of this 'late development' hypothesis. (Indeed, some of the standardised reading tests still in use today continue to 'adjust' scores according to gender on the same grounds.) The gender politics which underpinned this hypothesis attracted very little comment. When the 11+ exam and the two tier education system it sustained were abandoned in the UK in favour of a predominantly comprehensive model of secondary education, the changeover was certainly represented as an equality issue. Yet the predominant terms of reference were the greater equality the new educational contract would give to children from different social backgrounds. Equality in this context was presaged on social class, not gender.

Access and equality in a comprehensive system

In Britain, the re-emergence of feminism as a significant political movement in the 1960s coincided with the introduction of comprehensive education. This soon led to renewed interest in the extent to which schooling either helped or hindered greater social equality. Concerned by girls' continuing under-representation in key curriculum subject domains and their lower attainment in the education system as a whole, feminists began to explore how the apparent equality of access which comprehensive schooling promised masked continuing discrimination. Feminists began to identify both those institutional constraints which seemed to mitigate against girls' full participation within the school curriculum and examine how dominant conceptions of femininity might hinder girls' educational progress. To this end, some named and then studied the hidden curriculum: those aspects of school life which lay outside the subject content of schooling but which seemed to have a role in determining gender-differentiated outcomes. This included the ways boys dominated classroom interactions and playground space; and the ways school procedures themselves (lining up, the register, uniform) often reinforced gender differences, giving girls a less powerful place from which to speak (Clarricoates, 1987; Stanworth, 1981). Others identified bias in the existing curriculum content, the vantage point it encapsulated and its modes of delivery (Spender, 1982; Whyte, 1986). Such work became a means of explaining girls' lower levels of achievement in the areas of Maths and Science as well as the mechanisms through which boys and girls came to predominate in different subject areas, without recourse to concepts of 'natural aptitude' driven by biological determinism (Kelly, 1987).

Such social explanations fostered the possibility of social redress. Ways of overturning the status quo were explored through different kinds of curriculum intervention. Some of these concentrated on urging girls to step beyond the traditional gender boundaries expressed in current subject choices and enter areas of the curriculum traditionally viewed as masculine. Others attempted to make 'masculine' areas of the curriculum more girl-friendly by adapting the content to suit girls' presumed interests and expertise. Still others challenged the lower validation given to those aspects of the curriculum traditionally seen as 'feminine' (see for instance, my own earlier work on the romance genre, Moss, 1989a). The potentially conflicting logics of these approaches often led to heated debate within the feminist community. For instance, was it more appropriate to support Home Economics teachers in claiming higher status for what they did, or demand the abolition of Home Economics as a subject which reinforced gender stereotypes and acted as a poor substitute for science, needlessly diverting girls from other areas of the curriculum (Attar, 1990)?

The more debate on these issues continued, the harder it seemed to be to find neutral ground from which questions of value might finally be settled. How could feminists dissolve the distinction between masculine and feminine subject domains without adopting the values associated with one side rather than the other? Davies, drawing on Kristeva, refers to this question in terms of breaking out of the dualistic thinking associated with patriarchy, towards 'multiple genders and multiple subjectivities' (Davies, 1993). In her own work, she begins to outline how this might be done at least in part by underlining the extent to which questions of values are contingent: it may be strategically appropriate to blur the distinction between masculinity and femininity at one moment, identifying similarities of interest; and draw attention to sharply defined underlying differences at another. Fluidity becomes the name of the political game.

Gender identities as a focus for feminist action

This kind of post-structural analysis had most immediate influence in the study of gender identity. Girls' enculturation into femininity was increasingly represented as an inherently unstable project, full of contradictions and uncertainties, and incorporating few safe spaces immune to potential challenge (Hey, 1997; Davis, 1994). Acknowledging that teachers and pupils, girls as well as boys, made use of the range of resources they had at their disposal, both to assume positions of power and oppose and resist others who would position them as less powerful, set the scene for a new kind of exploration of the relations between gender, identity and education (Walkerdine, 1981; Williamson, 1981/2). Gender identities emerge from this kind of analysis as actively constructed, rather than as givens (Butler, 1990). They also multiply. There is more than one way of doing femininity or masculinity. Children in classrooms 'try out' different gender identities. They may adopt identities which are easier or more difficult to incorporate into the value system of the school, converging with or resisting the identities they are offered through the education system itself, often by drawing on a wider range of resources, including those associated with peer cultures and popular media (Cherland, 1994; Gilbert and Taylor, 1991). Social class and ethnicity here intersect with gender. Different forms of masculinity or femininity win different kinds of recognition, approval or challenge from teachers in different subject areas (Gilbert, 1993; Lee, 1996). They also do different kinds of work in binding children into existing patriarchal values, remaking or even subverting them. In this kind of context a good deal of feminist attention began to focus on how and when best to intervene in the formation of gendered identities, and how to judge the aptness of any such interventions (Gilbert and Taylor, 1991). The English curriculum seemed the main arena in which these issues could be tackled.

Valerie Walkerdine and her colleagues' study of girls' underachievement in Maths took the debate in another direction by linking the fluidity of gender identity specifically to questions of educational underachievement (see Walden and Walkerdine, 1985). The 'Girls and Mathematics' projects set out to examine why, although girls often outperformed boys in certain aspects of the Maths curriculum, they were much less frequently entered for the higher status examination and then did less well within it. In seeking to understand how this could happen in an educational system explicitly committed to meritocratic principles, Walden and Walkerdine argued that the dynamic of the classroom depended upon the creation of two contrasting subject positions for 'weak' and 'able' girl students (ibid.). Girls variously took up one or other position in the social interactions which represented the handover of mathematical knowledge. These subject identities in turn established the girls' overall place within the classroom economy as a whole, and so steered differentiated access to the curriculum content. The cumulative effect was to reinforce differentiated outcomes. For Walden and Walkerdine, questions about achievement within the curriculum are therefore less about who gains access to a given curriculum content than about how claims to knowledge are continuously defined and then (unequally) exercised in classroom settings:

> The characteristics displayed by girls and boys in classrooms lead teachers to read their performance in different ways and therefore to do different things about it ... It is not simply a matter of teacher bias against femininity. Rather it is a complex relation

between theory and practice of learning and teaching, leading to gender-differentiated production of success and failure.

(Walden and Walkerdine, 1985, p. 12)

This kind of work changed the terms of the argument in so far as it showed that who does well and who does badly within the system as it stands cannot be deduced straightforwardly by assuming a preordained relationship between a given curriculum content, and fixed gender identities, or indeed gendered aptitudes. Rather, Walden and Walkerdine argued, 'successful' or 'poor' curriculum attainment is tied to the way teacher judgements are made in practice about who is knowledgeable on what kind of terms and what then flows from this (ibid. p. 15). This kind of feminist analysis highlighted the contradictory outcomes that education affords girls as well as boys. Some would succeed where others failed. Nevertheless, none of this seemed to prepare feminists with the immediate means to tackle the story the attainment data began to tell in the mid 1990s about boys' uneven performance.

Gender and the curriculum: changing patterns of performance

By the mid 1990s, greater emphasis on the crucial role education was expected to play in producing a skilled workforce equipped to deal with the new knowledge economies had made the measurable outcomes of education much more visible, both nationally and internationally. Government-sponsored reform in many countries had seen an increasing emphasis on tracking pupil performance at different levels of the system, and making the results public through school performance league tables. As the supply of data built up, so more of the available evidence began to show girls' levels of educational attainment substantially improving in all areas of the curriculum. In the UK by the mid 1990s, girls either matched or outstripped boys in the available public measures of performance, at least up to age sixteen (Arnot *et al.*, 1998). Girls emerged as a school success story; boys did not.

The initial feminist response to news of girls' educational success could best be characterised as surprise, if not in some quarters downright suspicion. This is not what feminists were looking for, or indeed expecting. The kind of detailed examination of schools and classrooms which had for so long rightly preoccupied feminist scholars did not show that feminist perspectives had triumphed in schools. On the contrary, many of the targets for feminist intervention and challenge remained firmly entrenched. Whilst feminists paused to reconsider the nature of the evidence and what it might really mean, other commentators leapt into the discursive gap. Accounts of the narrowing gender differential in key areas of the curriculum began to gain increasing prominence within the media. These were not feminist voices lauding women's achievements. On the contrary, much of this commentary appeared to be part of an anti-feminist backlash which lambasted feminists for creating girls' success at the price of boys' failure (Gilbert and Gilbert, 1998). Press reports took on all the characteristics of a moral panic (Cohen, 1973). Stories about boys' comparative educational failure fed into stories about the threat to traditional family values, the redundancy of the male breadwinner, whose position within the family and the broader society was being fast eroded, and the dire consequences for social cohesion which must inevitably follow. What was happening in schools came to stand for what was happening in society at large. But whilst an account of the larger social picture might indeed have included the way in which manufacturing jobs and particularly the opportunities for unskilled labour and employment of the young were dwindling as economic restructuring gathered pace, the focus on schools contained this discussion, laying open the way to find other targets to blame. Women themselves, teachers, a curriculum bias towards girls, certain kinds of macho masculinities (for which read social class), single parent families, inadequate dads – all took their turn in the firing line. In this discursive context it swiftly became obvious that feminists needed to have something to say about boys' failure. At the very least, boys' failures needed explaining in ways which would not work to the detriment of girls.

Girls' success – boys' failure:
looking for a new feminist discourse

Boys have always loomed large in feminist accounts of the curriculum, generally in the role of obstructions, standing in the way of girls' progress. Early feminist critiques assumed that boys benefited from a curriculum largely predicated on their interests, which seemed to disproportionately bolster their confidence and sense of self-worth, unequally distributing power in their favour (Kelly, 1987; Spender, 1982; Stanworth, 1981). If the school played a part in gendering identity, then it did so through relegating girls to a subordinate role, whilst encouraging boys to see themselves as pre-eminent. Feminist interest largely centred on challenging or finding ways round this state of affairs. In this kind of analysis, boys and men are read as potential winners, not losers. Such work as there was on the formation of male identity within education, generally undertaken by male sociologists, largely shared this assumption. At the same time it focused more attention on the differences between groups of boys, often constructed round hierarchies determined by social class. For instance, Willis' *Learning to Labour* demonstrates how those young men whom the education system dubs as failures are simultaneously pursuing strategies which enable them to do power in other contexts (Willis, 1977). They escape with their masculinity intact. In this respect, losing is indeed cast as an intrinsically feminine attribute, whilst boys' response to the threat of failure can be exemplified as 'hyper masculinity' (Mac an Ghail, 1994). The losers' masculinity really wins out.

Not surprisingly, the assumption that all boys are winners remains a strong one within feminist discourse, even when tempered by the view that any hierarchy of losing will be intercut by social class and ethnicity too. This is such a powerful impulse that news of girls' improved educational performance continues to be treated with caution in some feminist quarters. Comparatively few accept it as a sign of fundamental social change. Yet this is precisely the position put forward in *Closing the Gender Gap*, one of the first feminist accounts to take at face value what the quantitative data on student performance seemed to be saying (Arnot *et al.*, 1999). Building on analysis of the available performance data in the UK, originally undertaken for the Equal Opportunities Commission and later the government inspections agency, Ofsted, *Closing the Gender Gap* accepts that educational outcomes for girls have changed. It also links girls' recent educational success in the UK context very strongly to the elimination within the education system of subject choice at fourteen (Arnot, David and Weiner, 1999). Ironically, as the authors comment, it was a Conservative government, loudly proclaiming the virtues of Victorian family values, and roundly condemned by feminist critics on many counts, which achieved this outcome at a stroke when they imposed a centralised National Curriculum upon the school system. Gendered subject choices at fourteen, predicated on views of 'natural' aptitude, disappeared overnight, and with them to a large extent their attendant gendered outcomes for girls. This, they contend, is why the closing of the gap is most dramatically demonstrated at the age of sixteen. More equal curricular access has ensured girls' improved performance in Maths and Science, whilst maintaining their lead in English and the arts and humanities. They concede that after sixteen the picture remains more complicated, as individualised curricular choice still leads to much more uneven entry patterns for boys and girls in different subject areas, with more boys still favouring Science, and more girls favouring arts as they self-select according to gender norms.

Closing the Gender Gap sets the new pattern of girls' educational achievement primarily in the context of educational policy-making, whilst also signalling larger-scale changes in the social worlds of work and family responsibilities. Both are seen as impacting on the educational pathways girls' choose to follow. But if equality of access has remained key to understanding girls' changing patterns of educational success, it cannot be so easily used to explain boys' failure. For the single area where the greatest discrepancy between boys' and girls' performance remains is in English, a subject which has always been part of the core curriculum, and yet whose curriculum content, feminist analysis insisted, brought boys the privileged place (NATE, 1985).

Boys and English: fixing failure
the managerial way

Boys' weaker performance in reading and writing is not a recent phenomenon. On the contrary it has long been regarded as an educational 'fact', largely explained in terms of boys' comparative 'late development', a concept assigning a biological basis to maturity, understood as both a physical and mental process (Millard, 1997). Biologically-driven explanations for boys' or girls' relative failings are inherently conservative. They speak to an economy of fixed aptitudes in which everyone finds their place. In this model the education system exists to deliver the 'natural aptitude' to the right location. Schools simply find who can do what, then take them to the appropriate destination. In practice, as feminists well know, the process of finding who can do what has never been neutral, but always loaded in favour of the more socially powerful. In the UK, adjusting boys' scores in the 11+ exam ensured they got to their rightful place in the face of, rather than because of, the educational evidence. Such judgements are always intersected by representations of gender, ethnicity and social class.

Yet in the current managerial climate this kind of discursive explanation for educational failure no longer finds a resonance. The 'rediscovery' of boys' comparative failure in English, made visible by the new means of assessing educational outcomes at every level of the education system, has not led to calls for a return to the kind of positive discrimination towards boys exercised in the 1960s. This kind of intervention would no longer win discursive legitimacy. Yet neither is the current state of affairs expected to be tolerated as a reflection of 'natural aptitude'. Rather, it has led to calls to teachers to redouble their efforts and do everything they can to improve boys' levels of performance within English. This time round the assumption is that educational failure can and will be fixed.

In the past decade, fixing educational failure has become a central aim of government policy in many jurisdictions. In the UK, following the election of the New Labour government, and the high priority it has put on reforming the literacy curriculum, local education authorities (LEAs) and individual schools have sometimes been encouraged to make raising boys' achievements in English an explicit part of their school improvement plans. Indeed, the government's intention to drive up educational standards across the board, itself seen as fundamental to sustaining Britain's long-term economic well being, depends upon substantially improving boys' performance. However, unlike the press in the late 1990s, the discrepancies between boys' and girls' educational achievements represent for the current government less a challenge to traditional values than a lack of consistency in educational product. The notion that the raw materials (biological aptitude) might be responsible for the outcomes, rather than the processes of manufacture (teaching), is anathema to the managerial vision which in many ways now dominates the political landscape.

In many respects, the dominant approaches to reform of the public sector now in play stem from business principles which seek to exercise control over the quality of outcome at every level of the system (Morley and Rassool, 1999). Adopting a managerial approach means in the first instance assessing what is going on using quantifiable input, through-put, and output figures for a given area. These act as measures which can then be used to benchmark current standards and establish room for improvement. The room for improvement is spelt out as targets to be met. When such targets are met they act as both the sign and the assurance of improved quality. Such measures act as a cornerstone of many governments' formula for running public affairs. They can be used to demonstrate that the administration has delivered on improved quality, thereby winning the political argument in favour of retaining public services.

In the new managerial context, target-setting is the main mechanism which drives the system from the centre. Provided central government can demonstrate that the aspects of the service it is targeting are appropriate to improving quality (something that the Labour party in the UK has actually found much harder to accomplish within health than within education), all it then has to do is insist that the targets it has set will be met. Exactly how this promise will be fulfilled is then to a large degree devolved to others who themselves can be called to account for any progress made (or lack of it). Thus within education in England, ambitious targets for improving Standard Assessment Test results have been devolved to the National Literacy and National Numeracy strategy teams (since reorganised as the Primary National Strategy) (see Moss, 2004). These bodies in turn progressively devolve responsibility for action further on down the system till we reach the level of the individual school, and even the individual teacher. The imperatives to do better are heavily centralised and closely monitored to the point where it is almost impossible at the level of the individual teacher to escape this general trend.

In political terms this is the strength of the approach. It is indeed the means of achieving a political quick-fix as devolved responsibilities for change bring everybody within the system into pursuit of the same goals. At the same time, such an approach is underpinned by an almost total eclecticism about what works and how to get the desired results. Provided standards go up, and targets are nearer to being achieved, nobody much minds how this happens. Such a context for educational improvement reconfigures what it might mean to fix gender differentials in educational performance. In the current educational climate the assumption is that fixing boys is about fixing educational product. The goal is not greater gender equality per se, but more homogeneity in output.

This is quite distinct from most feminist work in education which sought to change girls' patterns of achievement as a prelude to, or part of, changing the political status quo. The current concern with boys' performance within the education system directly sidesteps these broader issues. By way of example, *Can Do Better*, a government publication on raising boys' achievement in English which was sent into all secondary schools in the UK in 1998, drew explicit parallels between its concerns and those of earlier initiatives focused on girls' performance in Maths and Science, in the following terms:

> In the 1970s and 1980s the main gender issue in education was the performance of girls. In particular, there was anxiety about girls' achievements in subjects like mathematics and science, since relatively few chose to study these subjects beyond the age of 16 and their attainment in O level and GCSE lagged behind boys. Considerable work was done on this, and the girls' performance in these subjects at GCSE now matches that of boys. This clear improvement in the performance of girls shows what can be achieved when effort is carefully targeted.
>
> (QCA, 1998)

It presents as the lesson to be learnt from earlier (often feminist inspired) interventions that targeting teacher-effort works. In one sense, the maxim is perfectly legitimate, and wholly appropriate. Yet at the same time, any sense of a wider gender politics, which made such a strategic intervention on behalf of girls necessary in the first place, has been stripped out of the discourse. This makes it harder to bring back in any way of judging the remedies suggested for improving boys' performance in terms of their impact on gender relations, their consequences for gender identities or indeed the gender politics of the classroom, let alone gender relations in the wider social sphere.

In current official thinking represented in a range of government documents (Ofsted, 1993; DfES, 2005), advice about the routes to improving boys' performance dwells on two main themes: boys' motivation and the benefits of explicit teaching. Putting motivation at the centre of debate suggests that good learners are positively engaged rather than merely diligent, and thereby constructs a virtuous circle in which those who are personally committed to a curriculum which reflects their interests have good reason to learn. In many respects this is consistent with progressive views of the educational endeavour, which start from the child and see the pedagogic process as committed to enriching the personal voyage children make through the realms of knowledge (Walkerdine, 1990). This partly explains the wider constituency for this perspective which in many respects had previously underpinned feminist interventions into the curriculum on girls' behalf (Barrs and Pidgeon, 1993; Millard, 1997; QCA,

1998). But a curriculum committed to boys' interests should at least give feminists pause for thought. A feminist analysis assumes that boys' interests often work directly against girls', and indeed may precisely entrench a disequilibrium of power.

Lauding the virtues of explicit teaching chimes with a rather different agenda. On the one hand, it strengthens a commitment to a publicly-funded education system by insisting it can work for everyone, whilst on the other it suggests a reason for why the system has failed so far, namely poor teaching (Ofsted, 1993). Explicit teaching becomes the cure-all which will turn the current state of affairs round, a new pedagogic practice for new times (Bourne, 2000). There is much to be applauded in the democratic impulse which underpins this view. However, the reasons why boys might benefit from explicit teaching more than girls are rarely fully articulated. Indeed, this kind of approach runs the risk of invoking and valorising a fact-orientated, transmission style of teaching, in which the teacher holds all the authority and the pupil none – in contrast to a style of teaching encompassing affect, individual creativity and a democracy of interests between teachers and pupils. It is hard to avoid gendering such distinctions and reading the shift as away from teaching as nurturing, and therefore women's work, to teaching as more overt regulation, conducted in a 'masculine' style (Bourne, 2000; Walkerdine, 1990). Once again, questions about gender politics creep in.

Boys, literacy and underachievement: developing a feminist response in the new managerial climate

The changing political context has made the gender inequalities in the performance data on literacy visible once more and at the same time has re-geared the nature of the argument over that data. This has set feminists new challenges. Some have chosen to respond by focusing on the new managerial conditions which have given the performance data such prominence. Often this has meant taking issue with what might be called the politics of erasure, which treat the differences in achievement as a matter of mechanics to be quickly fixed without reference to wider social inequalities (Gilbert and Gilbert, 1998; Rowan et al., 2002). Others have concentrated more specifically on identifying curriculum interventions which might help redress the discrepancy in girls' and boys' performance (Barrs and Pidgeon, 1998; Millard, 1997). Much of this literature builds on themes already identified as important in educational work with girls and then extrapolates from this to see what might be most usefully applied to boys. When developed from an explicitly feminist perspective, any such assessment is made with the intention that girls should not lose out as a result, and is wary of endorsing stereotypic aspects of masculinity in the process (Gilbert and Gilbert, 1998, p. 21).

The interventions feminists have suggested for the literacy curriculum vary pretty much in line with the range of earlier work on girls' educational attainment (see above) and according to the logic of the social explanations for educational underachievement that they imply (Barrs and Pidgeon, 1993). One approach has been to extend from girls to boys the notion that gender stereotypes limit educational attainment. From this perspective the responsibility of the literacy curriculum is to challenge the boundaries gender identities set to educational aspirations. Applying this approach in the new context means remaking masculinities in ways which are less destructive for boys, as well as reshaping femininities, so that both boys and girls hold less fast to narrow conceptions and assumptions about who they are and what they can do (Rowan *et al.*, 2002). Undermining gender stereotypes on both sides is seen as a key to opening up more educational possibilities for all. In these respects the school offers hope of a solution to problems which have been apparently created elsewhere. Literature circles have certainly been used in this way. Originally intended as a means of promoting wider reading, some practitioners argued that their real value lay in the space they created for teachers to extend boys' emotional range by ensuring that they engaged with a greater range of texts than they might choose for themselves (Fokias, 1998). By creating a context where boys were then required to articulate their response collectively in a small group, they effectively had to step over boundaries otherwise set by stereotypic views of masculinity (Barrs and Pidgeon, 1998).

Other interventions were designed to change the content of the school literacy curriculum rather than pupil attributes. These approaches often draw on the assumption that educationally successful children feel more included in the existing curriculum dispensation whilst, conversely, those who feel excluded do less well. Girls' relative success at literacy is read as a measure of their inclusion in the literacy curriculum (despite previous feminist analysis of sex-role stereotyping in children's fiction which had argued the opposite). The grounds on which boys might feel excluded from the literacy curriculum are then variously defined: the absence of role models provided by enough older male readers (Hodgeon, 1993); a feminised curriculum grounded in narrative which overlooks the pleasures of non-fiction to which boys are more drawn (Millard, 1997); or the absence of the new technologies which have captured boys' imaginations (Rowan *et al.*, 2002). Of all of these, placing a greater emphasis on non-fiction in the literacy curriculum has had the greatest uptake. This is widely interpreted as re-balancing the curriculum in a more gender-neutral way by both matching boys' existing interests more closely whilst offering girls access to more powerful linguistic genres (Martin, 1985). Some of the difficulties with these approaches will be explored in later chapters, in particular the assumption that narrative is itself intrinsically gendered. (See also Rowan *et al.*'s critique of the assumption that boys will inevitably already know more about new technologies.)

However, at this stage in the book I want to turn to two rather different analyses of gender inequalities in attainment which explore the issues in other ways: Bente Elkjaer's work on gender and information technology and Judith Solsken's work on gender and literacy learning (Elkjaer, 1992; Solsken, 1993). Written ahead of, rather than in response to, the re-emergence of the gender gap in literacy attainment made visible by the new performance data, these writers suggest an alternative approach to understanding uneven educational performance. Both identify what is potentially problematic as well as advantageous in the opportunities that the curriculum affords both girls and boys. Both are able to show that whilst boys' responses can be meaningfully differentiated from girls', they are neither uniform nor monolithic. There is indeed more than one kind of boy, just as there is more than one kind of girl. Finally, for both writers the social relations embedded in schooling emerge as the central issue.

Gender differentiation in practice: a view from the Information Technology classroom

Writing from within a feminist research tradition, Bente Elkjaer's main interests focus on the learning potential of new technologies, and their adoption and adaptation in the workplace. Her 1992 article, 'Girls and Information Technology in Denmark – an account of a socially constructed problem', provides an insightful description of children's use of computer technology as a socially situated and gender-differentiated practice, which is highly suggestive for understanding the gendered outcomes of the literacy curriculum.

Elkjaer collected her data from a group of Danish Eighth Grade classrooms where pupils had opted to study Information Technology (IT) as part of their schooling. Elkjaer was interested both in the motivations of the girls and boys who had opted for this subject and in how they fared in the classroom once their studies had begun. The enquiry itself stemmed from her sense of unease that all too often girls were presumed to have a potentially problematic relationship to IT, whilst boys were considered to have an automatic affinity with the area. From her own perspective, such unquestioned assumptions about gender-specific aptitudes for IT amounted to little more than empty stereotyping which effectively construed boys' relationship to the subject as the norm against which girls' responses could be judged and found wanting. By contrast, her own intention was to 'introduce light and shade into the stereotypical perception of gender and IT' (Elkjaer, 1992, p. 27) by making it a priority in her research to scrutinise boys' relationship to the subject at least as much as girls'.

Data were collected by interviewing pupils about their subject choice and then closely observing a sequence of IT lessons. The groups Elkjaer observed contained roughly equal numbers of girls and boys. In analysing her interview data, Elkjaer found that at first sight many of the girls' reasons for choosing IT seemed to confirm general expectations that they would find its technical side more off-putting and feel less comfortable with this aspect of the subject. Their answers seemed to show that they opted for IT in spite of, rather than because of, its technical content and were motivated mainly by its longer-term usefulness to them in the post-school jobs market. Yet, as Elkjaer points out, the priority we give to girls' motivations here actually detracts from their willingness none-the-less to take the technical scientific aspects of the subject on board. In effect, she argues, we simultaneously collude with a view that girls don't really belong in science, even when the hard evidence from their actual choices is precisely that girls are stepping into this domain.

Taking this kind of positive reading of the relationship between what the girls said and what they did led her to scrutinise more carefully the ways in which the boys articulated their own subject 'preferences'. Here she found that by contrast in their own account they seemed almost compelled to take scientific subjects, representing themselves as exercising little active choice in this arena. The boys' own view of their gender identities and the subject matter appropriate to them seemed to have made the choice for them. With these different kinds of orientation to the subject content in mind, Elkjaer turned her attention to the IT classroom.

Hosts and guests – how boys and girls position themselves in the IT classroom

Elkjaer's observations of the teaching and learning activity in the IT classroom showed that it encompassed two very different domains of social interaction. On the one hand there was the public domain of whole-class work where boys largely dominated the discursive space and actively competed for the floor. On the other hand there was the more private domain of pair-work around the computer screen. The curriculum content of IT was divided between these two domains. Elkjaer observed that the more technical aspects of the subject, predicated on acquiring the necessary IT skills, were largely handled in the private domain, whilst the public domain tended to be reserved for whole-class discussion of the social impact of IT, an additional part of the curriculum content. The main thrust of Elkjaer's article is on the very different use girls and boys make of these domains and their orientation to the subject content handled there.

The picture she paints of the public domain is a familiar one: boys compete to assert what they know, marginalising and barely acknowledging any contributions girls make as they jostle for space to be heard. Yet in her data, the boys do fall silent when the teacher uses the public domain for direct instruction in computer skills. One of the incidents Elkjaer cites is when the teacher goes over a programming exercise in the whole-class setting. During this phase the main interaction takes place between the teacher and the girls 'partly because the teacher appeals to the girls more extensively, and partly because the boys withdraw from the public sphere of learning' (ibid., p. 34). In other words, the presumed lack of knowledge on the girls' part makes them an explicit target for the teacher's attention in this kind of context, attention which they are prepared to play to. By contrast, the boys actively scale down their own participation at this point. Elkjaer speculates that this is precisely because the context focuses on what pupils have not yet grasped or might find difficult. The one boy who does raise a problem with his work does so almost inaudibly and is reluctant to expand the point, whilst at the end of the session, when the pupils are asked to choose between working on their own or receiving additional tuition from the teacher, all the boys go off to work independently, whilst the girls cluster round the computer with the teacher. From this kind of data, Elkjaer begins to develop a hypothesis: that the girls benefit from their ambiguous status in the classroom, actively garnering support and subject input from the teacher, something which works in their long-term interests. By contrast, the priority the boys give to maintaining their own public standing as those who already know effectively cuts them off from much of this additional help. Data collected from the private domain of paired work around the computer begins to show why this strategy may be problematic for at least some of the boys.

In the context of the classrooms she observed, the acquisition of the necessary technical skills in IT happens primarily in the paired work round the computer, where children try their hand at the variety of programming exercises the teacher has introduced. Here Elkjaer documents clear differences in the ways in which the boys and girls operate in this segment of the lessons. Elkjaer observes that the girl pairings are far more likely to be working from a similar level of relatively modest expertise. Where the exercises are new to both partners, they seem to find no difficulty in seeking the help they require from other pairs or from the teacher. They share the tasks equally, each struggling to get things right, and are more inclined to laugh and commiserate if they get things wrong. By contrast, the boy pairings often encompass quite different levels of computer skill. Where this is the case, Elkjaer observes that the more competent member of the pair does the work, whilst the less competent member is reduced to being an inactive bystander with few opportunities for picking up the skills they do not already have:

> John does all the keying. They do not talk together about the exercise. When Finn makes a proposal, it is rejected, or John knows it already ... John writes the programme very meticulously and carefully, while Finn does all the 'heavy' work, such as counting sections on the display unit ... John works independently and does not discuss his next steps with Finn. He may order Finn to get the print outs.
>
> (Ibid., p. 36)

Neither the boys themselves, nor their teachers, seem to have any way of recognising what might make such arrangements difficult and, indeed, the weaker boys in effect cover up for their lack of knowledge by claiming as their own what their more competent pair does:

> The boys seem to get along well but Jan remains the spectator ... Morton controls the keys ... At the end of the session ... Jan contacts one of the other boys in order to 'boast' of their splendid programme ... It is also Jan who contacts the teacher, so she can admire the programme ... Although the teacher invites Jan to go over the programme with the class he lets Morten do it.
>
> (Ibid., p. 36)

Elkjaer comments: 'It is debatable how much the boys who have a weak foundation in computer science benefit from the teaching, but no matter how much they in fact learn, they rarely miss an opportunity to "boast" of their knowledge in front of the teacher and their friends'. She argues that the mistake commentators make is to conflate boys' dominance of the public space of the classroom with their actual subject competence. The two are not the same. Indeed, in her view, whilst jostling amongst each other to hold the floor may well secure boys' own position in a social hierarchy, it does little to promote the best conditions for their learning. In this sense Elkjaer perceives the boys' determination to adopt the status of 'hosts' in relation to IT as limiting who amongst them can succeed in this arena, whereas girls' willingness to be cast as 'guests' actually opens up the terrain for them on a much more equal footing.

By paying close attention to the different uses boys and girls made of the varied contexts and associated resources for teaching and learning within IT, Elkjaer reiterates the importance of understanding teaching and learning as culturally shaped activities, and prioritises the means of identifying the gender-specific logics which underpin them. Her analysis also begins to suggest ways of reconciling the apparent advantages which masculinity seems to confer on boy students with poorer educational outcomes for at least some boys. From Elkjaer's perspective, learning IT does not primarily mean coming to grips with an abstracted body of knowledge, or a free-standing technology, so much as participating in social contexts where beliefs about gendered competence shape differential access to the resources which are available, and do so in both unexpected and contradictory ways. In these respects she uses her work to directly challenge some of the most conventionally held views about how a gendered competence is built and who might be the biggest winners and losers on what terms.

Gender differentiation in literacy learning:
a view from the kindergarten

Writing from within a literacy as social practice tradition, Judith Solsken's study focuses on children's acquisition of literacy at home and in school. Unusually for work in this area, she gives particular prominence to gender rather than community as an organising principle which helps shape children's literacy learning.

Solsken's data stem from a longitudinal study of a single cohort, drawn largely from middle-class suburban families who entered kindergarten in the same year. The study continued to monitor these children in their local primary school up until the end of Second Grade. In the first instance, data were collected through home visits with selected case-study children in the summer before they joined kindergarten. These visits were then supplemented by parental interviews and, during later phases of the research, parental questionnaires. In school, each of the case-study children was documented over the three-year research period through a cycle of classroom observations designed to focus on their reading and writing activities. These methods were chosen to create a view of literacy learning from the participants' perspective. From the outset Solsken recorded literacy as a social activity, in which the actions of adults or older family members helped define what literacy might be used for, its purposes and values, but children then struggled to take on and accommodate themselves to or rework these definitions as they participated in particular reading or writing tasks. In analysing the individual differences she found between the children in terms of their orientation to the literacy activities they undertook at home and in school, Solsken focuses on the extent to which literacy can be represented alternatively as adult-sponsored work or self-regulated play and the part gender has in deciding this. These conflicting perspectives and the way they are resolved by individual children are teased out through what Solsken calls learning biographies.

Viewing literacy as work or play
– a gendered equation

Solsken's learning biographies reconstruct the stance children adopt as they pursue literacy activities in different settings. Written in the first instance as simple narratives, based largely on field notes, they combine evidence of what children do and how they participate in a range of activities at home and school with a description of the context which generates those activities, and the motivations of others involved. For instance, in the initial home interviews Solsken would arrive at the child's house with a bag of children's books and a variety of paper and writing implements in order to elicit from her interviewees what they already knew about reading and writing in the context of their home environment. Her questions alternated between asking children about objects in that immediate environment – their own toys and favourite books – and encouraging them to make use of the materials she had brought with her. She invited them to write or draw on the paper, and choose a book to listen to from those she provided. In her account of these interviews, she simultaneously paints a picture of the social relations in the immediate family environment, drawing on the way in which the interview itself seems embedded in the ebb and flow of family life, as well as detailing what the children actually did. To take as an example the biography she presents of a boy called Luke, she records not only his actions during the time she spends in the house, but also the way in which his elder sister follows them around, adding her own commentary to what is going on:

> I noticed a Star Wars comic on the floor and asked Luke about it. He responded by showing me his favourite part and naming the characters. His sister, who had been observing with a proprietary curiosity, announced that Luke couldn't read. He darted off to get another book to show me, a Star Wars activity book in which he had completed mazes and dot-to-dot pictures.
>
> (Solsken, 1993, p. 23)

In these respects she pays attention to where participants' views of literacy seem to converge and where they diverge. She strengthens this picture of the home literacy environment and the different kinds of views of literacy's purposes and the values it encompasses by subsequently interviewing parents about the range of reading and writing activities in the home in which family members participate, and their own attitude towards their child's activity. The interview Solsken conducted with Jane's mother, for example, is integrated into her learning biography like this:

> Jane had known her letters and numbers since she was two, and her mother had taught her the sounds related to letters. Although Jane recognised the printed names of all the children at day camp by sight, she did not consider herself a reader. 'She can't read,' her mother said, 'can't remember *and* and *the*, has a block ... She wants to learn to read but she's not ready.' Jane loved being read to, however, and enjoyed looking at books on her own. 'She would be read to for hours if you'd do it,' her mother observed.
>
> (Ibid., p. 41)

These initial snapshots are later added to from the detailed observation of these children's patterns of literacy activity in school as they unfold in kindergarten and then First and Second Grade.

The main characteristic of the school classroom environments that Solsken observed is that they were structured in the first instance around integrating literacy activity into children's play and, later, around presenting literacy as meaningful work. All three classrooms from kindergarten to Second Grade stressed pupil choice and self-directed participation in a wide range of activities. The potential for children to steer their own way round the literacy environment of these classrooms was one of the main reasons Solsken based her research in these sites. Solsken considers that in many ways each of these classrooms operated with what Bernstein calls invisible pedagogy, that is the pedagogical relationship between teacher and taught was masked rather than made immediately visible through the social organisation of the classroom (Bernstein, 1996). This leads to a particular form of curriculum:

> Play is identified as the central concept in invisible pedagogies. Almost all of the child's activity is considered play and is observed and interpreted in terms of developmental learning. Teachers' arrangement of the environment and their response to children's activity are based on these interpretations and implicitly shape children's activity. Thus children's play in such pedagogies is their work.
>
> (Solsken, 1993, p. 61)

Taken in relation to both school and home, Solsken shows how children are often given contradictory messages about what literacy is for and how they are positioned in relation to it which each child then has to resolve for themselves. In her analysis, the extent to which literacy is represented as work or play, by whom, in which context, becomes key to understanding the dynamics of this process. For Solsken, literacy is exemplified as play in contexts where reading and writing are integrated into purposeful and self-directed activity which children engage in for themselves. Such activity has no external sponsor, or the external sponsor's and the child's interests converge sufficiently strongly that they establish a seamless joint purpose, in which the child appears to exercise the main ownership over the task. Literacy as work is much more clearly externally imposed, and serves a narrower set of purposes, often acting as a means to someone else's end. Outcomes are judged according to adult-imposed standards.

In the interview with Jane's mother we can see traces of reading as play and reading as work both being invoked. On the one hand, Jane's relative knowledge of print and her capacity to decode text are judged according to a particular set of standards, more often associated with formal schooling. This is reading as adult-sponsored work. On the other hand the more diffuse interactions with texts which Jane enjoys through hearing others read or looking at books herself are much more characteristic of literacy as child-sponsored play whose merit rests with the child's own pleasure. In

Solsken's view, family members may well invoke both frames of reference, but in and through their own activities will give added force to one or the other. That leaves the child to position themselves in relation to these contradictory stances. Solsken argues that the way in which individuals resolve this for themselves will be structured in and through the gender dynamics of their social relations at home and in school.

She goes on to demonstrate this point through her analysis of the children's learning biographies. In Luke's case, she draws attention to the way in which the gulf between what he as the youngest in the family can do with literacy and what his older sisters can do is evaluated in terms consistent with the view that literacy is work. His sisters can apparently apply themselves to the task of reading and writing, whilst he flits aimlessly from one thing to another, not settling down to the real business. Solsken comments:

> [Luke's] mother and sisters ... were clearly involved in, and concerned about Luke's reading and writing. They modelled a whole set of behaviours around literacy that included quietness, relative immobility, and interest in conventionally female topics, certainly not monsters and space wars. They regarded Luke's literacy behaviours as somewhat out of bounds and certainly immature.
>
> (Ibid., p. 30)

For Solsken, Luke has two choices: he can either buy into the view that literacy is work of a particular kind, then buckle down and apply those values to himself, or he can resist. She argues that he takes the latter path precisely by consistently invoking play-centred definitions of literacy which lead him into different forms of behaviour from those his family members value.

> Luke's mother and sisters did not regard Luke's play-based encounters with print as fully appropriate literacy behaviour and sought to engage him in the activities they valued. Luke, in turn, regarded these attempts as impositions of adult goals and plans in conflict with his own. In treating this conflict as a kind of competitive game, Luke came to invest in play not only as self-selected and pleasurable activity, but also as a form of mitigated resistance to adult-sponsored work, and in this case, female identified literacy.
>
> (Ibid., p. 31)

When Luke started school, Solsken watched him transferring this set of attitudes over into the new setting, and there re-working them. Whilst he sometimes incorporated aspects of literacy into his play, he resolutely resisted forms of literacy activity which seem to fulfil the function of work. This was despite the fact that the kindergarten environment itself was structured round integrating literacy into play activities:

Even though his teachers tried to link writing to his interests by focusing on his drawn story and spoken description, Luke treated writing as a visual artifact required by teachers, not as a vehicle of expression or communication. And his general response to adult requirements was boredom or insurrection. Observing his apparent lack of interest in writing, his teachers continued to show their interest in the stories expressed in his drawings and periodically engaged him in conferences focused on expressing his stories in writing. Luke's interest in print in the classroom was strong [only] when the print connected to his play: ... he was very possessive of signs a teacher had written to label his block space towers and vehicles.

(Ibid., p. 98)

Luke resisted the hidden work agenda in the classroom by insisting on taking at face value the invitation to play in ways which continually pushed literacy to the margin of his activities, or allowed its inclusion only on his own terms. Solsken links these responses in school to the ambivalent position Luke holds at home as the youngest of three siblings with two older sisters and a mother who have converged on work-centred definitions of literacy. By refusing to play the literacy game by their rules, he asserts his difference from them. Rather than lose on their terms, by being judged as less competent than them, he aims to win on his own. This sets up new kinds of tensions in the classroom for him and for his teachers.

In describing early literacy interactions in this way, Solsken argues that the acquisition of literacy is always part and parcel of carving out a social identity in relation to others. For this reason she calls her own approach to understanding literacy acquisition 'literacy as social status and identity'. Just as gender relations are structured into the home and school, so they thread their way through literacy. However, amongst the cohort of children she studies as a whole, there is no necessary correlation between masculinity, femininity and a work- or play-centred view of literacy activity. Luke's case can be contrasted with that of Jack, whose two older brothers have also assumed work-centred definitions of literacy, which in this case Jack co-opts for himself. (Indeed in her data, older siblings, whether girls or boys, almost invariably operate with work-centred definitions of literacy, derived from their experience of schooling.) This sets Jack a different set of challenges in a play-centred classroom.

The tensions that Solsken identifies round literacy emerge in both home and school settings. Individual children manage these tensions in different ways. Gender asserts itself not as a wholly predictable element in the mix, therefore, but through the claims children make to similarity with, or difference from, salient others. Yet the choices individual children make are inevitably responsive to the broader regularities which stand behind individual families and classrooms, shaping common ground and jointly held literacy practices. In the households she studies, women play a disproportionate role in actively preparing children for and then supporting them with the literacy work of school, a factor which itself is clearly linked to patterns of gendered work within and outside the home. How women manage this role by adopting a work- or play-centred view of literacy therefore becomes more central to understanding how children negotiate their way into schooled literacy than the part men play in other kinds of literate activity in the home. Indeed, from her perspective it is precisely women's management of children's entry into schooled literacy which provides a prime source of tension, particularly sharply felt by many of the boys on her database, as they struggle to assert their own gender identities around these practices in relation to family and peers.

Gender differences in attainment: setting a new research agenda

A number of common themes emerge in Elkjaer and Solsken's work. Both are quite clear that gender is one of the key mechanisms through which differentiated uptake of the curriculum happens but that the material on which gender operates is often contradictory or ambivalent. Both conduct close studies of specific contexts in which the interplay between masculinities, femininities and schooled learning are worked out, without assuming they already know which issues or conditions will matter most for whom as children grapple with a particular subject matter. Schooling clearly constructs a hierarchy of knowers, but how gender fits within a particular hierarchy cannot be decided in the abstract. Neither author starts their exploration from a sense of fixed gender identities. Instead of presuming that gendered learning derives from putting on a fixed set of attributes, or reproducing a narrow range of existing stereotypes, they concentrate on how gendered outcomes are constructed in relation to something else, as children negotiate their way through schooling and the difficulties and tensions it presents them with. There is no single way of being a boy or being a girl. Rather, girls and boys do femininity or masculinity with the resources to hand, in a given context. As the available resources change so what it means to be masculine or feminine within a particular context will change too. This process creates both winners and losers.

Both writers therefore offer a potentially dynamic account in which any investment in gender differentiation is always socially structured, yet is also open to change. There are differences between them too. Elkjaer suggests a more difficult interface between masculinity and schooling. She sees femininity as having a broader canvas to play on, for girls can to some extent move into boys' territory, whereas boys' masculinity remains more fiercely policed. In her account, there is a high price to pay for masculine success. Some boys do well but only at the expense of their peers. By contrast,

35

Solsken sees risks for both boys and girls as they make choices over how to position themselves around literacy. For her, becoming literate holds a particular social charge which all children must negotiate. In her account girls are more likely to 'play safe' and occupy territory which is more closely defined and proscribed. She sees a price to pay for such caution, just as there is a price to pay for the risks boys take too. These new ways of looking at gender-differentiated attainment in specific areas of the curriculum through a focus on socially situated interaction in the classroom are core to the rest of this book.

Conclusion: examining the literacy curriculum and the social distinctions it creates

New managerialism and the emphasis it places on performance data has brought boys' relative underachievement in literacy back into the spotlight. It has also generated a context where fixing the problem seems urgent, even whilst there is little consensus over the exact nature of boys' problem with literacy. Feminists find themselves caught between, on the one hand, the task of rebutting anti-feminist explanations for boys' underachievement and, on the other, the difficulties of rapidly finding remedies which can apparently address boys' attainment, yet without jeopardising girls'. Dealing with this dilemma at speed has often meant unpicking what can or can't be transposed from existing understandings about the social roots of educational underachievement derived from working with girls for use with boys (Gilbert and Gilbert, 1998). One of the ideas to have been most commonly transposed is that the root of the problem of unequal achievement lies with the formation of social identities and the space such identities then find for expression, incorporation or opposition within schooling. Whilst advocates don't always agree on which aspects of masculinity should be challenged and which incorporated within school settings, the general assumption is that boys' educational failure stems from a mismatch between these two. To remedy boys' underachievement in this light has meant looking for new ways of remaking masculinities or incorporating hitherto 'hidden' aspects of masculinity into the literacy curriculum on new terms (Gilbert and Gilbert, 1998; Rowan et al., 2002; Millard, 1997).

This book adopts a different approach to understanding gender-differentiated patterns of failure and success within the literacy curriculum. Rather than look for the best match between the literacy curriculum and aspects of masculinity, it begins the other way round by examining the social organisation of literacy in the classroom and the social distinctions it creates. This resets the scope of the enquiry in line with the work of Elkjaer and Solsken. In their respective studies of the IT and literacy curricula, Elkjaer and Solsken do not focus on what the curriculum has to say about gender identity per se; rather they show how the formation of schooled knowledge in these two specific domains offers alternative subject positions to students, created in relation to something else – assumptions about technical expertise in IT which create the roles of host or guest in the classroom; or assumptions about literacy learning and its trajectory which distinguish between learning as play or work and so present different possibilities for pupil engagement with the literacy curriculum. These contrasting subject positions then intersect with children's negotiations over gender identity in complex and sometimes contradictory ways.

The distinction Elkjaer and Solsken make between the explicit content of the curriculum and the role the curriculum plays in creating gender-differentiated outcomes amongst the student body is important to the argument I will develop in this book. It takes me closer to the work of Basil Bernstein and his theorisation of pedagogic discourse (Bernstein, 1996). Bernstein argues that the role schooling plays in social reproduction is determined not by any specific content that school knowledge either covers or excludes, but by the part/whole relations 'within' a given curriculum, established and enacted through pacing and sequencing rules (framing) and the strength of insulation between one body of knowledge and another (classification). These different aspects of pedagogic discourse combine to establish boundaries to knowledge in its different forms, and at the same time delineate who can access that knowledge and under what terms, conditions which schools as institutions both set out and then effectively police. For Bernstein, social reproduction happens indirectly through the recontextualising rules of pedagogic discourse and the different subject positions it creates rather than directly through the explicit messages the system carries about gender, ethnicity or social class.

With these perspectives in mind, this book sets out to look afresh at the social organisation of the literacy curriculum, and how children engage with what it says literacy is. To do so the book draws, in the first instance, on research tools associated with literacy as social practice perspectives. What those tools are and how they might be relevant to the current endeavour is the focus of the next chapter.

2

STUDYING LITERACY WITH
MORE THAN GENDER IN MIND

Introduction

For different reasons, the discourse of new managerialism and a feminist discourse on educational underachievement have converged on 'failing boys' as an object of concern within the literacy curriculum. The terms of the discourse help set the boundaries to the problem, and what will be explored within that remit. Attention largely falls either on what 'failing boys' themselves lack by way of particular skills or attributes, or alternatively what the school curriculum itself lacks in terms of its capacity to address such a group. The hunt is on for whatever is deemed missing.

But the objects of all this attention, 'failing boys', stand at the end of a large number of social processes which have helped create them. Where and how are such boys produced? If the attainment data show that boys disproportionately underachieve in literacy, then a social explanation requires evidence of where and how this happens in and through social interaction. To date these processes are not well understood or documented. Solsken's research remains the most complete attempt to explore these issues through the collection of empirical data. Most other work in the area selects from existing theories that identify a likely cause for the formation of this group, extrapolates from that to argue the case for a particular kind of intervention, and only then tracks in close detail the relative success of particular initiatives designed to deal with the problem.

This leaves relatively unexamined the initial explanations used to determine such a focus for action in the first place. This makes it more difficult to assess the appropriateness of the forms of action taken. The urgency of the need to find immediate solutions in the current climate seems to preclude operating in any other way. Under precisely these circumstances I would argue that there is every reason to slow down, rather than speed up, thinking about gender and literacy and how they intertwine. In this chapter I outline what 'slow thinking' (Richard Quarshie, personal communication) about the gender differentiation of literacy might look like using tools associated with literacy as social practice perspectives.

Research from a literacy as social practice perspective

Literacy as social practice perspectives study literacy not as a finite set of mental skills but as a social practice which is defined and shaped through use in culturally specific contexts. Drawing on a variety of different disciplines including anthropology, sociolinguistics, and sociology, such approaches assume that what counts as reading and writing (Heap, 1991) is socially constructed, and will vary over time and according to setting (Heath, 1983; Street, 1984; Barton and Hamilton, 1998). Sometimes referred to as the New Literacy Studies, they stand in opposition to traditions that conceive of literacy as a purely cognitive phenomenon which can be studied as an abstract set of skills (Street, 1984). For literacy as social practice perspectives there is no single way of doing literacy which transcends the specific social and cultural setting in which literacy happens.

This kind of research has developed in two main ways. One strand sets out to identify and describe distinct forms of literacy which have developed and are deployed within particular communities for those communities' own purposes and on their own terms (Street, 1993; Barton and Hamilton, 1998). The preference is for studying communities which are often socially, politically or economically marginalised. Such studies then act as a challenge to normative conceptions of what literacy is by offering an alternative means of valuing what different communities do with the resources they have at their disposal. Much of this work has been developed as a counterweight to official literacy programmes targeted at segments of the population deemed to be illiterate.

A second strand of work focuses more closely on literacy learning, whether at home or in school. Studies examine how adults induct children into particular understandings of what literacy is and how it should be exercised. Differences in how this happens are of keen interest. Some of this research then also considers whether children experience either continuity or disjuncture between literacy and its instruction at home and in school, and whether this impacts on children's progress as readers or writers. Both strands of research recognise that the ways in which diverse communities within a given society gain access to specific forms of literacy and exercise their entitlement over them are often politically charged. And that school literacy holds a privileged place in arbitrating between different versions of what it means to read and write.

The insistence on looking for evidence of different conceptions of what literacy is, for whom, and the attempt to understand how one version of literacy might come to dominate over others, make such approaches particularly suitable for examining how gender differences in literacy attainment might emerge. Yet to date, gender has rarely been at the forefront in these kinds of studies. Instead, the closest exploration of uneven outcomes from the literacy curriculum is premised on differences in community membership defined by ethnicity or social class. By reviewing how this work has developed, this chapter considers what these traditions might contribute to a study of literacy, gender and attainment, in particular through the research tools they provide.

Although researchers working within this tradition use a variety of ethnographic research tools to study literacy as a social practice (Green and Bloome, 1996), most steer by the concept of the literacy event. This provides a key focus for both data collection and analysis. This chapter will review the different ways in which this key concept has been taken up and applied in discussion of literacy learning, both at home and in school, using the work of Henrietta Dombey, Shirley Brice Heath, Carolyn Baker and Janet Maybin as key points of reference.

What is a literacy event?

A literacy event can be broadly defined as any occasion where a piece of written text plays an integral part in what is going on (Street, 1984; Baynham, 1995; Barton, 1994). As a research tool, it can be regarded as a bounded moment in time where the role literacy plays in the immediate social interactions between participants becomes available for study alongside the particular competence which is being exercised. Any one event can be studied in its own terms or linked to other kinds of literacy events associated with the same participants or setting, thus revealing common orientations to literacy within a given community. This analytic move from the specific to the general is signalled through the concept of literacy practices, a term now widely used to designate the ways of thinking about or doing things with literacy which characterise and shape reading and writing in a given community (Street, 1993).

Using the literacy event as the unit of analysis allows the researcher to both explore how literacy acquires a specific social and cultural value and resonance through the immediate interaction and to track any underlying continuities which typify its use within a given community. To take an example: in British primary schools 'reading aloud in class' often takes place as a distinct literacy event whose conduct is relatively well specified. That is to say, participants would recognise what kinds of role they are expected to perform during this kind of event and would adjust their response to the text accordingly. There are different possibilities: for instance, in a whole class setting, the teacher could be the sole reader; that role might devolve turn by turn to individual pupils; or pupils and teacher might read aloud together in unison. But there are also limits; some things are permissible or likely within this kind of event, and other things are not. Thus teachers and pupils are unlikely to jointly read aloud a school letter being sent home to parents. Equally, during unison reading of a given chunk of text – reading a big book aloud together in class for instance – individual readers would not be expected to speed ahead, taking off at their own pace, nor break off to ask questions about the text's content. By contrast, the teacher will have the right to orchestrate the pace of such reading and its pauses as well as determine the moment when it will halt. The teacher's orientation to this event is therefore different from the student's.

Steering by the event leads the researcher to these kinds of social expectations about how reading will be done at any particular time. From a literacy as social practice perspective, these social expectations help determine the array of skills and competencies brought into use in dealing with texts in any particular context. Documenting the event, rather than simply recording and/or assessing the skill, guarantees that the social shaping of literacy gets into the frame as part of the object of study. Variation in how literacy takes place can then be analysed in relation to the specific social and institutional context which generates these kinds of expectations about what it means to read or write well here. Reading aloud in Koranic schools, for instance, where this practice is used to induct children into knowledge of the Koran, may well be underpinned by different kinds of social expectations about how that activity should proceed (who joins in, when and how), and determine the ensuing mix of individual and unison reading, even as the activity itself will be mediated and bounded through different social relations (Baynham, 1995, pp. 170–173). From a literacy as social practice perspective, reading aloud in these two different contexts – the primary school classroom and the Koranic school – is not the same thing, even though a psychological approach to literacy might well regard them as demonstrations of the same processing skills. And indeed, the same children might well experience both events.

Of course, not all literacy events are quite so distinctly delineated as reading aloud in school. What about glancing at a bus timetable to work out where the bus is going and when the next one will arrive? Is this a literacy event which is amenable to the same kind of analysis? In one sense it still fits the opening definition of a literacy event, given above, but it is less certain whether any social expectations about the character of the occasion as such come into play. What are the means for assessing whether the bus timetable has been read well or read badly? Perhaps one might say that some literacy events are more closely defined than others within a given community, and may be more tightly regulated. And that the researcher's job is therefore to find out which kinds of literacy event have what kinds of salience for whom. This underlines the importance of steering by the participants' perspective in trying to understand how any literacy event works and the competencies it brings into play. This principle holds when looking in detail at the inner workings of any given event, and when looking at the pattern and range of literacy events as they occur for a particular community in the broader flow of everyday social activity.

Using the literacy event to study literacy learning: the concept of the 'telling case'

For literacy as social practice perspectives, a given literacy event often acts as a 'telling case' (Mitchell, 1983). That is to say, analyses of the structure of a specific event and the way in which reading or writing takes place within it are used to elucidate more general theoretical principles which underpin the social construction of literacy within a given community. Analysis may well involve paying attention to: the requisite knowledge needed to participate 'well' in a given event; the social relations between participants; how what they do or say relates to the text in hand; the social meaning of the event for participants; the structuring of the event in and through its relationship to other possible events; the necessary material or discursive resources which are integral to the activity; and the social means through which such resources are distributed. Although the particularity of the individual event is often the immediate concern, the specificity of the action this time round can by these means be related to the wider continuities of time, place and institutional or community membership which generate them. To take this discussion forward I turn now to authors who have used the literacy event to throw light on the social construction of literacy more broadly, both at home and in school.

The bedtime story as a telling case

In the following example, Henrietta Dombey uses a few minutes' tape-recording of a mother and child reading a bedtime story to reflect on what is being learnt through the conversational exchange between these participants, as well as from the text itself (Dombey, 1992). In her analysis the particular example comes to stand for the more general principles which underpin this type of event and give it value.

Example 1: Reading *Rosie's Walk*

This extract comes from a bedtime story session in which a mother is reading to her three-and-a-half-year-old daughter. As this extract opens, the mother is about to start reading their third book of the evening, Pat Hutchins' *Rosie's Walk* (1970), a picture book in which the pictures act as an important counterpoint to the written text. Only a small portion of the whole session is quoted below. In the transcript, Henrietta Dombey lays up what was said in parallel with an account of what was on the page of the book, so that the reader can follow the unfolding relationship between talk and text. M is the mother, A her daughter Anna.

Transcript	Text
M C'mon 'cos I want to go and have my supper. Hurry up. Rosie's Walk	ROSIE'S WALK By PAT HUTCHINS *Picture of carefree hen walking through cluttered rural scene, followed by watchful fox* *Cover*
M Rosie the hen went for a walk	*Picture of hen setting out across picturesque farmyard*
A A fox is following her	*with fox eyeing her greedily from under the hen-house*
M Oh!	Rosie the hen went for a walk
M Across the yard	*Picture of hen walking past fruit trees, unaware of fox jumping after her* across the yard
M Boum ****	*Picture of hen walking on unaware while fox bumps his nose on rake he has landed on*
M Around the pond	*Picture of hen walking beside pond, unaware of fox jumping after her.*
A **** fish in the pond	*No fish in picture.* around the pond
A Splash! How they, how the fox just don't get out?	*Picture of hen walking on unaware of fox landing in the pond. No fish in the picture*
M Oh I expect he'll climb out	
A Why?	
M Why will he climb out?	
A Yeah	
M Well, why do you think he'll climb out?	
A Like when he wants, when he, the hen to eat	
M Yes, he wants to eat Rosie	

(Dombey, 1992, pp. 30–31)

Part and parcel of the daily routine in many middle-class households in North America and the UK, and easy to recognise as a distinct kind of social occasion, the bedtime story in many respects seems an ideal focus for examining how adults induct children into specific kinds of literacy practice. Relatively easy to capture and document as a naturally occurring literacy event, study of the bedtime story can lead to a closer understanding of the role social interactions have in enabling young readers to make sense of texts, as well as an examination of the value such practices might have either within specific communities or more generally (Teale and Sulzby, 1986; Heath, 1982).

Dombey opens her analysis with the following observation:

> There are only two sentences in the printed text, but the reading of these is surrounded and interspersed by thirty-nine conversational utterances. These merit examination. They are not an irrelevant distraction, but the means through which Anna takes on the narrative they surround.
>
> (Dombey, 1992, p. 30)

Dombey's commentary highlights the important role given to talk about text in many studies of literacy learning from a literacy as social practice perspective. The talk about text which accompanies the act of reading or writing, or which indeed may also precede or follow it, is seen to play a fundamental role in inducting children into what is meant by literacy in a given context. Talk is one of the main vehicles by which children learn to be literate and enter a shared notion of what literacy is. It provides evidence of the intrinsically social nature of learning and of 'the true direction of the development of thinking ... from the social to the individual' (Vygotsky, 1962, p. 20).

In this instance Dombey argues that the mother–child interaction both structures and makes possible the child's ownership of, and apprenticeship into, a sense of readership closely associated with the kind of text they are perusing. For Dombey, one of the most striking features of the talk is the extent to which the conversational initiative rests with Anna. Yet the child's talk remains sharply bounded and focused within the story world. Neither mother nor child venture far outside the question of 'what will happen next?'. In posing that question together and then answering it, they rely on what they already know about this story, as they read the clues to what will happen next which each picture provides. But this is not a case of recalling in some simple sense the real answer, so much as exploring how the narrative itself plays with that question. Indeed, Dombey points out that the comments mother and child make 'represent the actions and characters as operating in the present, not the past' (Dombey, 1992, p. 33). On each page it becomes possible to ponder what is happening now, and what might happen next, replaying the drama of whether the hen will really escape from the fox this time or not. The finality of the story structure, its fixity, is both known and recognised yet also actively postponed. In this way, Dombey argues, the conversation that takes place in this literacy event reproduces the field of play potentially open to the reader of narrative fiction. Accordingly, the event itself does indeed teach this child what it means to be a (fiction) reader. Mother and daughter converge on the same criteria.

In her analysis, Dombey renders strange the already familiar so that she can examine what this kind of literacy event really teaches its participants. Dombey's analysis shows that the search for meaning rather than the drudgery of decoding or accurate recall lies at the heart of this kind of conversational exchange about texts. She uses this insight to argue for a richer literacy curriculum in school, as well as a wider recognition of the important role talk plays in learning to read (ibid., p. 35). Her answer to the question 'Do such literacy events have a value?' is a pretty straightforward 'yes'.

But whose literacy event is this?
Putting the event in context

Many middle-class communities in North America, the UK, Australia and New Zealand consider the bedtime story to be a crucial part of children's initiation into literacy. But this is by no means true elsewhere. For some researchers, this raises questions about precisely whose way of reading this really is and the terms in which 'good literacy preparation' is being defined here (Gregory, 1996; Heath, 1982). The recognition that the bedtime story is a culturally specific practice, enacted in particular communities, at particular times, with particular effects, strengthens the expectation that other settings and other social domains may yield alternative ways of doing things. The hunt is on for evidence of other kinds of literacy events taking place outside the institutional context of the middle-class home and mainstream schooling, which may be of equal significance for the children who participate in them (Freebody, 2001; Heath, 1983; Williams and Gregory, 1999). This kind of endeavour has resulted in descriptions of much more diverse sets of literacy practices which may seem far less obviously geared to explicitly inducting children into literacy (Maybin and Moss, 1993; Moss, 1993b).

There is a general principle at work in this shift in the focus of research which is worth pausing over. On the one hand, the commitment to seeing literacy as differently shaped in relation to the context in which it is enacted pushes researchers to consider in some detail the particularity of the here and now, and the kind of stance towards literacy which is being constructed (Bloome, 1992). But it also enables researchers to recognise and acknowledge the limits of that particularity: where its writ will run, as it were.

One way of summing up this dual focus quite concisely is to borrow and adapt James Heap's phrase 'What counts as reading?' (Heap, 1991). Heap uses the question 'What counts as reading?' to direct analysis of the means by which children learn to read in specific social settings. For Heap, the question 'What counts as reading?' cannot be decided in the abstract.

Instead, he is quite clear that it can only ever be determined procedurally, by recourse to the social interactions between participants in the particular literacy events which make such judgements visible. From his perspective, it is precisely these forms of social interaction between significant others which induct children into knowing what literacy is by showing them what counts as literacy in this context. For Heap, reading well is always a context-specific achievement.

Borrowing and rephrasing Heap's question as 'What counts as literacy, here?' provides a steer to the study of literacy events in which equal weighting can be given to the examination of participants' interactions, the views of literacy that such interactions validate and the context such interaction is angled towards, which indeed gives it life. As I have argued elsewhere, to know what counts as literacy is therefore also to recognise which setting that version belongs to, and indeed whose version it is (Moss, 1993a; Moss, 1993b). Disentangling what belongs here from what belongs there leads to a review of the relative prestige or social power which accrues to some practices associated with one setting rather than another. It also raises questions about the consequences such different valuations have for children's learning and indeed who is in a position to arbitrate between competing versions of 'what counts as literacy' in any one event (Heath, 1983; Michaels, 1986; Moss, 1993b).

Participating in literacy events both within and across community boundaries

Some of the complexities involved in studying literacy in this way can be demonstrated from a brief look at Shirley Brice Heath's *Ways with Words* (1983). Shirley Brice Heath set out to demonstrate how the contrasting shape and function given to literacy events within three distinct communities in the Appalachians helped create different stances towards literacy learning within those communities. She did this by carefully documenting any moments of social activity between adults and children, or children and their peers, which seemed to show different orientations to the act of reading or writing being created. For Heath this meant throwing the net wide, rather than only looking for explicitly didactic moments when the skills conventionally associated with literacy seemed to be being directly taught. Indeed, comparatively little of her data appears at first sight as if it has very much to do with the acquisition of the skills associated with reading and writing. Instead, her accomplishment as an ethnographer lies precisely in her ability to tease out how the 'ways with words' which are integral to each community, and which provide the backdrop to its uses for literacy, shape the patterns of children's literacy learning within the home and finally impact on or interact with the patterns of literacy learning embedded in the curriculum of the school.

An idea of the scope of her analysis can be gleaned from her treatment of storytelling as a social practice within two of these communities and its relationship to the literacy practices which schools explicitly value. A good deal of her data show how children in the white working-class community of Roadville and the black working-class community of Trackton grow up into very different oral storytelling traditions, through their immersion in the range of social occasions which elicit stories within their communities. Heath argues that these kinds of literacy events induct them into a particular range of communicative strategies and sanctioned story forms. Within Trackton great stress is placed on the verbal dexterity associated with developing and elaborating stories as the occasion demands, often within quickfire conversation where the skill of doing something new or imaginative is duly recognised. By contrast, within Roadville, primacy of place is given to telling factual narratives with a clear moral message. Heath details how this happens through the form of literacy events which encompass storytelling within this community:

> Children in Roadville are not allowed to tell stories, unless an adult announces that something which happened to a child makes a good story and invites a retelling. When children are asked to retell such events they are expected to tell non-fictive stories which 'stick to the truth'. Adults listen carefully and correct children if their facts are not as the adult remembers them. In contrast, fictive stories which are exaggerations of real life events, modelled on plots or characters children meet in story books, are not accepted as stories but as 'lies' without 'a piece of truth'. Children grow up being taught to tell true stories on themselves.
>
> (Heath, 1983, p. 158)

This hard-and-fast line between telling the truth and making things up is challenged in the context of the school, which places a very different value on fictive storytelling through the organisation of the literacy curriculum. In school, the ability to demonstrate an imaginative reaction to fictive storytelling is highly prized, and actively used to develop both the reading and writing curriculum through the choice of materials children are given. For Heath, this disjuncture in approach to storytelling at home and at school has the potential to hamper Roadville children's attempts to catch onto the school literacy curriculum as it develops. She suggests that children from Trackton are similarly excluded from fully participating in school literacy, but for reasons which are almost diametrically opposed. The high value this community places on the ability to elaborate and extemporise in oral discourse does not match with an early years reading curriculum which is geared to teaching children how to follow a given text and stay within its boundaries. In

Heath's account only middle-class children, whose home literacy practices much more closely resemble those encountered in the school environment, will find the transition from home to school easy.

The ethnographic tools Heath employs lead her to argue that under-achievement in literacy amongst children from non-mainstream communities stems from the contrast between their experience of what literacy is and how it works at home and the practices they subsequently encounter in school. In her view, any discontinuities are further compounded by teachers' lack of understanding of what non-mainstream children know about literacy as well as how such knowledge could be valued. Part of her argument is that schools need to be far more alert to the cultural specificity of the literacy practices they themselves employ, and make greater efforts to understand the potentially different repertoires children from other communities may bring to school. In all these respects, *Ways with Words* became a strategic intervention into the 'difference' or 'deficit' debates which dominated educational thinking in the late seventies and early eighties (Rosen, 1988).

Making sense of more than one perspective

Shirley Brice Heath's work significantly expanded the scope and range of what might usefully be considered a literacy event. By redescribing the literacy practices associated with the communities of Roadville and Trackton in their own terms she was able to show how far they diverge from practices more familiar from mainstream settings and at the same time highlight what is at stake when schools privilege some ways of doing literacy over others. Many of the underlying assumptions about the social roots of educational failure to be found in Heath's work are consistent with the analysis of boys' educational underachievement made within the feminist community. In both cases particular emphasis is put on the potential damage caused by a perceived mismatch between the affiliations and experience of a particular social group and the culture of the school.

But in fact there are good reasons for pausing over the terms of this argument. In particular, does such analysis overstate the case for the homogeneity of experience within those communities or social groups which are chosen for study? Put simply, will a boy from Trackton always have more in common with a girl from Trackton than with a boy from Roadville? Will ethnicity always trump either gender or social class in forming a stronger group identity amongst those regarded as excluded from the culture of the school? Or does the strength of any one group allegiance inevitably hide other social fractures which leave their own mark? In a way, the very strength of the feminist argument has been to draw attention to social difference within groups as well as between them. Indeed, my reasons for highlighting Elkjaer and Solsken's work in the previous chapter was precisely because of their insistence on differences within the firm boundaries of subject knowledge, social class and gender.

In Heath's account, adults induct children into the 'ways with words' which are characteristic of a distinct community. The particular version of literacy they acquire arises within and belongs to that setting. But I have argued elsewhere that as they travel from home to school and back again children will always participate in more than one community and come to know more than one set of values (Moss, 2001c). Moreover, even within a given community there are different ways of knowing what to do and how to do it. Adults' induction may be less uniform and coherent than might at first appear, whilst part of children's task may well be to make sense of contradictory and multiple possibilities. This is certainly Solsken's argument. Indeed, Heath's own data provide just such a telling example. Towards the end of the book she reproduces an exchange between two Roadville children in which they consciously reflect upon and manipulate their knowledge of the differences between the rules for 'storytelling' (i.e. making things up) at school, and 'telling stories' (i.e. lying) at home for their own purposes.

Example 2: Storytelling or telling stories?

The following dialogue took place as two children from Roadville travelled home together after a day at school. The actual speech seems to be a direct quotation from field notes, though Heath doesn't comment directly on this. This is the complete episode as quoted in the book. The contextual information included below is presented alongside the extract in Heath (1983).

On the school bus on the way home from school, Wendy had regaled her friends with a tale about how she was going to bring her dog to the end-of-school party. When they got off the bus, Sally ... decided to invoke home-knowledge on her friend.

SALLY: That story, you just told, you know that ain't so.

WENDY: I'm not tellin' no story, uh-er-ah, no I'm tellin' the kind Miss Wash [her teacher] talks about.

SALLY: Mamma won't let you get away with that kinda excuse. You know better.

WENDY: What are you so, uh, excited about. We got one kinda story mamma knows about and a whole 'nother one we do at school. They're different // *looking at Sally*// and you know it=

SALLY: =You better hope mamma knows it, if she catches you making up stuff like that

(Heath, 1983, pp. 294–295)

Heath describes this exchange as 'a rare description of how the girls recognized the differing conventions and moral values home and school attached to stories', before turning on to other matters (ibid., p. 295). I would want to add that it shows that children both assimilate to but also rework and use for their own purposes whatever adults delineate for them. In this instance, the two girls show that they are well aware of the disconti-nuities between home and school versions of what counts as storytelling and what its social value should be. They recognise the respective bound-ary-markers employed and use them to argue against each other. Indeed, Wendy wins herself some space by explicitly playing one version off against another in this exchange with her friend. The discontinuities between home and school as well as the continuities between one setting and another may be just as important in shaping participants' understanding of which version of literacy belongs where.

One possible conclusion to draw from this kind of data is that recogni-tion of difference, rather than similarity, is in fact the norm and that children establish for themselves, and as a matter of routine in social interaction with others, where the boundaries to one kind of practice end and another begin. This suggests a different kind of agenda for research. Before attending to this more closely, however, I want to turn next from literacy events which have been used to understand literacy learning in the home to literacy events which have been used to explore literacy learning in school.

Schools as the arbitrators of what counts as literacy

From a literacy as social practice perspective, the politics of literacy learn-ing hinge around the question of community and which community's ways of doing literacy are both represented and recognised in school. School acts as a gatekeeper, privileging some ways of being literate at the expense of others. The social power schools have to define what counts as literacy is encapsulated in their curricula and in their classroom practice. By deter-mining the pace and sequence in which the component parts of literacy are taught, schools in effect decide who shall get access to which form of literacy, when and under what terms. Indeed, many would argue that the characteristic end result of official schooling is both an increasing special-isation in sanctioned forms of literacy and their uneven distribution (Cazden, 1988). From this kind of analysis schools emerge as a conserva-tive force, largely wedded to maintaining the social status quo as much by virtue of what they determinedly exclude as well as what they include.

Research on literacy learning in schools takes up these points in differ-ent ways. Some studies closely examine how schools rule some forms of literacy in or out (Baker, 1991; Michaels, 1986); others focus more posi-tively on how good teachers and pupils can converge on the same territory or appropriate from each others' repertoire (Dombey, 1988; Mills, 1988; Bourne and Jewitt, 2003). Still others demonstrate how the boundaries to schooled literacy can be contested or redrawn through pupils' own actions whether they take place within the public space of the classroom or at the margins of official events in the less formal contexts provided by peer inter-action (Bloome, 1992; Shuman, 1993; Maybin, 1994; Sola and Bennett, 1994). The next two sections explore some of the methodological issues involved in selecting from the range of literacy events that take place in school and how the choices researchers make in this respect help shape their findings.

Defining what counts as literacy from above

I begin with Carolyn Baker's research on the Australian early years literacy curriculum. Published in an article called 'Literacy Practices and Social Relations in Classroom Reading Events' (Baker, 1991), Baker's interests led her to focus on storybook reading sessions in kindergarten and First Grade classrooms. These are formal literacy events, easily identified as highly structured encounters within the school day. For Baker they represent clear examples of how teachers establish the ground rules for what counts as lit-eracy in school, and marshal children's attention accordingly.

Example 3: Reading *Smarty Pants*

In the following extract from her published data, a kindergarten class are reading a picture book called *Smarty Pants* with their teacher. During this literacy event, the teacher turns over a succession of pages to reveal a series of illustrations which she invites the children to comment upon. In the original article, no further contextual information is given about where the children and teacher are, precisely how big the group is, nor indeed, exactly which text was used. (Its title is recorded, but no other biblio-graphic details are given.)

T: Okay, friends, just turn your eyes to the front cover of this book. First of all, how many of you can tell me what you think this story is going to be about, just by looking at the front cover, Barry?

B: Sma:arty Pa:ants

T: Smarty pants, right. And who is Smarty Pants, do you think? Just by hav-ing a look at him on the front cover. Who do you think he is, Rachel?

R: A clown

T: A cu-lown, right. Well, turn over the front cover until we come to the first page. What can you see on that page? What is he doing, Linda?

L: ((no response)) (3.0)

T: What is he doing? (1.5) Is he standing up like we're standing up? His two feet? What's he doing, Sally Fraser?

S: He's he's he's standing upside down.

T: He's standing upside down. What do you think he's doing that for? What might he be doing?
(Original transcript omitted)

T: What might he be doing, John?

J: A handstand

T: Right. Why do you think he's doing that? (2.0) Why do [you think he's doing a handstand, Kylie?

P: [(I was)

K: Because he's smart

T: Right. Because he's doing a trick or he's being smart. What, what can we see him doing here? What is he doing in this vehicle do you think. Billy?

B: Um he's his he's racing, in it.

T: Right! He's racing in it what sort of a car is it then do you think if he's racing in it, Jennifer?

J: A racing [car

T: [a racing car, okay. Have a look at the next page. What do we see in here Timothy?

TIM: He's driving a racing aeroplane with a dog in the back that doesn't like (...) up in the air

T: He doesn't, how do you know he doesn't like being up in the air?

TIM: Because he, only it doesn't look like, doesn't, the puppy isn't looking very uh

S: Happy

TIM: Happy

T: He's looking rather pale to me! He's sort of thinking we're a bit far up in the air I don't like this very much!

(Baker, 1991)

Like Dombey, Baker's analysis focuses on the talk which accompanies the act of adult and children reading the text together. But whereas in the bedtime story session, which Dombey described above, the child led the conversational exchange, here control rests firmly with the teacher. Baker argues that the primary function of the teacher's talk in this instance is to make clear to the pupils 'what "reading" is taken to be and ... document that "good" or "correct" reading has been achieved' (Baker, 1991, p. 163). The teacher's talk has an explicitly evaluative role. Baker argues that the discursive mechanisms the teacher uses to achieve this end are those familiar from linguistic analysis of classroom discourse more generally. That is to say the discourse is dominated by initiation–response–feedback sequences (or question–answer–evaluation sequences, as Baker calls them) in which the teacher takes the lead and the children follow. The exchange is teacher-driven, and the children fit into the discursive spaces the teacher leaves for them. For pupils, the available space is the space to answer the questions the teacher poses by supplying whatever the teacher already has in mind. Convergence on that space meets with positive evaluation:

T: Why do [you think he's doing a handstand, Kylie?
K: Because he's smart
T: Right. Because he's doing a trick or he's being smart.

Where there is less immediate evidence of convergence, the teacher may rephrase the question, or elicit further responses from other children.

T: What is he doing, Linda?
L: ((no response)) (3.0)
T: What is he doing? (1.5) Is he standing up like we're standing up? His two feet? What's he doing, Sally Fraser?

Part of Baker's argument is that these kinds of discursive structures both establish and reinforce a pattern of social control in which the children yield to the teacher's point of view. This is perhaps to say no more than one might of any such classroom discourse structures. But Baker's real interest is in the work such linguistic features do in relation to the texts which are being shared. What lessons does such a discursive strategy give about read-ing? This takes her in several different directions.

Baker's starting point is that, procedurally, 'what counts as reading' is being decided by the teacher, in and through the ways in which the con-versational interaction with the pupils is conducted. The teacher in effect controls and mediates what the children will make of the text. She does so by the ways in which she paces the group's discursive process through the book: pages are turned only after the required responses to each teacher question have been made. And by the strategies she uses to ensure they fol-low her conversational lead: whilst they are free to look at the pictures the teacher's questions and evaluative responses signal what is actually deemed salient on each page. Teacher control over the talk ensures pupils learn to look at the text through her eyes. The teacher's talk about the text makes the text what it will be, in effect closing down its meaning potential.

To establish this point more fully, Baker homes in on the kinds of ques-tions the teacher asks. Of particular interest to Baker are the predominance of 'wh' questions posed by the teacher: What?, Who?, Where? These lead to the sanctioning of single 'right' answers, which are treated as self-evident matters of fact. For the pupils, the multiple possibili-ties of responding to such a text are pared down to finding the answer the teacher has in mind. By fully endorsing only the one answer amongst the many, the teacher turns the fictional text into a repository of apparently factually correct information, which the children must find by 'just look-ing'. The information is self-evidently there, if only they can put their finger on it. Baker comments: 'The fictional story is thus colonised by the reading practices of the information paradigm' (ibid., p. 171). This is one of the lessons about reading which she argues this literacy event provides.

In this event, the right afforded the teacher to pose the questions and adjudicate when they have been sufficiently well answered also sets up another discursive contrast: between the provisionality of the answers the children are expected to offer and the finality of the judgement about their aptness which the teacher makes. In this respect the children are perennially positioned as novice readers of the text, making uncertain judgements based only on the particular segment of the text they are being shown now. The provisionality and uncertainty of the pupil responses contrasts with the authority of the teacher to know things absolutely. The event therefore also endorses a disequilibrium of knowledge. The children are construed as knowing less, the conversational position they occupy being that of good guessers. Baker comments that the discourse which accompanies the reading of child-appropriate texts therefore marks out 'not only the superior knowledge of the teacher, but the students' difference and distance from adult culture and adult knowledge' (ibid., p. 174). The adult-sponsored talk both creates and sustains the subject position of a (tentative) child reader.

The conclusions Baker comes to about 'What counts as reading here?' leave little room for pupil agency in the face of overwhelming teacher control. Both the choice of this event and the analysis of the social interactions which take place within it lead to a view of school literacy as powerfully normative and hard to resist: there is no space in this encounter for pupils to contest the teacher's reading or offer up their own. In Baker's account, schools come to stand as an institutional mechanism for endorsing a single authoritative view of the text which will brook no opposition. This leads her on to argue for a different kind of pedagogy which would indeed create room for more critical and divergent responses. If the focus on a single type of well-orchestrated literacy event is integral to establishing this position, then by choosing a different kind of event a different picture of schools as a site for literacy learning can emerge.

Renegotiating what counts as literacy from below

In contrast to Baker, Janet Maybin set out to document children's informal talk in British primary school settings. The literacy events she captured were incidental to this project, rather than its main aim. In much of the published data she eschews the kind of formally orchestrated literacy events characteristic of whole-class settings which Baker chose in favour of events with a looser structure which mainly take place in small group settings (Maybin, 2006). In many cases the written texts involved are worksheets, which children are expected to work through independently in order to complete tasks the teacher has set. This kind of activity provides the context for talk which is both on and off task (Dyson, 2003). The texts weave their way into this on-going stream of talk.

Example 4: *'He's got thousands of teeth'*

The extract below was collected from a class of ten-year-olds who were working in small groups. Some of the class had just returned from a scavenging hunt in the playground. The class teacher was moving around the room from group to group. The group Maybin was taping consisted of three children, Julie, Kirsty and Sharon, and a parent helper, Mrs Reilly. Mrs Reilly and Kirsty had brought a book on snails back from the library to the classroom. They joined Sharon and Julie who were preparing to display the snail the group had found out in the playground. During the course of this event Julie also talked to a pupil in another group who was doing a word puzzle. No further details are provided about the texts in use.

JULIE:	I'll just write 'This was drawn by bla, bla, bla'
KIRSTY:	It's got thousands of teeth {reads} 'Its long tongue is covered with thousands of tiny teeth.' He's got thousands of teeth.
JULIE:	He has, he's got thousands of teeth, that little snail has
SHARON:	Look at its trail {teacher comes over}
JULIE:	Miss, it's got hundreds and … it's got thousands and thousands of teeth/
KIRSTY:	/on its long tongue
TEACHER:	It's got what?
KIRSTY:	Thousands of teeth. It says here.
MRS REILLY:	Those are tentacles. It's got four tentacles.
JULIE:	Yea, teeth, teeth.
MRS REILLY:	{Reads} 'to touch, feel and smell, and it breathes through [the hole in its side.'
JULIE:	[Teeth
MRS REILLY:	So there must be a hole somewhere
JULIE:	eat {a suggestion to the pupil doing the word puzzle}*
MRS REILLY:	We saw its eyes, didn't we? At the end of its tentacles and it can only see light and dark
JULIE:	tune {to the same pupil}*
PUPIL:	It can only be three letters/
JULIE:	/{reads} 'or more'. Three letters or more
KIRSTY:	Miss, it's got a thousand, thousands of teeth on its tongue
SHARON:	Yes, cause we went into the library, Mrs Reilly and Kirsty went into the library to look it up
TEACHER:	What's that, the snail?
SHARON:	Yea
PUPIL:	Miss, where's the sellotape?

SHARON: And it breathes through its side
KIRSTY: It breathes [through its side
SHARON: [It's got this little hole/
KIRSTY: /It breathes through a hole in its side

(Maybin, 1994)

{* additional contextual comments added here}

Maybin (2006) describes this event as part of the pattern of overlapping classroom activity known as topic work, which at the time the data was collected was a characteristic feature of the organisation of British primary schools. In effect, the setting is multidimensional. The teacher is circulating the room, dealing with the demands of different pupils, whilst the groups themselves are busy on a number of tasks, conducted simultaneously. Even within the single group, Mrs Reilly and Kirsty are dealing with the library book; Julie is alternately writing a card for the group's display, listening to the readers, and talking to another pupil doing a different activity; whilst Sharon is observing the snail as well as listening to the readers. All three pupils take turns competing for the teacher's attention as she moves nearer where they are sitting.

This literacy event looks very different from the formally orchestrated encounters between teachers and pupils which Baker documents. There is a far less ordered approach to the texts in use. Attention chops and changes, as one voice is superseded by another. Indeed, Maybin uses this example to highlight the provisionality of informal dialogue and the meanings and knowledge constructed within it, as well as point to the struggle over authoritative discourse which she sees as symptomatic of children's relationship to the adult world (Maybin, 2006).

A key theme in her work is the way in which individuals borrow from others' speech, often directly quoting or revoicing others' words, and in the process reformulating what they mean. She uses the extract to demonstrate how different participants in this literacy event appropriate the language of the text for different purposes. Maybin argues that Mrs Reilly uses the language of the library book as a means of trying to steer the children's unfolding activity into something that might look like purposeful educational enquiry in this context. That is to say, she takes the text and the information it contains as her starting point, and then sets out to relate the contents of the text to the actual snail the children have in front of them. Accordingly, she reads aloud part of the text and borrows its language as she encourages the children to look for the features the text identifies as salient.

MRS REILLY: Those are tentacles. It's got four tentacles.
JULIE: Yea, teeth, teeth.
MRS REILLY: {Reads} 'to touch, feel and smell, and it breathes through
              [the hole in its side.'

JULIE:	[Teeth
MRS REILLY:	So there must be a hole somewhere
JULIE:	eat {a suggestion to the pupil doing the word puzzle}*
MRS REILLY:	We saw its eyes, didn't we? At the end of its tentacles and it can only see light and dark

(Maybin, 1994)

The children use the text as a different kind of reference point. Kirsty alights on a single sentence in the book which explains that the snail has thousands of little teeth on its tongue. She summarises this information as 'He's got thousands of teeth' and announces this fact to the rest of the group, both before and after reading the relevant sentence aloud. 'Thousands of teeth' then becomes a newsworthy piece of information in its own right, which is exclaimed over and passed on within the small group. It also becomes a way of attracting teacher attention: Julie calls the teacher over to tell her what they've found out, treating the information as a matter for public display. In the conversation with the teacher the children also seem to use what they've found out as a means of demonstrating how hard they have been working. Laying claim to information in this way establishes their credentials as good pupils. The value of this kind of knowledge relay in this context is shown by the way they compete amongst themselves to get the most newsworthy bits of information to the teacher first.

KIRSTY:	Miss, it's got a thousand, thousands of teeth on its tongue
SHARON:	Yes, cause we went into the library, Mrs Reilly and Kirsty went into the library to look it up
TEACHER:	What's that, the snail?
SHARON:	Yea
PUPIL:	Miss, where's the sellotape?
SHARON:	And it breathes through its side

(Ibid.)

Where Baker's data seem to represent well-marshalled convergence on a single way of doing reading, this event demonstrates different versions of what counts as literacy, running side by side in the same setting. In part, this is because the kind of discursive strategies the teacher in Baker's data used to marshal attention to and win consent for her point of view are absent from Mrs Reilly's talk, perhaps reflecting both the latter's uncertain status in the classroom as parent helper, and the more informal context in which this interaction takes place. But even when the teacher hoves into view the relative status of these different versions of what counts as reading is not settled. Amongst these participants what counts as literacy looks much more contingent, dependent on the immediate social interactions and the way they pan out. And in this event there is no moment of closure or resolution in which one version wins out over others.

Structure and agency in the classroom

Baker and Maybin focus on different kinds of literacy events. In her analysis, Baker represents a teacher-directed storybook session as the means of enfolding children into a selective, authoritative and ideological world-view which relentlessly positions the pupils in relation to the text. By contrast, Maybin represents more informal talk about texts as a means of contesting and struggling over others' discourse, including the language of the text itself, in a context where there is always more than one voice present, waiting to be differently mobilised. In some respects their very different analyses of ways of doing literacy in school can be read as a political disagreement in which these authors either prioritise social reproduction or social agency, homing in respectively on the mechanisms which deliver social conformity or on the spaces which remain to voice alternative points of view. Yet Baker and Maybin's data are not necessarily incompatible. Nor do they need to cancel each other out. In their divergence they represent equally valid impulses in the social structuring of school.

Indeed, although their respective analyses give a different weighting to one over the other, structure and agency are both there in each of the two episodes quoted above. Thus towards the end of the interchange Baker quotes from, the teacher prompts the class about the vehicle Smarty Pants is pictured driving until she elicits the noun phrase 'a racing car', from Jennifer, at which point she turns the storybook page and poses the next question, 'What do we see in here?' In answering this next question, Timothy picks up and adapts Jennifer's phrase:

> He's driving a *racing aeroplane* with a dog in the back that doesn't like (...) up in the air
>
> (Baker, 1991, p. 171. My italics)

By modelling his answer on Jennifer's, he generates a new noun phrase 'racing aeroplane', before going on to add his own commentary about the dog. In the real time social interaction, the teacher overlooks the expression 'racing aeroplane' to pursue another line of enquiry, as does Baker later in her commentary. Yet Timothy's answer shows an active appropriation and refashioning of the teacher's discourse into something new. There is agency here. Equally, in Maybin's account the space in which the girls jostle over different versions of what it means to be literate is itself an established part of the school structure. Although they may use the information text in a different way from the parent helper, they do so in order to demonstrate to the teacher what they understand by 'working well' within the school's structural constraints.

Conclusion: resetting the agenda for research into gender and literacy

In one sense literacy as social practice perspectives are quite right to identify schools as uniquely powerful cultural institutions, able to privilege certain forms of literacy at the expense of others. Yet different ways of being literate persist. To understand how this can be, it is not enough to polarise school and community as if each were the guarantor of only one way of doing literacy that belongs wholly to one group and not another. There are differences within, as well as between, communities. And individuals both encounter and appropriate competing versions of what it means to read or to write, across as well as within many different settings. It follows that in any literacy event participants may well have to negotiate over what will count as literacy this time round even as the interaction proceeds. A good deal therefore depends not only on who is in a position to judge between competing versions this time round, but also on what others make of how that judgement is exercised. For the same lessons are not necessarily learnt about where or how the boundary to a practice should be fixed, as the argument between the two Roadville girls quoted earlier makes clear.

Judith Solsken's work on gender and literacy has a particularly important contribution to make here (Solsken, 1993). Her research differs markedly from others within the literacy as social practice tradition by explicitly documenting different ways of reacting to a range of literacy practices within the same community. Her argument is not about the inclusion or exclusion of one community's way of doing literacy within schooled settings, but rather about how participants deal with the conflicts between different practices which resonate in the same setting. In her work, therefore, gender does not substitute for community, redrawing the line around a different homogeneous practice. Rather, distinctions made round gender interact with distinctions made about literacy as part of an on-going process which is not fully resolved. This represents a different way of thinking about structure and agency and the relationship between home and school (Moss, 2002b).

To take these issues forward, this book will use the concept of the literacy event to examine in more detail how 'what counts as literacy' is defined in school. Rather than expect the school to operate as a single homogeneous site, geared to privileging only one kind of literacy practice, this book will look for evidence of how different versions of literacy manifest themselves within this setting. It will consider how boundaries between practices are perceived and managed by pupils and teachers. Gender-differentiation will be sought at this level, as children appropriate and rework the resources they have at their disposal.

3

LITERACY EVENTS IN THE CONTEXT OF THE SCHOOL

Rethinking how literacy, gender and attainment intertwine

Introduction

This chapter sets out to document 'what counts as literacy' for 7–9-year-olds in the context of the British primary school. The focus is on reading rather than writing. The chapter draws on research conducted over a two-year period in six classes in four different schools, using a range of ethnographic research tools. Collected immediately before the introduction of the National Literacy Strategy in England, the data captures a particular moment in time. Yet the characteristic features here identified in the social organisation of literacy over the school day persist, and continue to structure relations between different aspects of 'what counts as literacy' in British schools. The chapter will argue that the distinctions observed in play have a profound impact on setting the terms of the relationship between gender and literacy. They also help explain why boys' performance in literacy seems particularly sharply polarised between those who do well and those who do not. But not in the sense that one might most immediately expect. The crucial distinctions that schools make about 'what counts as literacy' are not in themselves constructed with reference to gender. The literacy curriculum is primarily geared to making fine distinctions between students based on their relative proficiency as readers and writers. Gender and literacy intertwine here as boys and girls struggle to make sense of the social positions they come to occupy in a hierarchy of skills which is both externally imposed and made highly visible through schooling.

Rethinking the terms of the debate: is inclusion crucial to understanding the development of literacy practices in school?

When boys' attainment in literacy emerged as a key topic in the 1990s some of the immediate explanations put forward as to why their performance might be weaker than girls' revolved around the potential lack of fit between boys' own interests and the content of the English curriculum.

One of the most frequent ways in which such a lack of fit was expressed was in terms of the absence of non-fiction texts from the literacy curriculum. The predominance of narrative texts as the main vehicle for teaching literacy, particularly in the early years, and the association of these texts with imagined or personal responses was contrasted with boys' presumed interests in non-fiction and the accumulation of impersonal information from such texts. Boys were repositioned as excluded from the literacy curriculum in these terms and the under-representation of their preferred genre then seemed to offer an explanation for why boys might do less well (Millard, 1997).

Boys' preference for non-fiction seemed to be borne out in the available quantitative data on children's reading, which showed marked differences in girls' and boys' choice of reading material, the time they spent on reading, and their attitude towards that activity as well as their attainment (Barrs, 1993). Having identified an explanation for boys' underachievement, the proposed remedy was to introduce more non-fiction to the curriculum thus re-balancing the potential advantages which might accrue from focusing on one kind of text rather than another. In some quarters it was argued that such a switch away from narrative would benefit girls too by ensuring that they also gained access to the more socially powerful genres which non-fiction symbolised (Martin, 1985).

Look more closely at the explanation though, and a number of problems arise. Such perspectives treat differences in genre preferences between boys and girls as a given, and ask few questions about why or how such preferences develop. Instead, genre preferences are understood as an expression of gendered identities which already exist fully fledged and largely independent of the social contexts in which literacy learning takes place. Once in place such preferences then predispose the child to take more or less from the literacy curriculum. So the argument goes. Yet this assumption hinges on the notions that the contrast between fiction and non-fiction texts is self-evident and their association with either male or female readers straightforward.

In fact, at the level of content such contrasts are often painted in the most stereotypic terms: narrative fiction stands for the (feminine) world of affect; non-fiction stands for a functional (and masculine) world of hard facts devoid of emotions. Yet much of the non-fiction that sustains the adult market is actually structured as a prose argument, which takes a stance, and engages the reader with that position, rather than reciting a list of indisputable truths. Whilst the news is almost entirely sustained by narrative structures, as are the 'true stories' which populate women's magazines. In addition, an increasing quantity of non-fiction revolves around visual rather than verbal text, thereby primarily using the spatial resource of the page, rather than the linear resource of written language, to achieve its effect (Kress, 2003). Take these conflicting characteristics together and it is hard to see quite what criteria are really being invoked when non-fiction is cast as intrinsically masculine or its forms as inherently more powerful.

The assumptions that boys prefer non-fiction and that we know what kinds of non-fiction these are begin to look more like empty stereotyping. Even if taken at face value, there is little attempt to track where such a different orientation to ways of making sense of the world might emerge. At best, boys' preference for non-fiction is assumed to be created by young boys modelling their genre preferences on the reading tastes of their fathers (assumed to be non-fiction) and against the reading tastes of their mothers (assumed to be fiction). There are few attempts to check how far these assumptions actually represent what children see and understand about adult readers. Certainly data collected as part of this research in the form of parental questionnaires or as photographs that children in each case-study site were invited to take of reading in the home, showed a much less clear-cut picture (see Moss, 2001a for a detailed account of the children's photographs). Many of the women who filled out the questionnaire reported that they were mainly reading for study as they pursued better qualifications. Whilst children's pictures of adults reading at home often showed both men and women hunkered down with the newspaper. In fact, regardless of the text in question, the pictures mainly seemed to demonstrate that when adults read to themselves their attention does not waiver or become easily engaged elsewhere. Readers are absorbed in a way that puts others at a distance. Children seemed to understand this through the shots they composed (ibid., 2001a, p. 287). Returning to the quantitative data with these points in mind, it becomes clear that only a small minority of boys and girls claim to prefer reading non-fiction over fiction anyway. Boys just form a larger percentage of that minority than girls making the same choice (Hall and Coles, 1999).

One of the consequences of so confidently naming non-fiction, or indeed any other topic such as competence in new technologies, as the area where the greatest mismatch between community and school resources lies is that other kinds of questions about the potential causes of boys' underachievement in literacy then disappear from sight (Rowan *et al.*, 2002): not least, questions about the social organisation of the existing literacy curriculum in school and its impact, rather than what is presumed to be missing from its content. It is with the social organisation of literacy in school that this chapter begins.

The literacy event as a methodological tool: putting texts, contexts and readers in the picture

The research this chapter draws on began with a remit to explore the emergence of children's genre preferences, how they might materialise within school settings as well as at home, and what their salience might be for boys' development as readers. This influenced the way in which the concept of the literacy event was theorised and applied as a methodological tool.

The exploration of variation in literacy practices linked to text type rather than community membership or social setting is relatively rare in literacy as social practice research (Moss, 1996; Moss, 2003b). It is more prevalent as an organising principle in audience studies where the fan base for particular kinds of texts and the texts themselves are a more common object of study (Moss, 1993a; 1993b). Although the research here began with an interest in exploring how specific texts might be linked to specific practices, it left open the question of which kinds of texts might prove decisive for whom. Rather than set the parameters to the enquiry by focusing in on just non-fiction, or the range of texts represented on the reading curriculum, or even the kinds of texts children chose for themselves, the enquiry instead set out to map which kinds of texts got into which kinds of contexts for which kinds of readers over the course of the school day (Moss and Attar, 1999). What were the salient distinctions participants made between the range of texts they had access to? As a means of tracking this, literacy events were always treated as consisting of these three elements: a text, a reader and a social setting in which that reading took place. The different possible kinds of combinations of texts, readers and contexts observed were then analysed to identify salient contrasts between them.

To map the distinctions that participants themselves made in each of the classrooms that we visited, fellow researcher Dena Attar and I paid attention to the salient attributes of the texts, the context and the readers which were highlighted during the course of each literacy event through the participants' own words and actions. One of the points to emerge quite fast was that the teachers in the classes we observed made clear distinctions between different kinds of literacy events, and that at least at the beginning of the school year they made it part of their business to explain directly to pupils which texts were expected to be used in which contexts by whom as well as what should be done with them there. This was an expected part of inducting children into their classroom's routine. In a way we entered the classrooms alongside the pupils and set out to acquire the same kind of knowledge of 'what counts as literacy here'.

Literacy events in school: tracking combinations of texts, contexts and readers

So as not to prejudge which kinds of texts might be most germane to establishing literacy as a gender-differentiated practice, the research documented the full range of texts which came into use during the school day in each of the case-study classrooms. The texts documented included writing on noticeboards, letters being sent home, pictures children had clipped out or drawn and were circulating amongst themselves, as well as the many print texts supplied by teachers to keep the work of the class going. (At the time the data were recorded there was comparatively little use of electronic media, including computers, in any of the classrooms. Nonetheless, media texts were certainly included in the study when they appeared.) Field notes recorded literacy events by identifying which kind of text was being used, with which kind of reader, in which kind of context, and what was being done. Some of the literacy events documented in this way took place as part of the official curriculum; others happened more informally.

Recording texts

As far as the texts were concerned, texts in use were initially logged by recording publication details (title, author, date) if they were available; and by noting the time and place in which the texts were used by whom. Samples of texts supplied for classroom distribution were collected, especially if they were worksheets or letters. More ephemeral texts such as writing on blackboards or flip charts were copied into field notes. As it became apparent that there were many more texts in classrooms than found their way into literacy events, the research team began to pay attention to the larger range of texts that were potentially available as well as those that were observed in use. A variety of audit techniques were used to record them. This included taking photographs of the places where texts were stored or displayed in class. As a result the researchers began to realise that the different places texts were stored in themselves signalled salient distinctions between the texts and their anticipated use (see Chapter 5). Classrooms routinely sort and label texts. Often they did so in ways we hadn't anticipated. For instance, participants regularly distinguished between texts in a terminology that seemed particular to schools, and drew attention to the function of particular texts in that setting. The home-reading book, the worksheet, and the class library are all good examples of this. In the first phase of the research, the researchers privileged the language in use by the participants over other possible ways of grouping and sorting texts that belong to other settings.

Recording readers

As far as readers were concerned, the researchers began by logging which individuals used which texts but also noted how those readers were designated for the duration of the literacy event and the role that designated participants were expected to follow. In many classes, for instance, children would be ability-sorted for particular literacy events. Pupils assigned different ability labels would then get different texts to work with and would sometimes be asked to use those texts in different ways. Some such groups might also relocate to a different part of the classroom or even the school and work with a different teacher or helper. In this instance, the ability label seemed to take precedence in shaping the rest of the event and the resources in use within it. By contrast, in other settings readers would be positioned quite differently. For instance, at the beginning of a lesson or during story time teachers would often read a specific text aloud to the whole class, expecting them all to show their active participation in the event in the same way, by listening attentively without fidgeting or inter-rupting except when asked. The pupils 'read' the text by paying attention to the teacher's voice. Different events were predicated on a different view of what is required from the readers and who can perform that role in rela-tion to which resources. The researchers noted how readers were positioned in each interaction. This was recorded in the field notes.

Recording contexts

As far as the social context was concerned, the researchers noted the imme-diate physical setting for the text's use (which part of the classroom the text appeared or was deployed in) as well as the discursive context for the liter-acy event. The discursive context included the information participants used to recognise what kind of event this was and what kind of activity would therefore follow. At its simplest this might mean noting down the way a particular literacy event was referred to, for instance, quiet reading time, or in the case of some events the way in which the curriculum slots, where they occurred, were labelled. For instance, there were different ways of dealing with texts during assembly rather than in Maths. Field notes recorded the kind of ground rules about how the event would proceed which those taking part seemed to share, and the criteria participants drew on to establish whether such events had happened well.

These procedures for tracking literacy events and their component parts were developed and refined over time in relation to the four schools and the six classrooms where the research was conducted. (See the analytic matrix in Appendix 1, pp. 200–201.) In addition to the observations recorded in field notes and the various ways of documenting the texts themselves, some typical literacy events were also taped. This made the talk which accompanied the activity and which seemed part and parcel of the social organisation of these events available for analysis.

Sometimes the forms of knowledge participants drew on in the course of particular events were made quite explicit in classroom interactions; some-times they remained implicit. The researchers were alert to both possibilities. To take one example, at the beginning of the year in Bluebird School, the teacher explicitly inducted the Year 3 class being observed into the structured way of organising reading time known in that school as 'Everybody Reading In Class' (ERIC). For this group this involved a carousel of activities: teacher reads to whole class; children read in pairs; children read in small groups; children read silently on their own; children read non-fiction. These took place over the week. All of this was new to the class so, turn by turn, the teacher explained the routines which would allow this kind of activity to happen later on in the year with a minimum of teacher intervention. This involved knowing which books you should be using when and where, how to get and return them to the same place, and what the expectations were about what to do with them: whether children should listen or read aloud, take turns or work on their own and so on.

Whilst I and they learnt about this together, I also observed things happening which no-one had spoken about, but which everyone else seemed to understand already and to expect. The child who left the classroom without asking and returned about ten minutes later with a book I hadn't seen her with before turned out to be returning a reading scheme book to the place outside the classroom where they were kept and picking up another one, a routine already familiar to her from a previous year. Asking what she had been doing revealed the connections between text, context and reader made in this instance. In effect this was routine knowledge already embedded in this setting. The researcher's job was to track both the spoken and unspoken assumptions about which resources belonged in which setting and what would therefore be done with them. The research proceeded on the basis that cultural meanings are often embedded in the fabric of the event and the resources it garners within it, rather than fully articulated. To this end, the classroom observations were complemented by both formal and informal interviews with participants.

Using the language of the researched to see what they see

The research process generated detailed accounts of individual literacy events which included details of the text involved, who its readers were and the context in which the reading took place. The language participants themselves used to describe particular aspects of the events they were involved in and/or the resources they deployed provided an important starting point.

For instance, one of the research activities which the team instigated at the start of the research was to try and log who was reading what during quiet reading time. Whatever this activity was called and the precise way in which it took place, sooner or later in each school site children would be given the opportunity to freely choose from a range of books in class which they could settle down to read to themselves. During this time the researchers would frantically circulate, trying to jot down the individual titles particular readers had chosen. The logic of the exercise was to find out if more boys than girls were reading non-fiction at these times. In fact, what frequently happened was that the researcher would approach a particular child with the question 'What are you reading?', at which point the child would put down their book and go and find, or gather up, a different text altogether, with the words, 'I'm reading this.' What they were showing us was a distinct category of text, known on the ground as their reading book.

In school a reading book has a precise definition, not in terms of the type of book it is, but in terms of the contexts it is associated with. It can be fiction or non-fiction (though we documented far fewer of the latter in this role, and those almost exclusively from reading schemes). It can come from home, or from the school or class library, or from reading stock designated for this specific purpose (schools varied, with some restricting what could count as a reading book more than others, and for a smaller or larger percentage of their pupils). It is meant to travel home, though it may not necessarily be read there (schools differed in their expectations on this point, as did parents and children in their willingness to undertake this task). But the child absolutely must have it when an adult in authority asks him or her to read aloud, be they classroom helper, parent or teacher. Moreover, to enable such an event to pass off successfully in school, the book has to be seen to match the reader's perceived level of proficiency. Those who struggle to read their 'reading book' on the appointed occasion can be interrupted mid-text and sent off to change it for another one more closely matched to their ability. Reading aloud to a figure of authority in this kind of context leads to a public evaluation of reading competence. This is signalled by the way in which such judgements are noted down in the 'home reading record book' (the document the child uses to log the book they are reading), and in the teacher's records.

The following example of the reading book in use comes from field notes. A child is reading to a parent helper in an area adjacent to the main classroom where the rest of the class are working on a science topic. She is taking her turn to read aloud before another child is called to take her place. The book she has brought with her is a large hardback picture book called *Mr and Mrs Pig's Evening Out* (Rayner, 1976), which had been chosen from the class library. The incident was recorded in the field notes like this:

Example 1

> 10.15 Mini-link area outside classroom
> Parent (?) helper with girl. She has *Mr and Mrs Pig's Evening Out*. Helper sitting quietly correcting the words as the girl makes mistakes. The girl doesn't look up from the book but just keeps on going. The helper has asked her to stop and is writing on the sheet. The girl puts the book away and helper says 'Can I have your home reading book to just write in darling?' She writes in her comments whilst girl sits quietly. 'Well done, Ella. Next? Um Nadia?'
> (Bluebird, Year 3)

The use of the text in this context is tuned to the judgement which will be made of the reader's proficiency. The adult keeps the child long enough to form a judgement on her reading and then record it. Both child and adult understand what this event is for and orientate to it accordingly.

Moving beyond the language of the researched

In the account given above, the categorisation employed at local level for a particular kind of book ('the reading book') led the researchers to identify and follow these texts into their designated contexts of use, noting the social relations between participants embedded in those contexts, the kinds of activity they were associated with, and finally the particular orientation towards literacy those events produced.

The particular role the reading book plays is signalled by the textual company it keeps (the public record of its reader's proficiency which accompanies it from one context of use to another); by the structuring of the events it finds its way into; and by the roles allotted to participants there. Its distinctive character is underscored by the way in which it is (temporarily) stored separately from other texts, too. Reading books travel from place to place in pupil book-bags. This helps emphasise their peculiar status. Reading books are always linked to judgements about an individual reader's competence. This role takes precedence. Thus in the example quoted above, a text categorised and stored as a picture book in the library becomes a reading book by virtue of its introduction into a proficiency context.

Because reading books help define their reader's proficiency at reading, the researchers named the literacy events which produced and confirmed the peculiar status of the reading book 'proficiency encounters' and the orientation towards literacy which such encounters embodied 'reading for proficiency'. In effect, this meant going beyond the participant's language to find new ways of describing the inner logic which made such events cohere. This is consistent with Bernstein's definition of languages of description and their role in theory building (Bernstein, 1996; see Moss, 2003a for more detailed commentary on this point).

Different ways of reading in school

From tracking how the range of available texts were mobilised in classroom settings, it soon became apparent that teachers marked out and choreographed different kinds of literacy events through their designation of the appropriate use of space, time and resources. Movement from one part of the room to another – from the mat to the tables, for instance – would signal a different order of social relations, a different conceptual take on the task in hand, and a different focus for activity. Observations of this kind showed that there was not just one single school literacy being constructed in these classrooms but, rather different versions of 'what counts as literacy here', whose context-specific patterns participants seemed to recognise and then use to steer their own actions accordingly.

Analysis of the data suggested that what happened where, when and how was more dependent on the immediate context and the resources it provided participants with than any over-arching set of beliefs and values which individual teachers might bring to their classrooms. (In fact, in interview teachers' accounts of their own values and beliefs in teaching reading seldom matched the balance of their practice as documented by the researchers.)

This grounding of practice in the contingencies of the classroom and its resources was in many ways exemplified by the ways in which teachers introduced pupils into the routine sequence and choreography of the literacy events which typified their practice. Children would be given an explicit set of instructions to follow and know, rather than an explicit set of values they were meant to adopt. The values remained embedded within the ways things worked.

Focusing in on school literacy in this way led to the identification of three different ways of doing reading routinely invoked in classrooms, each with its own distinct set of ground rules. The research team called these: 'reading for proficiency' – where how well the child reads is of prime importance; 'reading for choice' – where what gets read matters most; and 'procedural reading' – where reading is not considered an end in itself but is incidental to accomplishing something else. Evidence for these different ways of doing reading and being a reader could be found in each of the case-study sites.

Of these three ways of reading, only two – reading for choice, and reading for proficiency – would generally be recognised as part of the reading curriculum. The third way of reading – procedural reading – was seldom the focus for explicit reflection on the part of either teachers or pupils, and was mainly associated with other areas of the curriculum or aspects of the work of the classroom.

Defining three ways of reading in school

Reading for proficiency, reading for choice, and procedural reading group together literacy events which seem to be driven by the same set of underlying principles. They can be defined like this:

Reading for proficiency

Whilst such encounters could take place in a variety of settings (home, school), involve a variety of participants in the role of assessor (parent,

parent helper, classroom assistant, teacher) and include pupils designated poor or able readers; whilst they might encompass a wide range of texts, elicit different kinds of attention from the assessor, and generate different kinds of questions for the reader (focusing on decoding skills, comprehension, or even enjoyment) at heart, what united these different kinds of performance was an emphasis on the evaluation of individual competence. This clearly framed reading as publicly assessed work for which the individual can absolutely be held to account in contexts where relations between reader and listener are unequal. Whatever the criteria in play, judgements about the individual reader's proficiency would be passed. It is hard to think of any other area of the curriculum where such sharply individualised judgements are routinely made about pupils on the basis of a particular performance. There is a kind of calling to account here which simply does not happen anywhere else.

Reading for choice

Whilst proficiency encounters emphasise the relative competence of individual readers and the progress they make in their reading, reading for choice slots emphasise the range of texts available, and link reading to notions of enjoyment. The act of selecting this text rather than that becomes much more salient, and is construed as evidence of the readers' personal motivation and investment in the content of the text. Sometimes teachers make these kinds of choices on behalf of their pupils; more often pupils are expected to make them for themselves. Even though schools varied considerably in terms of the number and range of texts which were available to choose from, the research data showed that children consistently gained access to a greater variety of texts at these times. These might include fiction or non-fiction, predominantly verbal or predominantly visual texts, ephemera such as magazines or newspapers, as well as children's own writing. Reading for choice slots also gave children greatest freedom over what to do with the texts they had chosen: share with a friend, read in a group, listen to story tapes or even use the texts to play games. In many respects reading for choice slots seemed to operate as 'time out' from the disciplined working practices of the rest of the school curriculum. Often children were engaged in directing this activity for themselves. Provided children kept to the general rules for classroom behaviour, teacher monitoring of what had gone on was light. Criteria for assessing the outcome of such activity were often diffuse and predicated on levels of personal engagement and enjoyment rather than any more concrete end product. (The ebb and flow of activity in the book corner documented in the episode in the field notes below becomes justifiable in this way.)

In classrooms most reading for choice slots happened as part of the literacy curriculum and would be explicitly planned as such. At Bluebird

School part of the literacy curriculum was organised as a carousel of activities known locally as ERIC (Everybody Reading In Class). Each of the other schools programmed in 'quiet reading time' as a daily slot on the curriculum when children were expected to read on their own. But 'reading for choice' might also take the shape of relatively unplanned opportunities to read which happened during the day. For instance, when classes were finishing off work they had been set by the teacher, those who finished first would generally be allowed to browse the class library or read to themselves before their peers finished too. The researchers also included as 'reading for choice' those moments when the teacher read aloud to the class not as the prelude to some other task, such as answering comprehension questions or writing a story, but as an end in itself.

The extract from field notes below exemplifies this variety. It encompasses two literacy events which took place towards the end of the school day and began as the class started to finish some Maths work:

Example 2

MATHS, TABLES

Harold's finished – told he can sit in the book corner. Harold asks 'Can I listen to a tape?'

Martin and Terence in book corner too. Terence's looking through books right in the corner – takes picture book and flicks through. Does this with several books ...

2.45 Sam and Terence now putting headphones on too. Jim and Peter looking through football magazines. Jim annoyed that Terence had headphones he wanted – gets them somehow. Terence goes back to going through picture books. Colin has a picture book too, sitting next to Terence. Peter's taken *Players* to his desk ...

2.55 Peter's returned *Players*, has football sticker album.

3.00 In book corner and around the classroom: two football texts shared between four boys, plus one football text with one boy.

Catherine, Suzy and Lynne are talking, starting up a unison recitation with a finger-clicking introduction. Organised by Catherine ...

3.03 Class all in book corner except for 3 girls and 3 boys finishing maths work ...

STORY TIME, CARPET

Teacher has book on lap: *Roald Dahl*, [Chris Powling (1997) Evans Profiles Series].

Teacher: 'We read some historical fiction – extraordinary story called *Death of a City*.' Questions class about what happened. 'What happened when he got out of London?' ...

Teacher: 'So that was one kind of book based in fact. Then we read some short stories by Margaret Mahy from *A Necklace of Raindrops*

[Joan Aiken and Jan Pienkowski (1975)].That's two very different sorts of books. We're going to look at a different kind.' Explains biography. Questions and answers continue. Teacher shows class cover of book – *Roald Dahl.*
3.15 Teacher reads

(Farthing, Year 4)

Although story time here is clearly demarcated as a separate event, both episodes are structured round the selection of some texts from the many. In the second episode the teacher introduces the new book by trying to generate a level of interest in the text precisely because it represents one type amongst many. She positions the students as readers who will actively engage with and be interested by this variety of materials.

The kinds of literacy events the research labelled 'reading for proficiency' and 'reading for choice' are recognised by teachers, children and parents as an integral part of the school reading curriculum, even though they might well refer to them in different ways. Teachers planned for both kinds of activities as ways of fulfilling the requirements of the National Curriculum. However, reading for choice and reading for proficiency by no means accounted for all of the reading going on over the course of the day. In fact, the bulk of the reading that took place in class operated according to very different ground rules.

Procedural reading

Whilst reading for proficiency and reading for choice are clearly delineated as part of the official reading curriculum, from the point of view of its participants procedural reading happens as part of some other kind of curriculum activity or administrative task. This is reading to get (other) things done where, although reading takes place, it is regarded as incidental to some other purpose which holds the attention of both teachers and pupils. Reading stays in the background. Yet this kind of reading plays a crucial part in steering curriculum delivery. In the process it establishes very different relations between text, readers and context.

Procedural texts are generally non-fiction, often non-narrative texts. Worksheets, textbooks, writing on the board as part of the lesson, and letters home, are all prime examples. Such texts start their classroom life as the focus for joint activity between teachers and pupils. Teachers introduce these texts to the class, and take prime responsibility for making them accessible to pupils by reading them aloud and/or explicating them before they hand them over. Most of these texts are then designed to travel on into a second context where children will use them to accomplish something else, as they work on their own or in groups using the text to steer that subsequent phase of activity. In either setting if pupils find that they are struggling with the reading, they are entitled to ask for help either from their peers or the teacher. For the end product of procedural reading is not the reading itself but something else – some other kind of output, be it in the form of a spoken or written text, which the text will help accomplish. The individual child's performance will be judged against this secondary outcome, not the act of reading per se.

In this way, procedural reading becomes a collective and jointly conducted effort, in which the level of competence of any one reader is not seen as a bar to working with the text. Access to the text can be gained through networking your way there using others' knowledge. Children stand in a different relationship to their peers during this process and their status in relation to this activity is negotiated in different ways: through the relevant knowledge they bring to the topic; their attentiveness to teacher directions; their understanding of the requirements of the task ahead; the resources they have which can aid its accomplishment in other ways including knowing where in the classroom the best resources for completing the task are.

In the example which follows, one procedural text is first of all jointly constructed by children and teacher as the teacher scribes the pupils' answers to her questions onto the blackboard, adapting their answers to fit the purpose of the coming task. A second procedural text in the form of a worksheet is then introduced to the whole class as a way of more formally structuring the second phase of classroom activity. Both texts steer and support that activity which involves pupils in sorting out man-made from natural materials as part of their science topic.

Example 3

    * SCIENCE, CARPET

    9.40 Classroom. Whole class on carpet. Teacher seated in front of blackboard.

    Teacher: We're going to start our science topic which is about materials. Have a look at what's written on the displays. We're going to start as a class looking at some materials, different objects. We're going to think about what they're actually made from.

    Priscilla has shell to hold.

    Teacher writes 'shells' on blackboard.

    Zena and Bernice hold next objects. Teacher writes 'corks' on board. {Pupils continue to name items and the teacher to write them on the board}

    Teacher: Katy stand up, what have you got there?

    Katy: Paper

    Teacher: Paper, good girl

    Four hands up. Jude has plastic container, Heather glass jar.

    Teacher: Jenni as you're sitting so beautifully

Vera: Cotton wool
Teacher: Cotton actually (...)

TEXT ON BOARD:

cotton   wood
paper   coal
shells
metal   corks
glass jar
fabrics   tin can
plastic container   plastic cubes

9.50 Worksheets handed out
Worksheet on natural and man-made materials.
Pupils to fill in 2 lists – natural materials, and man-made, and decide which materials are which. Box at bottom of worksheet starts 'I have found out' followed by 4 blank lines.

* SCIENCE, TABLES

10.00 Pupils seated at tables. Heather walks over to book on win-dowsill and spells out 'metal'. Goes back to table, returns with Vera, repeats spelling out 'metal' and shows her book cover. Both go back to table. Bernice has collected 3 books and is sitting cross-legged on carpet with them, reading the top one *It's cotton*. Takes book to teacher, goes back to reading on carpet. Vera asks me how to spell material, another girl asks how to spell brick. Antoine asks teacher about cork.

(Kingfisher, Year 3)

*Designation of the context for the literacy event used in the field notes

The procedural texts are interwoven with the on-going pattern of activity as it unfolds over time in the classroom. They directly support and help struc-ture key phases of that activity. When working through procedural texts, children draw on a variety of resources to complete the task set. This includes help from peers and/or the other adults in class.

Variation in practice within and across sites: how different ways of organising reading are realised

Repeated combinations of similar texts, readers and contexts led the researchers to identify three common ways of organising reading and to label them: reading for proficiency, reading for choice and procedural reading. These kinds of literacy events made up the bulk of curricular activity in all four case-study sites. However, they did not quite account for everything. For instance, one of the schools had a religious affiliation,

74

which meant that prayers and religious observance formed a key part of the daily routine. These literacy events took on a different character because reading the texts in these contexts involved saying the words aloud and together, often drawing on memory rather than on any written document immediately to hand. The oral text thus created took precedence over the written form from which it stemmed. In some respects, this practice seemed to spill over into other parts of the curriculum. These kinds of oral texts had a prominence in the daily routine of the classroom not found in the other schools. Yet this way of doing reading seemed to act as an addition to, rather than a replacement for, the basic repertoire.

Whilst literacy events which exemplified reading for proficiency, reading for choice and procedural reading occurred in each of the case-study sites, there were differences in their relative prominence within the on-going stream of classroom activity and the depth of resources through which each way of reading was realised. Exploring those differences became the next stage in the analysis. The strong and well-motivated initial categorisation of events allowed for a subsequent and more subtle analysis in which the potentially contradictory pull of different elements within any one instance could be more fully explored. This is demonstrated below in the comparison of the ways in which reading for choice was managed in three of the case-study sites.

Reading for choice the pupil way: a comparison of quiet reading time

During the period of data collection each of the schools in which the study was based included quiet reading as part of its weekly routine. This activity was considered to be part of the official literacy curriculum. At its simplest, and as the name implied, it meant any period of time set aside for pupils to read quietly to themselves. Whilst most of the class were so occupied, the teacher might be listening to individual readers or getting on with some other task. The activity was expected to be self-sustaining and largely self-directed, as pupils chose what and sometimes how they would read. Yet although this seemed to imply convergence on a common set of principles, in fact the precise character of the event was hugely contingent on the resources available.

Reading for choice with few resources: quiet reading time in Shepherd School

In Shepherd, quiet reading time was timetabled alongside morning and afternoon registration. As a consequence it was interrupted by routine administrative tasks, such as taking the register and notices. In the morning session, reading could be substituted by finishing off homework or other classroom writing. This meant the majority of the children might well be doing other things besides reading. The books available for use during quiet reading time were shelved in the class library. By and large these were not books children could borrow to take home, as most pupils were still restricted to taking a reading scheme book home instead. These were considered to match their proficiency as readers more closely. With the exception of about five titles the class library was entirely composed of fiction texts that were long enough to be subdivided into chapters. Non-fiction was at that time kept in a central reference library for use in topic work.

The most popular books in use during quiet reading time were the few picture books the class library contained. These had the advantage of being easy to read in one sitting. Some boys smuggled in favourite non-fiction books from the school reference library which they kept in their trays and held over to the next session. Otherwise, books were expected to be returned to the class library when the time was up. In practice this meant most of the rest of the class library books went unread. The length of the texts didn't fit the length of the time available to read them in. If children started a book in one session, they could not guarantee finding it again at the next. Many children simply sat with their reading books in front of them. Provided they were quiet, not much actual reading needed to go on.

Reading for choice with lots to choose from: quiet reading time in Bluebird School

By contrast in Bluebird, quiet reading occupied a distinct slot on the literacy curriculum, alternating with paired reading, group reading, and the teacher reading to the whole class as part of the ERIC carousel. The class library contained a wide range of texts of different lengths, requiring different kinds of attention: fiction, non-fiction, picture books, topic books, pupil-chosen, teacher-chosen, pupil-made, newspapers, and sometimes magazines. The library itself occupied a different space, separate from the main classroom and away from the teacher's gaze. Pupils could congregate on the comfy chairs and soft cushions, or lounge on the floor, as they gathered to change books, or stayed to read. The official injunction was to read silently, but quiet talk was tolerated and friends would often look at books together. Books with a strong visual element – picture books, puzzle books, some kinds of non-fiction – were often used in this way. Sometimes the class would be asked to talk about their reading at the end of the session, but more often they would pack away and then return to the business of the curriculum proper by congregating on the mat in front of the teacher. The children could make use of this same space and resources whenever they had finished work earlier than others in the class. When a sufficiently large number of children were making use of the facilities, the teacher would draw the curricular activity to a close and bring all the children together again to start the next lesson sequence. Children were expected to borrow materials from the class library each week and take them home regardless of whether they were still using reading scheme books for their reader.

Different takes on quiet reading: comparing Shepherd and Bluebird

Both schools had a curriculum slot nominated as quiet reading in which notions of range and choice played a part. Yet the overall effect was different. Notionally speaking, children were free to choose what to read for themselves in both sites. During this slot they were also much freer to move around the class than they would be at other times, ostensibly because of the need to change books. They could also choose much more freely where they sat, and whether to read alone or with others. In these respects quiet reading time had the character of self-directed activity. This in itself set it apart from much of the rest of the curriculum. Once quiet reading time was over the teacher would take back control of the agenda again, allotting tasks, directing the pace, orchestrating the round of activities. These contrasts in both sites established quiet reading time as time for (child-directed) play, rather than time for (teacher-directed) work.

Yet in Shepherd exactly what kind of reading this was remained relatively low profile. This was in part because of the mismatch between the potential of the resources and the context for their use; and in part because of the way reading competed with other activities at the same time, rather than being the sole focus of the event. The occasion didn't strongly underline what reading for choice might be, or build a collective sense of its possibilities. From the pupil perspective, choice stayed at the level of choosing what to do in a situation which was lightly teacher-monitored. By contrast in Bluebird 'range' and 'choice' were materially underpinned in more substantial ways. The high level of individual responsibility which pupils enjoyed at this time was also part of a range of teacher strategies used elsewhere on the curriculum. This was part and parcel of how teachers expected children to manage their work at other times. The specific responsibility individuals had for directing their own reading during quiet reading time was thus more highly visible and well defined than in Shepherd, as were the resources which made exercising real choice possible.

Comparing these two events shows how literacy events geared to 'reading as choice' can differ in what they deliver to participants, despite the similarities in underlying principles of composition that they share. It also highlights the role that the resources available within any event play alongside the underlying conception of what those resources are for.

Reading for choice the teacher way

An example from Kingfisher shows a rather different means of implementing reading for choice, again with different consequences for those involved. In this classroom, choice of texts was largely managed by the teacher. She expected the class to cover the necessary range of texts at her direction, rather than through the choices they made. At first, during quiet reading time children were allotted a weekly turn to read a particular genre from distinct collections assembled for that purpose and labelled accordingly. The range presented in class included information books, poetry, plays, topic books and (story)tapes. Children were told to choose from the basket where their allotted collection was kept. Later they were restricted to their current reading books i.e. the ones they were required to take to proficiency encounters. Quiet reading time was thus integrated much more closely into reading for proficiency. From there on, choice increasingly became the range of texts the teacher taught during English curriculum time to allow the pupils to sample from a range of genres. A good example is provided by the extracts from field notes below, in which the teacher presents children with the opportunity to read some joke books as part of their English lesson:

Example 4

ENGLISH, CARPET

Teacher: This morning we're going to be looking at jokes. In your reading groups you are going to take a set of these [i.e. photocopies] and a couple of books from the book box. Everyone will have something to look at with the person sitting next to you or in your group. [10–15 minutes, sitting reading them. Can swap them round.] Think about which one is the funniest.

ENGLISH, TABLES (...)

Teacher: I've gone round – most people have found their favourite joke. You were reading them beautifully ... looking at all the work I gave you ... Just bring your favourite joke – sheet or book – and we'll read some of them on the carpet.

(Kingfisher, Year 3)

Here the activity of reading is dominated by the teacher's stated purposes and the point she is leading them to: the written outcome from the reading – a class joke book. Yet along the way the teacher continues to frame individual activities in terms of pupil choice. Pupils have to choose their favourite joke, even if that means no more than choosing between so many jokes on a photocopied page, where none are really more interesting than the others. They read a range of texts in order to select from the many. In contrast to the quiet reading times outlined above, this occasion remains strictly teacher-controlled. Yet there is an oscillation between teacher talk which frames the activity as monitored work, and teacher talk which frames the children's activity as self-motivated fun.

In part, what this occasion points to is the potential hybridity of different literacy events. Different elements within an event can pull different ways. In this instance teacher judgements on how well individual readers are doing are never far away. '*You were reading them beautifully*', edges the encounter towards a proficiency frame; whilst the end point of the activity – a class joke book – evokes the routines of classroom work, and a procedural frame. Yet the request to readers is to find and pool individual favourites, to stake a claim for oneself through the choices one has exercised, whilst the texts themselves suggest fun, not work, as the agenda.

Faced with such hybridity, the point is not so much to arbitrate between the combinations of different elements within particular literacy events, settling the argument between them, as it were, but rather to map out how the different elements interact in any one setting. The key analytic task is therefore both to explore the underlying principles that make one way of reading recognisably distinct from another – why this event belongs primarily to the category 'reading for choice', for instance – and also to examine the potential ways in which different elements associated with one way of reading can be recombined and with what effect. From the participants' perspective, different ways of reading can be distilled, but also remade anew.

Placing all these examples in the same category, 'reading for choice', highlights a number of key contrasts which run through the data as a whole: the extent to which teachers visibly manage the reading curriculum from the centre or, sometimes by sleight of hand, devolve that management to the periphery; the extent to which reading is cast as work or play (see also Solsken, 1993); the extent to which reading is conducted as a collective or individual activity; the extent to which reading itself is backgrounded or foregrounded; and the different subjectivities which are formed as a result.

Literacy events and the recontextualisation of resources

Analysing the data as the orchestration of resources within the parameters of a single event makes it possible to observe the oscillations, or even tensions, between different elements within a single literacy event and the ways in which they seem to sometimes pull in different directions. Sometimes the tensions between elements are greater than at others.

On the whole, literacy events that revolve around reading for proficiency show most homogeneity across the different sites, and their boundaries are most clearly defined. Literacy events that revolve around reading for choice show maximum variation within sites as well as between them. This is evident in the data presented above. Sometimes one or other of these ways of reading migrates out from one area of the curriculum to steer activity in another. For instance, in Bluebird the ground rules for reading for choice seemed to underpin the use of topic books in History and, to a lesser extent, in Science. Meanwhile, in each site procedural reading would happen within as well as outside of the English curriculum. Boundaries are permeable. By these means the distinctive character of each way of reading and the resources they are associated with can be brought into different kinds of relationship.

One way of dealing with this fluidity is to conclude that texts, readers and contexts are the semiotic resources that are drawn on in particular literacy events. But the semiotic potential of the resources may or may not be fully realised. This in part depends on how they interrelate, and the extent to which they reinforce each other or pull in different directions. To give an example, all of the classrooms where the research was based included a 'soft area', however vestigial, often close to the class library or book corner, usually carpeted and containing at least one comfy chair, and maybe fabric drapes. This setting was most strongly associated with reading for choice. Often this area would only become available to children during quiet reading time, when they would be allowed to lounge on beanbags, recline on a comfy chair or simply spread out on the carpet. The setting encouraged pupils to, as it were, take time out from the rigours of proper lessons where they had to sit up straight and pay attention, adopting a quite different bodily posture. The material and physical resources of the setting, through their invocation of the comforts of a well-furnished front room, reinforce notions of reading as (domestic) leisure, even if practically speaking they can only do so in a token way: there are never enough chairs for everyone to have one. But their potential to do this may not be fully realised: imagine the same setting used for a one-on-one proficiency encounter, with the child in the comfy chair sitting up straight and reading aloud to the teacher, whilst the teacher assesses the child's performance. Within a given literacy event, temporary alliances between elements happen through the mobilisation of resources this time round. All the different elements within a given literacy event can fall the same way, reinforcing each other, or they can begin to pull in different directions.

Continuities in practice at the level of the school

The potential hybridity of literacy events does not imply a free-for-all, where anyone can make reading whichever way they like. At the level of the school, it is clearly possible to push literacy more strongly in one direction rather than another by providing more contexts and resources which seem to push in the same direction. In Kingfisher, for instance, the reading for proficiency frame was particularly visible. In part, this happened quite simply because proficiency encounters were given precedence over any other kind of curricular activity. Thus every child was expected to be heard to read every day, and would leave the classroom when it was their turn to do so regardless of what else was going on. The school deliberately staffed for this aspect of the curriculum so that proficiency encounters were primarily run by specialist staff rather than parent volunteers.

Texts that were intended to be taken to proficiency encounters were also those made most immediately and publicly accessible in the school. The school's entire stock of reading books were arranged serially along the full length of the school corridor according to their perceived level of difficulty or 'readability'. Their physical sequence reflected the judgements made about the proficiency of the reader who would go to pick them up. Choosing a reading book meant going to one's allotted space in the corridor. By contrast, the school library shelved its range of fiction and non-fiction resources according to different criteria (author; Dewey number) but was not open for borrowing and was rarely used by students.

This school was quite explicit about the emphasis it gave to reading for proficiency through its reading policy and stressed this in its communication with parents about reading and the use of the reading book. Parents' role in helping their children to read was closely monitored, with parents expected to listen to their children read every day and fill in the home-reading book to show that they had done so. Yet even so, notions of reading for choice persisted. If the choices teachers made for their pupils could be turned into work to be got through, pupils continued to exercise choice for themselves in other ways. Favourite texts from home found their way into class and were shared there. Children found ways to choose between reading books and found settings where they could choose what they would do with them, too. Thus one of the favourite pastimes of a group of girls observed in the class was to read aloud poems from their reading book in unison, giving a rap rendition which turned the text from work into play.

The case-study schools varied in the weighting they gave to one way of reading over another through the prominence they gave to certain kinds of events, and the different ways in which they resourced for them. In all of the sites, no one way of reading operated to the exclusion of the others. Rather, the relations between these different ways of reading remained unsettled and open to reworking by the different participants involved.

Reading for proficiency, reading for choice and procedural reading interact. Whilst on the one hand they offer competing logics for how reading should take place which are kept apart by the bounded nature of the events in which they occur, on the other hand they also represent a collective repertoire which has the potential to be differently invoked by both teachers and pupils.

81

Gender differentiation and the reading curriculum: the dynamic of proficiency versus choice from the pupils' perspective

Reading for proficiency, reading for choice and procedural reading do not speak directly about gender. This is not part of their explicit terms of reference. Indeed, close observation of literacy events in school of the kind outlined above provides little evidence for the belief that the reading curriculum in the primary school is feminised by virtue of its content, or through the close association of narrative fiction with a required personal response. But the complex interplay of resources which these three ways of reading map out does begin to suggest the means by which reading itself becomes gender-differentiated for children. Most importantly, this seems to happen in response to the proficiency judgements made in class about children as readers.

Perhaps the most unexpected finding from the research data was the strength of the proficiency frame which surrounded reading in school and the extent to which this permeated children's use of fiction texts in particular. This was so in each site, whether, like Kingfisher, the school emphasised reading for proficiency encounters in their daily curriculum or not. Indeed, one of the research's findings was that although reading for choice remained a strong frame at the rhetorical level, both in teacher talk about their practice and indeed as part of official documentation on the curriculum, it was harder to find it fully realised on the ground. The examples of reading for choice in action, quoted above, are quite typical in this respect.

The strength of the proficiency frame in part stems from the strong interplay between reading and the social construction of ability which runs through schooling in the early years. From the moment they enter school, how well children read and how quickly they build on their existing reading skills are key determinants of their place within the classroom. Although other areas of the curriculum clearly matter, none holds as central a role in sorting and discriminating between children. It is their perceived proficiency at reading, not their proficiency at maths, which sends children to sit at different tables during the length of the school day, and in some classrooms determines that they will be given different tasks to work at under different conditions. In effect, teacher judgements about reading generate ability groupings. Reading matters. Teachers know it and parents know it. Children know it too, even in those classrooms which try hardest to render such differences invisible to the pupils themselves.

Judgements about children's proficiency as readers are made about them as individuals in circumstances where the child cannot easily fudge or disguise what they can or can't do. It is a particularly visible calling to account where the outcome is relatively transparent to all those involved. This is particularly so in the early stages of schooling, where children are most likely to be moving through a structured reading scheme. Whether they move up a level or not depends upon the teacher's judgement of the pupil's skill. The child's own estimation of themselves will not carry much weight in this context. The extent to which the child has measured up becomes all too obvious from the kind of text they are subsequently allotted. The weaker the reader, then the larger the print size in the text will be, the fewer the number of words, and the bigger the space allotted to pictures. The text tells its own story about where this reader is and what progress they have made. One way or another, children cannot escape this judgement. They have to find a way to deal with it.

Distinctions between readers continue to be made on this basis as children make their way up the school. In the classrooms observed, those children who were deemed the weakest readers were still assigned to reading scheme books. They were unable to move from one scheme level to another without the teacher's say so. Matching pupil's competence to the texts they read remained a major preoccupation. Only those children who had been designated as independent readers were completely free to choose what they read for themselves. Others were supposed to stick to books that were appropriate to their level of skill, even when they had moved from reading schemes to a wider choice of texts. The proficiency criteria moved with them. From this point of view it is perhaps less surprising that pupils demonstrated their awareness of the central importance given to proficiency criteria when, during quiet reading time, they would put down the book they were actually reading in order to find the researcher their 'reading book':

Example 5

> When I asked Priscilla the name of her book she reacted just like
> before – didn't show me the book she was actually reading (her own)
> but reached into her bag and got out another book to show me.
>
> (Kingfisher, Year 3)

The fact that children so often gave precedence to the text associated with the proficiency frame, even though they were not at that point participating in a proficiency event, showed that this version of what counts as literacy could be readily mobilised, even in the contexts most strongly associated with 'reading for choice'.

Fiction, non-fiction, and the designation of reading proficiency

In classrooms, judgements about readers' skills at reading are based on what they do with fiction texts. In fact, almost all fiction texts for the primary age group underline the link between reading and proficiency through their design characteristics, including their use of typeface and lay-out, and the ways in which they combine verbal text and pictures. Whether they are producing reading schemes or 'real' books, children's publishers differentiate and segment fiction texts for the junior age range according to proficiency levels, and using agreed standards. The bigger the typeface, the larger the spaces between the lines of type, and the higher the propor-tion of picture to text, the easier the book will be to read. Libraries and bookshops sort and store their fiction collections by similar criteria: picture books, read-alones, junior fiction, will be housed on different shelves on the assumption that they are appropriate for readers with varying levels of proficiency. Together, these features construct a reading ladder, and, by implication, the reader's place upon it. Children, like grown-ups, can recognise an 'easy' book from a 'hard' book because of the way it looks. Children recognise these distinctions in the fiction books they are assigned, and in those assigned to others in their class. The fiction books they are seen with signal to others how competent they are at reading. They grade and sort the group.

Non-fiction texts are not subject to the same rules, either through design or use. These contrasts matter. Looking at the choices children made dur-ing quiet reading time, the most consistent differences emerged not between (all) boys and (all) girls in respect of the particular genres they chose, but between boys and girls designated as more or less able readers. The choices of boys designated as less able readers stood out because only this group consistently chose certain kinds of highly visual non-fiction texts over and above anything else that was on offer. This was so even in class-rooms where non-fiction was hard to come by and no official provision was made to ensure its ready availability. Other children, regardless of their des-ignation as readers, spent more time on fiction.

Subsets of texts and subsets of readers: managing gender and social status in class

What was the attraction of these kinds of non-fiction texts for this partic-ular subset of readers? A review of the texts concerned suggested that the kinds of non-fiction which boys designated as weak readers chose shared a number of key features. First, they were highly visual. Page layouts were constructed on a double spread, with the visuals leading the written text, rather than vice versa. Paragraphs were often linked to particular images, and would be relatively free-standing of the rest of the verbal text on the page. They could therefore be read in any sequence, with the visuals steering the selection individual readers made from the page as a whole. Moreover, unlike the bulk of fiction texts, the most popular non-fiction texts eschewed carefully graded point size of typeface as a way of sig-nalling the level of proficiency of their intended readership. Instead, the size of typeface varied according to the prominence given to the verbal text on the page: large typefaces for headings; smaller for subheadings; smallest for the individual paragraphs which accompanied the visual images. The bulk of the print on the page would therefore be in a point size most often reserved in fiction for lengthier texts pitched at the fluent reader.

These design characteristics immediately set these texts apart from much of the rest of the book stock the school provided, and indeed caused some concern about their suitability amongst many of the teachers in whose classrooms these materials circulated. They were unsure how far the verbal text matched the reading proficiency of the children in the class, let alone the underachieving boys who seemed to make a beeline for them. Finally, such texts were almost always large, bound hardbacks. Again, this was in distinct contrast to the predominantly paperback, small size fiction texts, or the stapled, soft-backed reading scheme books. Take these attributes together and these non-fiction texts signal 'adults' as their intended readership, both as material objects and in terms of their internal characteristics (layout, visual style). At a stroke they remove their readers from the stigma associated with reading 'easy' fiction.

One of the advantages of the design features associated with this group of non-fiction texts is that they obscure whether these are 'easy' or 'hard' books, or indeed what kinds of competencies readers would need to make the most of them. At the same time, they also give weaker readers plenty to do precisely because it is possible to steer round them using visual images alone, or by browsing the headings and short paragraphs without having to wade through the whole text from beginning to end. The pictures alone can act as prompts for readers to announce what they already know about a particular topic. Outside of any context of official evaluation, boys who would struggle with the print could steer their own way through these texts for their own purposes and simultaneously establish their credentials as knowledgable experts. Whilst these kinds of books found little official sanction within proficiency encounters, and were unlikely to form the backbone of the tasks undertaken via procedural reading, they could be appropriated in reading for choice slots to reposition their readers and in effect redo their social standing amongst their peers. By choosing non-fiction texts, boys designated as weak readers solved a dilemma which their difficulties with reading seemed to pose them. Girls designated as weak readers did not make the same choices.

Gender, text choice and reading attainment

Approaching the genre preferences children make through the range of social contexts for reading which frame texts in school suggests a new way of understanding gendered text choices, in which the turn to non-fiction on the part of boys designated as weak readers increasingly looks like an escape from the proficiency judgements associated with fiction texts. Boys designated as weak readers seemed to be in flight from negative proficiency judgements in ways in which girls were not.

Girls designated as weak readers did not react to their lowly position in the classroom hierarchy in the same way. Even during reading for choice time they seemed quite prepared to keep to the level of fiction books that they were allotted, and to choose according to proficiency criteria. The following extract from field notes shows one girl placed in the lowest proficiency group doing exactly this during quiet reading time:

Example 6

> Hannah swapped the first book (she tried) 'because there are too many hard words in it'. [Note*: To date I have no record of weak boy readers using similar criteria to guide their choice in this way.]
>
> *Reflection made by the researcher in the field notes at the time of observation.
>
> (Bluebird, Year 3)

Looking across the data it was possible to see that girls designated as weak readers were generally happy to go along with teacher judgements about their proficiency, both in and out of proficiency encounters, whilst many of the boys designated weak readers were not. Thus even when readers had most opportunities to direct their reading for themselves, girls designated as weak readers often chose to spend time on fiction texts whose print size either matched or even fell below their competence. They seemed quite happy to turn this kind of reading into a collaborative exercise with their friends in which they helped each other through the pages (see Chapter 5 for examples of this kind of interaction).

By contrast, observation showed that boys designated as weak readers seldom settled with texts that were pitched at their proficiency level when they could choose something else. In the same class as Hannah and positioned in the same group of low attainers, Morris often spent quiet reading time lurking by the class library, rather than settling to read at all. In the following episode recorded in field notes he was standing in the book corner holding a small size paperback, 149 pages long:

Example 7

> Morris is clutching *Dirt Bike Racer* by Matt Christopher (1979). I asked him about the book and he said it was too hard for him, thumbing through the pages to show the number of words per line and lines per page. I asked if somebody else could read it to him and he said no. I said could he get someone else to read it to him

at home. He said he would like his mum to read it to him. He likes the book as it has a picture of a bike just like his.

(Bluebird, Year 3)

The field notes showed that Morris quite often picked this book out from the class library during quiet reading time. A chapter book with few illustrations, he never borrowed it to take home, and did not seem to try to tackle the text in class either, instead using the cover illustration to talk about dirt bike racing with his friends.

Low proficiency rankings seemed to conflict more with these boys' sense of self-esteem than they did for girls. Unable to reconcile the conflict between their standing in the reading hierarchy and their standing in the hierarchies of peer relations they often tried to escape judgements about their skill at reading altogether by either spending as little time as they could on reading in class, or by choosing texts which rendered their status as readers inconspicuous. Non-fiction texts gave them somewhere to go. Indeed, precisely because of the prevalence of illustration in these texts they provided one of the few arenas where more and less able boys could meet on a level, as it were. Boys designated as weak readers could muster their expertise in response to such a text without having to stumble through the print to identify what was going on (see Chapter 5). This was an advantage in relation to boys' status politics. It seemed to work less well in terms of making progress with their reading. For one net result of the strategies they employed was that many such boys simply spent less time on verbal text.

This analysis suggests a new way of thinking about the wide disparity in boys' attainment in literacy and the gulf between their performance and that of girls. For it reveals a route by which the distance between more and less able boy readers will increase, and conversely a mechanism by which girls at the bottom of the reading hierarchy may carry on keeping up with their peers. In effect, low-attaining girls gain more practice dealing with texts that are within their competence whilst low-attaining boys strive to avoid texts that reveal an unfavourable place in the social hierarchy. There seems to be far less at stake for girls in dealing with what the reading curriculum tells them about their place in class, whether high or low. This in turn raises some interesting questions about the terms on which help with reading is offered in the classroom to whom, and what is at stake in receiving such help, or indeed refusing it (see Chapter 5).

Conclusion

The research recorded in this chapter set out to track the salient contrasts schools make between fiction and non-fiction texts in their contexts of use as a way of understanding the social construction of genre preferences. What soon became apparent was the extent to which what counts as reading in school is bound up with the social stratification of readers. This happens via the classroom processes which sort children into those who can read and those who can't, with the appropriate gradations between. These processes can be seen at work in reading for proficiency slots. But their effects leach out into the rest of the curriculum, not least through the common use of the teacher's assessment of pupils' reading abilities to assign children different places to sit in class. Even in the 7–9 age group such distinctions continue to matter and indeed in many ways colour access to the curriculum more generally.

At the same time, reading for choice and procedural reading offer other ways of constituting readers and delineating their potential relationships to texts. In this sense schools simultaneously stress the importance of reading as a core skill for which individual readers can be held to account and provide other means of thinking about reading, and readers' relationships to texts. Gender, reading, and the designation of ability intertwine as readers take up these various resources for doing reading and use them in different ways to reposition both themselves and others. Different consequences flow from the choices they make.

Viewed from this perspective, genre preferences are not choices made in the abstract by an individual reader faced with an indefinite range of texts from which to select; rather they are socially judicious acts exercised in specific contexts which carry their own constraints.

4

TEXTS IN THEIR CONTEXT
OF USE

Non-fiction, text design and the social
regulation of reading in class

Introduction

The previous chapter considered the ways in which the literacy curriculum constructs a social hierarchy of learners in class. The social hierarchy becomes visible both through where children are asked to sit, but more particularly through the kinds of fiction texts they are asked to read. The chapter suggested that the preference for non-fiction texts on the part of boys who were designated less able readers stems in part from their desire to escape from their place at the bottom of the reading ladder. They seem to have most to lose from being seen with fiction texts that match their competence.

This chapter turns to the official use made of non-fiction texts in the primary classroom and the rationale which sustains this. It considers the extent to which text design anticipates and speaks to the contexts in which texts will be read, and the extent to which texts can be remade as they are recontextualised in different settings. It begins with audit data collected in classrooms on the range of texts available and examines what this reveals about the working categories participants employ to distinguish between texts in school settings. The chapter concludes by arguing that in choosing between fiction and non-fiction texts children are choosing between different reading paths which make different demands on their readers and open up different possibilities for use.

Turning from context to text

The previous chapter used close observation of the literacy events that make up the official school curriculum to identify three main ways of reading that emerge from the regularities and routines of classroom practice. It considered some of the dilemmas these ways of reading pose for both teachers and pupils as they struggle to keep them apart as well as borrow and recontextualise resources familiar from one context into another. The chapter argued that this creates the conditions in which one group of readers (boys designated less able at reading) develop a distinctive literacy practice that acts as an alternative to the ways in which the school curriculum seems to position them. Yet this group exploit opportunities that the organisation of the literacy curriculum as a whole offers them. The logic of reading for choice provides and sustains the space in which these readers manoeuvre around the judgements made of them elsewhere through the logic of reading for proficiency. The design characteristics of the texts they engage with are also crucial to this process because of the possibilities they offer for a different kind of use. From the point of view of their readers, they fit the requirements of the specific events in which they appear. In this sense, the apparent preference for non-fiction shown by boys who are designated weak readers emerges in schools, not at home.

Observation of the ways in which this particular group of boys used a particular subset of non-fiction texts showed that this bore only a passing resemblance to the kind of organised retrieval of information from non-fiction texts that is taught as part of the official curriculum. Yet neither is it best understood as a community practice which has migrated into schools from elsewhere. Rather, this chapter will argue that it depends upon the recontextualisation of the resources that are available in classrooms under a given set of conditions. The logic of the text, including what its design says about how it should be read, plays its part in shaping this particular practice.

The influence of the text upon readers

The kind of relationship of text to context outlined above to some extent parts company with previous attempts to link gender and literacy through textual analysis from a feminist perspective. These have developed via two main routes: through content analysis which considers the text in isolation; or through audience studies which examine the relationship of texts to their audience. Both kinds of analysis set out to identify what texts tell their readers about gender. Where they differ is over the value they ascribe to the texts' contents and the kind of influence they assume texts wield.

Content analysis was developed early on within the feminist movement. In essence, it meant devising means of tracking down and identifying gender bias in text content without regard to the contexts in which such texts might be read. By the early 1980s, conducting this kind of analysis had become one of the main means of challenging the status quo from an anti-sexist perspective (Nate, 1985; Leggett and Hemming, 1984; Stone, 1983). Findings from content analysis of books used in school showed that female characters occupied a much more limited range of roles than male characters and that gender-stereotyping was widespread. As a result, many school departments reconsidered the kinds of books they purchased, whilst publishers set about changing text content to meet this new kind of market. The heavily gender-stereotyped duo of Janet and John, familiar from an early reading scheme and the object of much feminist criticism, lost ground to Biff and Chip, lead characters in a more self-consciously gender-neutral environment which was constructed as the backdrop for the *Oxford Reading Tree* reading scheme in the mid-eighties. (This is still the most widely used reading scheme in British Primary schools.)

This kind of anti-sexist approach was in many ways an effective political tool in changing unconsidered attitudes towards what constituted appropriate content in children's books. But it also proved a fairly blunt instrument, not least because it presumed that content analysis of this kind could be straightforwardly equated with readers' experience of the text (see Moss, 1989b for a critical analysis of this view). In fact, by looking at readers as well as texts, feminist studies of those narrative forms most closely associated with a female readership began to show that many of the assumptions derived from content analysis were actually quite wide of the mark. Viewed from the perspective of their (female) readers, some of the text types which had been most widely derided – soaps, the romance – appeared much less certainly ideologically loaded against women than had originally been thought (Ang, 1985; Moss, 1989a; Radway, 1984).

This second strand of feminist work began to explore the relationship between text and context much more directly. Yet often the point of such studies remained to assess the ideological impact of the text upon the audience (Radway, 1984). Such studies continued to be steered by the assumption that reading is primarily identity work: that in reading other texts readers make up their minds about who they are and what they will become; and that in these terms the possibilities texts offer remain strongly gendered for male and female readers alike. (See Moss, 1993a and Moss, 1993b for critical reviews of the way in which the object of study is constructed in much of this literature.) These assumptions are largely reinforced by the choice of texts to be studied and their apparent fit with the range of contexts in which they are consumed. For instance, the predominance of romances or soap operas as objects of study leads to a concentration on contexts of consumption which are peculiarly domestic and structured around women's role within the home. The content of the text seems intimately connected with the interpersonal flavour of the social interactions which belong to that domain. Contexts and texts converge on the same kind of territory. By contrast, this chapter keeps open the question of what the relationship between text and context is and how it should be understood. How far does the context in which the text is read filter the text, or the text itself shape what will be made of it? These are the questions which run through this chapter.

Which comes first, the context or the text?

There are some good methodological reasons for bringing the relationship between text and context under closer scrutiny. The research documented in the previous chapter began by working back from contexts to texts. That is to say, it used information about which texts got into which contexts for which readers to sort the texts observed into salient groups. The data collected in this way showed that most of the non-fiction texts which surfaced during quiet reading time shared a range of design characteristics including varying size of print, non-linear layout and a high proportion of image to written text. This made them stand out from other texts in school, including other kinds of non-fiction. Yet these shared features might have gone unremarked if the researchers had not grouped the texts according to the ways in which they were used on the ground. The salience of a specific set of design characteristics for the particular group of readers who made use of these texts only became visible in this light.

Contexts tell readers what to do with texts. But texts also have the capacity to speak back to contexts. Sometimes there is a strong fit between the intentions of the text and the intentions of the context. Reading scheme books and reading for proficiency slots, for instance, clearly converge on the same territory. The reading scheme, through its sequenced organisation expressed in its design, directly supports the purposes of assessment and progression associated with the early years literacy curriculum. Its structure and design allows carefully monitored movement from one kind of text to another in a purposefully constructed chain. The reading scheme is predicated on a particular context of use and anticipates finding its way there. It is planned with that use in mind. But the precise fit between text and context is not always so exact nor so well anticipated on each side. Some contexts quite clearly define and prescribe what will happen to any texts which enter their domain; others do not.

Proficiency encounters clearly have the power to remake almost any text to fit their own requirements. When Ella took her reading book, *Mr and Mrs Pig's Evening Out* (Rayner, 1976), to the proficiency encounter reproduced in Example 1 (p. 67), the context overruled those features of the text which in other settings would define it as a picture book and might lead to the kind of speculative play with narrative structure exemplified in Henrietta Dombey's account of mother and child reading *Rosie the Hen* (Hutchins, 1970; Dombey, 1992). But not all contexts will be as prescriptive as this. Some may themselves be less sharply defined and therefore more open to following the text's lead.

Texts can and do move from one context to another. They have the potential to be recontextualised elsewhere and accordingly be turned into something else. To take an example from a classroom in Shepherd School, where a large format children's atlas was kept up by the blackboard, its pages almost the size of a flip chart. Published on cardboard and resembling a big book, it had originally been purchased as a reference text for use in whole-class settings and must have been designed and produced with this context in mind. Although never observed in use for teaching purposes, it was much in demand during quiet reading time when small groups of children would make off with it together. The teacher was at a loss to know why. In fact, close observation showed that they were using it to play a particular kind of game. Each double spread included an image of a continental landmass along with animals or other objects associated with the particular countries or regions it contained. Those playing the game would take it in turns to select one of these objects, whilst the rest of the group would have to guess which object that person was thinking about. The publisher's intentions are unlikely to have run this far. In this instance, text features planned with one context of use in mind were successfully appropriated into another setting.

Other texts may offer more resistance to being remade in this way. A reading scheme book is much less likely to lose its associations with proficiency encounters as it travels from school to home than a picture book like *Mr and Mrs Pig's Evening Out,* for instance. This in turn raises new questions. How far does the form of the text constrain the use that will be made of it? How far can the context bend a text to its own purposes? How do readers judge which texts fit best into which contexts? And indeed, what or who sets the limits to where and how far a text can travel?

Here is an example of a Year 5 pupil working on this range of issues for herself. In the course of an interview about her reading, Sara showed the interviewer the three books she had in her book-bag and talked about what she did with them. They were all fiction books which, to the interviewer at least, looked broadly similar. Yet Sara expected to use them in different contexts. One she was reading at home to herself, another had been chosen specifically to take to reading for proficiency encounters, whilst she browsed the third during any odd moments when free reading was allowed in class. What made some of these texts easier to move into one context rather than another? The book Sara was reading at home was one of her favourites, and was part of a series which was popular with several of her friends. But it also contained some long words she knew she would stumble over when reading aloud to the teacher. She preferred to read it at home when she could settle down to it without interruption and could read without her competence being assessed. The other two fitted more easily into the contexts school offered, the first because she judged it *easy* to read aloud with confidence. This functioned as her 'reading book' which she would take to the teacher if called upon to do so; the other she chose to read on occasions set aside for quiet reading in class because she did not mind stopping and starting as she made her way through it. In this fashion she arrived at her own judgement of which text best fitted which context and distributed them accordingly. The judgements she makes show an understanding of the different logics which drive the social spaces where she might read, and how she positions herself between them.

What does all this mean for the conduct of research? In the first instance it gives point and purpose to examining the full range of texts that are present in any particular site, rather than homing in pre-emptively on what the researcher assumes to be the most salient categories. It also means finding ways of understanding how particular contexts signal what is important about the texts they contain. For instance, it is possible to note how texts are physically sorted and stored or the extent to which they are assembled into 'text collections', i.e. identifiable groups which are assumed by participants to share a common set of characteristics. Any such study also needs to take account of the relationship participants themselves draw between texts and different contexts and what they assume makes them fit together or not as the case may be. This establishes the basis upon which to judge how far texts either anticipate, facilitate, or indeed, resist different contexts of use and so understand the constraints on practice which either the context or the text exerts.

Putting the text into context: auditing the live and the dead

Methodologically, starting with the context of use and then turning to the text is designed to constitute the text as an object of study in terms of those features which are relevant to its users within a particular setting. The research undertaken for this book used three main ways of linking texts to contexts: conducting text audits, that is to say logging the texts that were present within particular environments; documenting text collections, in other words recording how the range of available texts were physically sorted, labelled and stored for use; and describing the texts which got into particular literacy events.

Because by no means all of the texts available within any environment were seen in use, the researchers began to distinguish analytically between live texts – those texts which entered a literacy event and were seen used in some way – and dead texts – those texts which were present and therefore technically accessible, but did not seem to be used at all. This analytic distinction became an important means of discriminating amongst the available texts. Those texts which were effectively 'dead' could safely be dispatched to the periphery of the enquiry whilst researcher effort concentrated on the 'live'. At the same time this distinction began to steer attention to text design, not least because the design characteristics of texts in the live or dead group were often strikingly different.

In fact, there were different degrees of deadness. Some texts had clearly started out alive and become dead as time went on. Thus in a corridor outside one case-study classroom there was a large noticeboard displaying a collection of maps of the United Kingdom grouped together under the heading 'Geography'. The display incorporated this text:

> The United Kingdom of Great Britain is made up of 4 separate countries. These are: England. Wales. Scotland. Northern Ireland.

Here are their capital cities. Can you match each city to the right country?
Cardiff. Belfast. London. Edinburgh.

Whilst on the wall opposite was another display headed 'Pattern', which announced:

Year 4 have been creating patterns using TRANSLATION and ROTATION. Can you see which patterns are which?

Although these texts must have been alive at the point of making and appeared to be structured with a future literacy event in mind, in fact there was no evidence that any such event ever took place. No child paused to consider these questions or to move the capital cards to the 'right' countries. Perhaps these texts required the presence of a school inspector, or maybe a parent, to bring them into use?

If these were texts looking for a context which might activate them, then other texts looked highly unlikely ever to find such a thing. For instance, in one classroom, tucked away right at the end of the shelves, were multiple copies of a range of Ladybird books dating from the 1970s including history titles such as *Joan of Arc* and *The Story of Marco Polo*, topics which have never featured on the National Curriculum. Alongside them were a few stray copies of a reading scheme long since abandoned, and a dusty copy of a non-fiction book entitled *Bridges, Tunnels and Towers*. These texts seemed maximally dead, long since forgotten and abandoned. Such texts seemed to have no purchase on the enquiry and could in effect be dismissed. By contrast, those books in the class library that were riffled through but never actually borrowed did have something to say to the enquiry, if only as a reference point against which to judge those texts which made it from the shelf to a child's desk. Logging the choices participants made over a period of time from the potential pool of resources they had access to provided a better basis upon which to analyse the kinds of texts that were co-opted into literacy events in comparison to those that were not.

Text audits and text collections: working backwards from the evidence on the ground

Text audits were used to identify the full range of resources potentially available in a given location. In schools this meant considering both the environment of the classroom and the other public spaces that pupils had access to during the school day, such as the school library or corridor displays. Different techniques were used to record the results. For instance, it might be most appropriate to count the contents of a school library, or amass bibliographic details of texts in a class library; to log the range of official paperwork which appeared or disappeared on the teacher's desk, or photo-graph the types of texts that were on display on the noticeboards or in other areas of the school or classroom. Recording the text in its location helped establish the differences participants see between different groups of texts, as well as the criteria by which different kinds of texts become accessible.

Schools sort texts in a number of ways. They are often housed in quite different places according to their anticipated context of use. Some may be named and defined as well-motivated collections: topic books that stood upright on the windowsill, for instance, may well have been assembled and placed together for the duration of a particular sequence of classroom work. Others may appear less permanent or go unremarked; the pile of papers and books that lurk at the front of the class by the teacher's desk may simply be the week's resources for English or Maths lessons, kept together temporarily for ease of use. Even if they are not kept separately, the way texts are referred to can highlight salient characteristics which are important in terms of a text's use. Thus teachers commonly refer to some of the fiction texts that children are expected to borrow as 'chapter books'. In one sense this is a purely descriptive term which signals any book that is long enough to be divided into chapters. But it gains its particular reso-nance in this context through its relationship to the proficiency judgements teachers make about children's reading. In school, a 'chapter book' signals both a particular kind of text and the proficiency threshold individual readers need to pass if they are to make use of them and thus begin to function as independent readers. In primary schools, only rela-tively skilled readers are assumed to be able to muster the combination of skills and commitment that this length and complexity of text requires. The 'chapter book' therefore has a particular significance for teachers as to them it represents an important point on the ladder of support for reading which schools offer children. The publishing industry have responded to this perception by creating short books organised into chapters that seem to represent this precise tipping point. The usage of this term highlights the way in which fiction is in part bound into proficiency judgements in school settings and distinguishes a category of texts with particular salience within this context.

Paying attention to how texts are sorted and labelled in any one site leads the researcher to the working categories employed in particular set-tings, embedded in the purposes of the users, and redolent of the contexts any texts will be co-opted into. Conducted in tandem with observation of literacy events, such research techniques also reveal the difference between live texts (those that find their way into particular literacy events) and dead texts (those which don't). This distinction provides a much firmer basis upon which to understand the salient characteristics of the texts which are chosen.

How schools spell out the potential of non-fiction texts

Non-fiction texts are not a unitary category. They appear in different guises in different contexts across the school. In one sense one might define work-sheets or letters home to parents as non-fiction. Yet this would be to work outside the way the term itself is deployed in schools. There seem to be two main organising principles. On the one hand, there are the non-fiction texts which are associated with the reading curriculum and appear as part of reading for choice. On the other hand, there are the non-fiction texts which are associated with the procedural curriculum, and appear in subjects such as Science, History, Geography or even English. Schools vary in the relative weight they give to each of these.

When the bulk of the research data were collected for this book, three out of the four schools kept almost all of their non-fiction texts in the school library as a permanent reference collection. They were intended to be used for schoolwork in school time, rather than to be borrowed and taken home on the basis of personal interest. In practice, this made it very hard for children to get access to such books not least because so few of them would make it from the school library to the classroom. The exception was Bluebird School. This school was particularly committed to fully resourcing reading for choice as part of its English curriculum. In Bluebird pupils were expected to help choose the contents of their own class library every half-term by each borrowing one fiction and one non-fiction book from the central school library stock for this purpose. In this context, fiction and non-fiction were treated as equivalents and subject to the same conditions of use. In one of the other schools, Farthing, one of the teachers had encouraged the boys in her class to bring in football magazines to the class library. But here the magazines acted less as representatives of the bigger category, non-fiction, and more as tangible signs of boys' particular interests. This was the basis upon which they took their place in the class library. (See also Chapter 6.)

Non-fiction reading as work: reference books, textbooks, topic books and information books

Although non-fiction texts sometimes found their way into contexts associated with reading for choice, they were generally stored in places which made clear their strong association with classroom work. Classroom stores of non-fiction appear in one of three categories: as reference books, text-books or topic books. These all bring to mind teacher-directed tasks. In tandem with worksheets, these kinds of texts constitute the backbone of procedural reading. Such texts are not intended to be read as an end in themselves, but rather in the service of another goal. Work produced through their use was often displayed on noticeboards around the class or in corridors as evidence of this endeavour (see pp. 94–95).

Reference books included dictionaries, thesauruses and sometimes atlases. These texts were generally hardback, and bound rather than stapled. They were relatively few in number, certainly less than one per child. Often consisting of a variety of different editions and sourced from different publishers, they would be kept together in an area accessible to children but distinct from the class library. These books could generally be used by children at their own discretion during the course of their work, for instance as an aid to their writing. At other times the whole set would be brought out for the class to use as part of a teacher-directed activity. Under these circumstances children would undertake the same tasks using different versions of the required format. The precise terms of access varied between classrooms.

Textbooks (multiple copies of the same text, most often paperback and stapled) would be shelved in a separate area of the classroom, generally one reserved for access by the teacher. Purchased with whole-class use in mind, textbook content varied from those designed to ensure curriculum coverage in particular areas such as History or Science, to those designed to help drill children in core skills associated with Maths or English language. The latter often adopted the same instructional form as worksheets. Of the textbooks stored on shelves in classrooms, few were seen in regular use.

Topic books (most often hardback, and of larger physical dimensions than the fiction stock) were a more transient grouping of non-fiction texts brought together for the duration of a given theme and to support work on a particular topic in the broader curriculum. Topic books carrying out that function in class would consist of a mixed collection of texts produced by different publishers in different series and formats, but covering the same topic or theme. In some classrooms they would be propped upright with their covers showing, or they might be placed on tables near the noticeboard designated for display work on that theme, or they could be kept in a basket or box ready for use as needed. Unlike reference books and textbooks, they were not permanent residents in the classroom, but acted as temporary visitors, brought in from outside, either from the school library, sometimes other classrooms, or more distantly, the school library service.

By and large, the most concentrated use of topic books occurred during History, when children might well be given extended opportunities to find information on a given theme from the range of texts in class. This kind of curriculum activity was generally organised as procedural reading, in so far as the expectation was that the end point of the reading would be the production of a piece of writing summing up the information to be found in the published texts. Topic books assembled for use in other areas of the curriculum seemed to play a less central part in curriculum activity. In one classroom a topic box collected to support work on the Science topic, Sound, only became briefly accessible for browsing when and as children finished a sequence of teacher-directed tasks and before they moved on to other things.

One of the defining characteristics of these kinds of non-fiction is that they are never read through in sequence from beginning to end. Instead, the reader is expected to sample or browse the contents with a specific purpose in mind. Teachers might organise such sampling themselves on behalf of the class, either by choosing and then directing the class to particular pages; or alternatively by issuing a worksheet which steered pupils' course through the text. If they gave children the opportunity to browse the texts more freely, then they would expect them to follow principles of selection that had already been taught as part of the curriculum. In school settings, these principles of selection are most commonly referred to by teachers as information retrieval, study skills or reading for information(see below).

These three different kinds of text collections could be found in each of the classrooms where the research was based. In addition, the one school with a religious affiliation made a distinctive text collection in each of its classrooms in the form of prayer texts or Bibles assembled on a small table alongside a candle and religious icons or statuary. These different sorts of text collections were all formed in anticipation of certain kinds of literacy events. Inevitably, the precise rules for use and the frequency with which these texts were co-opted into literacy events varied from site to site. Thus in some classrooms, whilst topic books were prominently displayed on ledges or shelves for the duration of study of a particular theme, there were few official opportunities for children to actually take them down and use them. They seemed to do another kind of job in the class, announcing to the children by virtue of their presence exactly which aspect of History or Science they should be paying attention to.

The categories reference books, textbooks and topic books represent ways of thinking about texts. Many of the non-fiction texts which find their way into schools can also be more loosely grouped together as 'information books'. Publishers use this term as a way of signalling the broader categories of non-fiction books which are to be found sitting together on the shelves in the non-fiction section of school libraries, or in the children's section of public libraries. They may share many of the characteristics of the topic book, but are less closely tied to classroom use, often by virtue of the fact that their subject matter does not feature on the official curriculum. Many of these books never find their way into literacy events.

Schools and non-fiction: when discourse and text converge

Within schools, the notion that non-fiction books contain information and that it is the teacher's duty to teach children how to access and make use of that information is a strong one. It permeated a good deal of what happened in those literacy events where topic books came to life as part of the official business of the classroom. It also underpinned a good deal of teacher talk about those practices and found its formal expression in the documents which laid down the content of the English curriculum (DfEE, 1995). Generally known as information retrieval, this approach to dealing with non-fiction has a long history within the junior school curriculum. The skills associated with this practice can be taught either as a free-standing unit on the curriculum or as part of a particular subject such as History or English. They are sometimes packaged together with library skills, which is regarded as a way of teaching children to use the library classification system to find the non-fiction books they want, as well as the information they are looking for. In each case the object for the learner is to identify the relevant part of the text or collection from the whole.

In the British context, information retrieval is closely associated with the EXEL project, a research programme which attempted to identify, support and promote a range of reading strategies considered essential to making good use of non-fiction (Wray and Lewis, 1997). These include the reading strategies of skimming and scanning, as a means of processing the text, and what has become known as the EXIT model (Extending Interactions with Texts), a carefully staged sequence of pre-, during- and post-reading activities which children are now routinely taught as a way of dealing with information books.

These strategies provide a means of directing the processes of information retrieval so that children can amass, unify and recombine what they have taken from one text into another of their own making. In this way information is transformed into learning.

As far as their protagonists are concerned these strategies do no more than fit on to and in many ways express what good readers already do with non-fiction texts. Yet there is a conundrum here. The kinds of texts that are used to promote this way of reading in classrooms are themselves designed with precisely this use in mind. They embody ideas about how information can be constituted and then transferred from one place to another in anticipation of precisely this practice. Because these strategies are then enacted in classrooms, they apparently confirm that reading non-fiction is indeed a process of finding and assimilating new pieces of information. A kind of virtuous circle is built in which 'good' non-fiction texts are deemed to be those which both allow and encourage readers to behave in this way (Neate, 1992). Publishers, especially those with strong links to the education market, produce the texts to match. Discourse, object and practice converge. The circle is complete. The model of reading produces a context in which that model will be put into place, thereby necessitating a kind of text which will fulfil these same requirements, thus confirming the model.

Margaret Meek, in a detailed review of the kinds of non-fiction texts produced for the junior age group, points out that information books of the kind found in schools actually form a highly specific genre. They are not representative of all types of non-fiction, and indeed in some respects are quite peculiar to schools as institutional sites. She defines them as 'books to be learned from in systematic rather than informal ways, where the contents are arranged for pragmatic purposes of instruction or to promote in their readers definable acts of understanding' (Meek, 1996). Meek herself argues that such close convergence between discourse, object and practice is constraining, and puts unnecessary restrictions on what we imagine non-fiction to be. She maintains that information retrieval over-generalises about itself to the detriment of other forms of non-fiction text and other ways of reading. By taking this discourse to task she challenges the perceived view of what and how readers learn from non-fiction, and in the process advocates the production of a much broader variety of non-fiction texts (Meek, 1996).

Since the initial research period, information retrieval has been joined in English classrooms by another discourse about non-fiction: genre theory. Genre theory emerged in Australia in the 1980s as a form of linguistic analysis that specified a range of different non-fiction text types: report, instruction, explanation, and so on. Having laid out the varying rules of their construction, those advocating this analytic approach to non-fiction then argued that children should learn to write across this range in accordance with the general model of text construction which their linguistic analysis proposed (Martin *et al.*, 1994; see Barrs, 1994 for a critical review of genre theory). Once again, this approach has impacted both on curricula – the range of non-fiction text types so specified have been incorporated into the National Literacy Strategy in England – and on the texts publishers make for classroom use. Publishers now provide texts which conform to the specifications the linguists have laid down so that teachers can teach these text types to children. In England this discourse about non-fiction has had most impact on books designed to be used as part of the Literacy Hour and within the English curriculum. It finds its expression in textbooks or big books produced for whole-class use by publishers who already specialise in providing teaching materials for these contexts, such as Heinemann or Longman (see below. See also Goodwin and Routh, 2000). Yet whether or how the rules which generate these 'model text types' relate to the more general run of non-fiction texts that circulate elsewhere remains open to question.

Making a text to do the job: designing information books for schools

Most of the non-fiction texts in primary school are produced by a small range of publishers who produce texts specifically for this market. Oxford University Press provide many of the most commonly seen reference books. Franklin Watts, Wayland (now known as Hodder Wayland) and A & C Black are particularly closely associated with the production of topic books, whilst publishers such as Longman and Ginn are geared more to the textbook market. All of these publishers participate in the Educational Publishers Council, a special interest group within the Publishers' Association whose members are committed to 'producing materials which can specifically be classified as publications for use in the course of instruction in school' (EPC quoted in Attar, 1996). They are specialists who play to their market's requirements and tailor their production to what will be needed where on the school curriculum and in school libraries in the light of current legislation and the dominant ideas in professional practice.

A very different set of publishers' names appear on the fiction shelves: Penguin, Red Fox, Corgi, Mammoth, Bloomsbury, to list a few. If publishers specialise within the domain of non-fiction, then they specialise between fiction and non-fiction too. Scholastic are one of the few publishers to cross both domains with their *Horrible Histories* and *Horrible Science* books, yet these are also rare examples of non-fiction texts which are packaged to look like fiction titles. They are not primarily targeted at the educational market but at the leisure market where they take their place alongside the rest of Scholastic's fiction imprint.

Information books in school: non-fiction
and the rise of the double spread

As designed objects the kinds of information books destined for the school market stand out. Their physical dimensions are different from fiction texts; the pages are of a larger size and in the case of topic books they contain far more illustrations than any other category of print text available in schools except picture books or books using a cartoon format. These kinds of texts adopt their own distinct rules of layout, dominated by their use of the double spread as an organising principle which subdivides the central topic of the book into a series of manageable sub-themes, each one given its own space (Moss, 2001b).

Two history books destined for the school market and published in the 1990s demonstrate these kinds of design principles: Heinemann's *See Through History: Ancient Greece* (Loverance and Wood, 1998) and Ginn's *Ancient Greece* (Forrest, 1992) which were both observed in classroom use during the research. According to the publisher's list, Ginn's *Ancient Greece* is strictly speaking a textbook, available for sale in sets or half sets as well as individually. Like other textbooks it has soft covers and is stapled rather than bound. But the page layout of the Ginn History series makes these texts look more like topic books. (They may well have been designed to function in either category. Indeed, during the period of observation this title was seen used by pupils for individual research as well as an adjunct to whole-class teaching.) Heinemann's *See Through History: Ancient Greece* is more straightforwardly a topic book in a series aimed at library rather than classroom purchase. It has hard covers and is perfect bound. Schools would be expected to own a single copy for individual pupil use, though it was on one occasion also seen used in a whole class setting.

Both books employ the double spread as their primary means of organising their content. The contents page for Heinemann's *See Through History: Ancient Greece* lists the following themes on consecutive double pages: The Origins of the Greeks; The Land of Greece; The Greeks and the Sea; The Greek People; Family Life. The contents page for Ginn's *Ancient Greece* lists in the same number of pages: The Greeks at Sea; The Cities; Athens; The Parthenon; Markets and Shops. Each double spread contains a number of shared features. The main heading is positioned at the top left of the double spread. Underneath the heading is a lead paragraph summarising the main theme. The rest of each double spread consists of a mixture of writing and illustrations that instantiate this theme. The relationship between the elements on the page is established via headings, subheadings and/or captions. So on the double spread headed 'The Parthenon', in Ginn's *Ancient Greece*, two subheadings, 'How was the Parthenon built?' and 'Inside the Parthenon', are used to demarcate the two subsidiary subsections that will be dealt with in this space.

In each text, illustrations have a prominent place on the page, with the largest often spreading across the gutter from one page to the other. They do not occur in fixed positions, so that each double spread looks slightly different in this respect. The illustrations carry some of the information the reader is expected to peruse. Captions used for the illustrations help explain rather than just name what can be seen in the pictures. Thus in Heinemann's *See Through History: Ancient Greece* on the page headed 'The Land of Greece', the following caption is laid up next to an illustration of the sanctuary at Delphi.

> The sanctuary of Delphi, believed to be the holiest place in Greece, was built high up on a mountainside under the cliffs of Parnassos. Pilgrims went there to learn about the future by consulting the oracle in the Temple of Apollo. They went in procession to the Great Altar to make sacrifices and say prayers before going inside.
>
> (Loverance and Wood, 1998, p. 7)

This is the only reference to the sanctuary on the page. The caption in effect acts as a mini-paragraph, carrying additional information that can be added to the general topic 'The Land of Greece' and linked to the picture it accompanies.

Given these broad similarities, there are also some differences. Loverance and Wood (1998) contains more writing in a smaller print size than Forrest (1992). More of the written text is laid up as a series of columns stretching across the page. The writing itself shows more cohesion over greater length, and in effect makes more demands on its readers.

However, the use of subheadings means it is relatively easy to see at a glance what kind of information can be found where. Thus the page headed 'The Land of Greece' contains these subheadings: 'A skeleton of a land'; 'A hardy people'; 'Natural defences'; 'A landscape for gods'; 'A record of the past'. None of these subsections is more than two paragraphs long. In Forrest, more of the information is carried in the illustrations, with the writing directly supporting understanding of what can be seen, rather than vice versa. Text cohesion is weaker. Elements on the page are less closely bound into a cohesive whole.

Teaching information retrieval means in part teaching pupils to recognise the help that the book offers in terms of what information can be found where via the contents page, the index and the use of headings, illustrations and captions.

Book design over time

Use of the double spread is now commonplace in topic book design. Yet this is a relatively recent phenomenon which has arisen within a particular timeframe in relation to the technologies available and publishers' application of those technologies to the perceived requirements of their markets (see Kress and van Leeuwen, 1996; Moss, 2003b). Criticisms that have been voiced about the use of the double spread have mainly focused on whether it has led to a reduction in the information content such texts carry. For when the double spread stops, the exploration of that theme stops too. Information shrinks to fit the size of the page.

Two examples I have to hand of history books produced for schools in the 1950s and 1960s demonstrate these changes. The same size and appearance as paperback fiction, instead of being organised around the double spread they are structured round chapter-length stretches of continuous prose. In Longman's *Elizabethan Citizen* (Reeves and Hodgson, 1962) the book as a whole is divided into two parts, called respectively 'The Elizabethan citizen in a country town' and 'The Elizabethan citizen in London'. Each part is divided into further subsections with headings such as 'The citizen at home' or 'Shops and trades' but these range between five to fourteen pages long and follow on one from the other, as part of a continuous flow of writing. The writing is chunked into paragraphs but these operate as links in a much longer chain. Although the writing is interspersed with a variety of images, some with captions and some without, these occur at the rate of less than one image per page, and follow on from information in the written text rather than contributing something in their own right. The captions do no more than describe what can be seen. Thus a line drawing derived from a Tudor print showing young men playing in the street with ball and sticks is simply captioned, 'A game like hockey' (ibid., p. 45) and accompanies this bit of text:

In the summer evenings, when work was done, people strolled out to play games or to watch them, for they could not shut themselves in a hot cinema or stay indoors to watch the television. The older men played bowls in a cool green bowling-alley. The lads practised wrestling or jumping or played leap-frog. Sometimes they played a game like hockey in the streets.

(Ibid., pp. 44–45)

A & C Black's *People in History 3: Great Tudors and Stuarts* (Unstead, 1956) is divided into more conventional chapters of between seven and fourteen pages long, each focused on a separate individual. The chapters are titled but there are no subheadings within the chapters. Each chapter incorporates between three and four lined drawings, roughly half a page in size. In addition, there are three full-page colour illustrations printed on separate pages and on a different kind of paper and spaced through the text. In the case of both these books, the reader's job is clearly to follow the text within each substantial section from beginning to end. Neither of these texts provide the reader with an easy means of sampling or browsing their contents. Instead, the reader must make their way through a continuous stretch of prose lasting over several pages.

In both older books the information that the reader might be looking for is woven into the fabric of a lengthy stretch of text. This makes it hard to immediately pick out. By contrast, in contemporary topic books the information sought is much easier to find. All the different elements of the design tell readers very clearly where to look for the information they seek. A different balance between the information load carried in the pictures and in the writing seems also to have weakened the cohesive relationship between individual written paragraphs (Kress and van Leeuwen, 1996; Moss, 2001b). Each paragraph or subsection is easier to read as a relatively free-standing unit acting independently of the others on the page, and therefore outside of a tightly fixed order. Taken together these design features allow for fast retrieval of the information that is sought within a comparatively short time. If the selection of information on any one page looks too insubstantial for the reader's purposes, it can also be repackaged into a new order by amalgamating and combining information on one page with information on another. New possibilities for use open up.

Information books in their context of use

The relationship between text and context will be explored in the three examples that follow of the use of non-fiction texts as part of the official curriculum. Each records a particular context in which the teacher expects children to retrieve and then represent information from the texts concerned. These are, broadly speaking, procedural encounters where the success of the children's engagement with the text will be judged through the completion of a written task. In each case the texts are remade in slightly different ways depending in part on the extent to which teachers take direct control over what children do with the text or alternatively create conditions in which pupils themselves can take the lead.

Making the textbook in History: co-opting texts into teacher tales

The literacy event below comes from a history lesson in Shepherd School. The Year 4 class had been studying the Ancient Greeks using both textbooks and topic books. Textbooks were used when the teacher talked the children through the relevant sections of the text herself, thus controlling the flow of information. Topic books were used when the children were expected to find and retrieve relevant information on a given topic independently.

In this lesson sequence the teacher used Ginn's *Ancient Greece* as a textbook. The available half-set of copies had been shared out amongst the class so that each pupil was in sight of a copy. The teacher maintained control over the text by deciding which passages to select, reading them aloud to the class and then explaining their relevance for the theme she was teaching. The children were expected to make use of the material presented in this way in the written task which followed. By and large the children looked at the teacher as she talked, not at the texts. (The prominence given to oral narrative in these sessions was typical of many of the other literacy events which took place in this school.)

The following extract gives a flavour of the progress the class made through the text together, as the teacher used the whole-class space by turns to guide pupils to particular pictures or paragraphs, involve children in discussion of particular elements in the textbook, or spell out the significance of what she was showing them:

Example 1: Teaching the story of Ancient Greece

TEACHER: So we've found out two things already/ on this page (pp. 6–7 in Forrest, 1992) we've found out where the two cities were, Sparta was and where Athens was, where Athens still is today ... we've found out how they were ruled and what it was like for people in those two cities, and we've found out about a man called Pericles and what it means to have a democracy. Now I want you to turn to page 8, you can see a drawing of a wonderful building of Athens called the Parthenon. Now the Parthenon, on page 8 and page 9, in the middle is a building that the people of Athens built, with, inside they had a statue of one of their goddesses ... called Athena, and if you turn over the page to page 11 ... you will see a beautiful statue of a woman, it was {teacher starts reading} '*The statue's face, arms and feet were covered in white ivory*' which is the tusks of elephants, '*and her clothes were covered with ... gold. Her eyes were made of precious stones*' and this was a beautiful statue they had in Athens, so going on a beautiful building like that, and they had a beautiful statue with gold and ivory and jewels, what does it tell you about the people of Athens?

PUPIL: They were rich

PUPIL: They worship a god

PUPIL: They were good at making things

TEACHER: Yes they were very good at making things. These people in Athens can build fantastic buildings and they didn't have mechanical diggers and hydraulic lifts and cranes that we have today but they still managed to build incredible huge buildings

PUPIL: Are they making it? {Looking at the pictures on the preceding page}

TEACHER: Yes, on that page you can see where they are digging up, where they go to dig the marble out on the mountain// Right, page 18 and 19 {And the class turn on to the section on life in Sparta}

(Shepherd, Year 4)

Woven together into the teacher's whole-class talk, these extracts were used to tell a story about the rise of the city states of Athens and Sparta and the differences between them. This led to a writing task where pictures taken from the different pages in the book were used to prompt children into telling what they now knew about the two cities. To complete the written task the children could consult the textbooks, which remained on their desks during this time, or rely on their memory of what the teacher had said. Some quietly asked fellow pupils for help.

In this classroom the teacher's own talk held an important role in mediating the contents of the text to the students. Over time the way in which the teacher staged the selection of topics that she covered turned the study of Ancient Greece into a narrative of its rise and fall which would conclude with the death of Alexander the Great. In these history lessons, the teacher was the official guide to the topic. The texts backed her up rather than substituted for her own voice and were interwoven accordingly into the spoken text she created. To a great extent this was achieved by working with the grain of the texts she had chosen. For instance, in the event referred to above each of the chosen pages contained a variety of text chunks – either images or writing – clearly delineated one from another and each relatively easy to abstract from the company it kept on the page (Forrest, 1992). This gave her room to edit, elaborate and rework that material into a new relationship through her spoken commentary. For pupils, following the story of Ancient Greece meant following this commentary and the relationship the teacher made between parts of the text rather than turning to the text itself as the primary source of information.

Making the topic book in History: pupil networks
and the competition for resources

The following example of topic work in History looks rather different. Here the pupils had been given the task of navigating their way through the available texts independently. Like the Year 4 class in Shepherd, this Year 5 group at Bluebird were studying the Ancient Greeks. But in this setting much of the job of finding out about Ancient Greece had been devolved to the pupils in a series of carefully managed tasks which they had to undertake using the sizeable collection of resources the teacher had collected for this purpose. Some came from the school library, others from the school library service. These had been supplemented with anything that children could bring in from home.

The unit of work was conceptualised by the teacher as an exercise in information retrieval. Before they started on the topic the teacher had asked the pupils to identify what they already knew about the Ancient Greeks, as well as what they would like to learn more about. This is consistent with the EXIT model of non-fiction reading formalised by Wray and Lewis as a means of enabling children to connect new knowledge to old in ways that are conducive to learning (Wray and Lewis, 1997). As the work unfolded the teacher also invited children to list and reprise strategies appropriate to the task in hand. These included note-taking, summarising and using keywords as well as reminders about the value of contents pages and indexes and how to use them well to find the information they wanted.

The sequence of tasks involved the children working in small groups to amass a range of information from the available texts on a given theme. The information they had retrieved would then be written up into a joint document incorporating individual contributions. Whilst the general task would be set by the teacher, the children could often choose the particular aspect of the topic they wanted to work on themselves. The precise subject didn't matter as long as the whole group were involved in searching for relevant information in the texts provided and could demonstrate their success by transforming what they had found into a written account.

From the children's point of view one of the most crucial aspects of the exercise was the struggle to control the best resources. Not all of the books were equally good at dealing with all of the topics and indeed some topics were not well covered anywhere. Getting the right topic as well as the right resources to enable adequate information retrieval to take place was a key part of successfully completing the exercise. The struggle over resources and how it could be resolved is revealed in the following episode, recorded in field notes. At this stage the groups had been asked to compile a Fact File about the Greek gods as a way of seeking out and then transforming the relevant range of information. Most of the class were looking for pictures they could draw as well as writing that could act as source material.

The notes read like this:

Example 2: Knowing how to find the right text

HISTORY, TABLES

David is finding good bits and showing them to John and Leo so that they can take them and draw. Dermot and Peter are using the index to find Hercules using the *Illustrated Book of Myths: Tales and legends of the world*. Hercules is on Peter's worksheet. The boys chat excitedly about the work. [They are] buzzing round the class ... Swapping books, comparing a whole heap, consulting David about where the best pictures are. David explains {to the researcher} where the *Illustrated Book of Myths* came from = Mum, as she's a DK [publisher's] Rep. 'I looked at *How would you survive as an Ancient Greek?*, thought not much there, got *Myths* book instead.' David knows the book and is glad to have it.

When I talk to Bella, they have a single copy of book with one [boring, highly constrained*] list of gods on their 'favourite page' {*Young Researcher: The Greeks*}. It is the only book they are consulting. They like it because 'all the information is there'.

[*These adjectives are the researcher's, not the girl's]

(Bluebird, Year 5)

One way of finding the information you want from a topic book is indeed to use the contents page or index to search the text. Two boys are observed doing precisely this. But in fact for many of the boys in this class the quickest and most reliable route to finding what they needed was to ask David. By virtue of his mother's job as a Dorling Kindersley sales rep, David had been able to bring the greatest quantity of resources into class from home and throughout this session acted as a kind of unofficial librarian to the rest of the boys, helping particular classmates get their hands on what they wanted. Someone in search of a good picture of a god could find it most efficiently with David's help. He both knew more about what was in many of the books and, because he got asked most often, he also knew who had made off with what.

What the boys above were looking for was not just information per se, but the kinds of information that were interesting enough to spend time on as well as allow them to complete their classroom task. In this instance that included good stories. The search for information about the gods also provided an opportunity to swap tales from Greek mythology that involved action and excitement (the Disney film *Hercules* was due out later that year, which may have accounted for some of their interest in Greek myths at this time). A dramatic illustration provided an opportunity to tell each other what they knew about the various characters involved and their deeds.

In fact, these boys spent a good part of this session tracking down resources from each other and brokering deals amongst themselves about who would use which book, when. In their groups they had often come to quite complex arrangements about who would do the necessary drawings and who would do the writing. Fulfilling these requirements might well take them to different text sources. All of this created a pattern of busy movement around the class amongst the boys' tables as resources were swapped and exchanged, the good ones identified and then passed on. A non-fiction task – create a Fact File – and non-fiction texts created the space to actively spend time on fiction, trading details of the myths they knew. The gods they chose were the ones who participated in the most interesting tales.

The two girls observed seemed to have come to the conclusion that it was not worth trying to compete with this hectic level of activity. Instead, they settled for using resources which were less in demand. Bella and her friend consistently made off with the same 'favourite' book (Dineen, 1991). As there was no competition for it, they knew they could always find it quite easily on the topic table. To the researcher's eye the reason for its comparative neglect seemed quite obvious, as the only information it had on the gods was a long written list of their names and responsibilities. There were no pictures on this page, and no details of any of the stories linked to the individual deities. But from these girls' point of view, as the list was long it was also comprehensive, so it meant that everything they needed to complete their task was all in one place. The book they had chosen made getting the job of work done easier. In this context these boys seem to have recontextualised information retrieval into playful social interaction, whilst these girls treated it as more school work, best completed most economically.

These two examples, from Shepherd and Bluebird School respectively, show both teachers and pupils making different use of the affordance of non-fiction texts and the combinations of writing and image which they contain as they tackle the same topic in History. The pupils exercise more or less control over their route through the text, depending upon whether the texts are used as topic books or textbooks, and whether the act of reading takes place in whole-class or individual settings. The fit between text and context alters accordingly.

Making the information book in English: learning where to go

The final example comes from a sequence of lessons designed to teach information retrieval as a self-contained topic to the Year 3 pupils at Bluebird as part of the English curriculum. Here the teacher sets out to teach information retrieval precisely as a transferable skill, a way of doing reading which readers need to know to be able to function in the kind of Year 5 classroom described above. Teaching and resources are designed to converge on a single view of what non-fiction is and how it should be used.

Organised under the heading 'Reading for information', these weekly sessions were planned round the use of a set of commercially produced worksheets. These were called 'Reading for information: Red set' and were published by Scholastic Literacy Centre. The worksheets were variously headed 'Cover story'; 'What I learned from my book'; 'Skimming and scanning'; and 'How useful is this book?'. Use of the worksheets turned each session into a closely monitored procedural event as the children leafed through the texts to answer the questions they were set.

The group observed here were designated low ability readers and were being helped during the lesson by a number of classroom assistants. This time round the children were using a worksheet headed 'Looking at pictures and captions'. A variety of 'information books' had been collected from the school library and then spread out around the classroom. Titles included *Minibeasts* (Royston, 1992); *Planes* (Bailey, 1988); *See How They Grow: Lamb* (Royston, 1992); *Small Animals* (Royston, 1991); *Does It Bounce?* (Bryant-Mole, 1995); and *Tropical Rainforests* (Silver, 1998). The main criteria for their selection seemed to be that they contained both words and pictures and that the writing was pitched at a level which made appropriate demands on this group of readers. Pupils were expected to choose one text to work on.

The extract which follows comes from the start of the lesson and is reproduced from the original field notes. The teacher begins by summarising the difference between fiction and non-fiction texts:

Example 3: Teaching the skills to read non-fiction texts

English workshop: Reading for information. Location: classroom mat

TEACHER: Today we're looking inside the book. Not like a story book. With a story book, start at the beginning cos won't miss anything. Information book it's not so important. Contents page is there to help us find the information we want.
{As the teacher does her monologue children look for what she flags up in their books.}
Something else that can help you is the index at the back of the book.
{The helpers are finding the relevant bits for kids.}

TEACHER: How does the index help us?

PUPIL: Tells us where the pages are and the numbers.
{Teacher shows items in alphabet order – helpers demonstrate.}

TEACHER: If you want to find information you can use the contents page.
{Teacher shows don't have to read whole book, can find bit straight away.}

(Bluebird, Year 3)

The teacher anchors the lesson by restating the principles this group should apply to reading fiction – start at the beginning of the text and then plough straight on – before suggesting that non-fiction offers an escape from this practice. To demonstrate the principles upon which such an escape should be managed, she then goes on to identify some of the special features associated with the organisation of non-fiction texts – in this instance, contents pages, indexes and alphabetical order – and their function in providing readers with a short cut to the particular part of the text they might be looking for. Escape from one set of reading rules is therefore managed by the introduction of another: the organised hunt for information. The event helps construct the category of 'non-fiction' as a distinct entity, subject to a specific kind of practice.

The worksheet itself required children to answer a series of more detailed questions about the role of illustration in the particular text they were working on, such as 'Are [the pictures] captioned?', 'Do they help explain the text? Why or why not?'. In many respects these are leading questions, predicated on an ideal view of what the relationship between writing and image should be in non-fiction texts. They are designed to draw the children's attention to the ways in which particular text features help encode and relay the information carried. The teaching point will be reinforced if children identify the general feature in the particular text they are looking at, or even recognise its omission. However, whilst some of the texts available for the purposes of this task did keep to the rules the worksheet was predicated on, others did not. *See How They Grow: Lamb* (Royston, 1992), for instance, does not have a contents or index page, whilst the relationship it expresses between image and writing cannot be adequately captured by the questions 'Are [the pictures] captioned?' or 'Do they help explain the text?'.

In fact, the text is organised as a sequence of double spreads which illustrate different moments in the life cycle of a lamb as it grows over the first twelve weeks of its life. From the perspective of genre theory, the writing is most easily characterised as recount, and consists of a series of paragraphs written in the first person and voicing what the lamb sees and does, laid up in loose association with the accompanying illustrations on the page. I would argue that this is a hybrid text which really operates as a non-fiction picture book. My local library certainly categorises it this way and keeps it with other non-fiction picture books for young readers. It looks as if it is predicated on a rather different context of use: an adult and young child sharing the book together, with the adult following the writing and the child following the pictures, in the manner in which Henrietta Dombey describes in Chapter 3. From the perspective of information retrieval this may indeed be a less-than-ideal text in this particular context of use. The fact that it breaks the rules means that it cannot help consolidate the lessons that are expected to be learnt in this context about non-fiction reading.

In this particular event, the teacher and the worksheet steer the children through the text with a particular intention in mind: that this activity will inculcate the requisite knowledge children need to transfer into their own reading of non-fiction on the curriculum. What counts as reading non-fiction here is the ability to understand and work with the signposts the text gives about what kinds of information can be located where. The appearance of lessons on reading for information as a specific unit signals the importance teachers attach to managing pupils' transition into this kind of non-fiction reading, and doing so well. From the teachers' perspective, children need to learn how to recognise and respond appropriately to the kind of text they have in front of them. Browsing, sampling and dipping in and out of the text become appropriate strategies to employ with non-fiction when they are mar-shalled to fulfil a particular purpose. The teacher's job is to make this sense of purpose clear. If non-fiction books contain information, then the teacher needs to teach children how to systematically access and make use of that information. But in fact to fit in with this view, part of what some non-fiction texts potentially offer has to be screened out.

Different contexts bring texts to life in different ways. Information retrieval positions the texts as repositories of knowledge to be carefully searched for precise nuggets of information which can be extracted, amal-gamated and turned into another text as proof that the reader has read in the approved way. The ideal texts are those which allow this process to go on with a minimum of distraction or disruption. Yet such a tight conver-gence on the discourse of information retrieval is hard to maintain. Classroom contexts are multi-layered. They and the texts brought into such encounters point in other directions too. Thus the boy who was working on *See How They Grow: Lamb* completed the final question on the worksheet which asked: 'As an illustrated information book, how well does this com-pare with others?', with the answer 'It is not so exciting as a book about motorbikes'. This comment effectively changes the text, the reader and the context for making sense of the text, too. If he were looking at a book about motorbikes he would not be answering these kinds of questions.

Design choices and reading paths:
fiction and non-fiction reconsidered

Working backwards from the contexts to the texts in the literacy events analysed above suggests different ideal versions of the text that would fit participants' purposes more or less closely. Who gets to define what that ideal text is and then has the means to operationalise it varies in the three examples given in this chapter. In the first, the teacher uses particular text features to remake the text in her own way. By contrast, the second exam-ple shows pupils largely deciding for themselves what the ideal text will be in the context of the task they have been set and the resources to hand to accomplish it. The girls and boys observed chose differently. In the third example both teacher and worksheet converge on a broadly similar view of what the ideal non-fiction text should be, following the discourse of information retrieval. Yet the texts themselves, and readers too, can be harder to pin down than the discourse would allow.

The problem with the discourse of information retrieval is not so much that it makes an explicit connection between text and context of use, but that it presumes that the context of use it specifies is the only possible one, and that the ideal text type cannot vary from its own specification. In fact, the analysis of what readers do with non-fiction texts in different contexts shows that these texts offer up many more possibilities. They do so largely through the reading paths they employ.

Linear versus non-linear reading paths in fiction and non-fiction texts

The term 'reading paths' stems from the work of Kress and van Leeuwen (1996). They use it to refer to the way texts encode the route they expect readers to take through them. They argue that different kinds of reading paths may constrain or determine what the reader does to a greater or lesser degree. The main distinction they draw is between what they call the linear structure of continuous prose which unfolds through the logic of time and the non-linear structure of compositions that use the logic of space. Non-linear structures work within the confines of the space of the page, the picture or the screen by bringing into contiguous relationship everything which can be juxtaposed there. This allows writing and image to be mixed in much more fluid ways (ibid., pp. 218–233).

> [Non-linear] composition sets up particular hierarchies of the movement of the hypothetical reader within and across their different elements. [In these texts] reading paths begin with the most salient element, from there move to the next most salient element, and so on. Their trajectories are not necessarily similar to that of the densely printed page, left–right and top–bottom, but may move in a circle ... from the most salient element ... to the text, and from the text back ... again, in a circular fashion. Whether the reader only 'reads' the [image] and the headline, or also part or all of the verbal text, a complimentarity, a to-and-fro between text and image, is guaranteed.
>
> (Ibid., pp. 218–219)

In the text world of the primary school, fiction and non-fiction texts encompass very different kinds of reading paths. The densely written pages of a *Harry Potter* novel stand as a good example of a linear text. The reader must start at the beginning and move through the text in a fixed linear sequence. The experience unfolds over time as sentence follows sentence, paragraph follows paragraph and chapter follows chapter. The book does not lend itself to being read in any other way. By contrast, the kinds of non-fiction produced as information books for the school market begin to work with the logic of space as soon as they adopt the organising principle of the double spread. Some of the non-fiction texts that find their way into classrooms take this move a step further by using the pictures rather than the written text to organise the page layout (Moss, 2001b). In so doing, they fully exploit the potential of non-linear design and offer up new possibilities to readers.

Non-fiction as picture-led non-linear texts

Dorling Kindersley's *Eyewitness Guides* stand as good examples of picture-led non-linear texts (Moss, 2001b). They were also amongst the first publishers to design in this way. Dorling Kindersley (DK) design works on the basic premise that the space represented by the double spread will contain and organise what can be said, and that readers will sample at their own discretion across the various elements, whether pictures or writing. Each double spread therefore holds a variety of images and an assortment of accompanying paragraphs that are held in a loose association with each other, depending upon their position on the page, their relative size, and therefore their prominence in the overall layout. There is no fixed sequence in which writing and images must be read. If readers can dip in and out of what is presented on the page, they can also dip in and out of what is presented in the entire text, for the pages can be read in any order too. Readers can be highly selective about which elements of the text they will attempt, and which they will ignore altogether. Such selections do not have to be made with a fixed purpose in mind; rather, readers can sample as they go according to what they deem most salient on the page. A different relationship with the text becomes possible. If reading a linear text such as *Harry Potter* means submitting to the exact order the author lays down, then reading an *Eyewitness Guide* allows the reader to combine different elements from the text in the order in which the reader chooses. The design represents a different pacing and structure to the reading experience, expressed in the material composition of the text.

Linear and non-linear design solutions necessitate very different time commitments on the part of their readers, and suggest different social contexts in which that reading will take place. In this respect a fiction text like *Harry Potter* and a non-fiction text like the *Eyewitness Guides* do indeed stand at opposite ends of the spectrum. Compared to other linear texts available in school, each volume of *Harry Potter* forms a particularly lengthy stream of continuous prose, with no illustrations to break up the whole. It requires a substantial time commitment to complete. It can only be shared simultaneously by more than one reader if the text is read aloud to a group. Both page- and print-size are too small to allow for anything else. Whilst parents might do this for children at home, the sheer length of the text would prohibit most teachers from making such an attempt in school, whilst reducing the larger text to extracts would not preserve the narrative thread. Under these circumstances it would be hard for two friends to co-ordinate their progress through the text, even if they started reading the same volume on the same day. *Harry Potter* in present-day England is an individual read which requires a considerable commitment of solitary time. Sharing the text comes afterwards, in discussion with friends as highlights are recalled, on bulletin boards and websites, or at *Harry Potter* parties, where episodes and activities are relived.

At the other end of the spectrum the non-linear composition employed in *Eyewitness Guides* offers very different possibilities. Gone are the kinds of linguistic markers so characteristic of linear prose that bind one paragraph into a fixed position between two others as the text unfolds. Instead, the individual elements on the page are brought into a much looser relationship, derived from the combination of images as well as writing. These kinds of texts are easy to share in real time precisely because the layout makes possible a number of entry points on any one page. The size and prominence of the images and the bite-sized chunks of writing mean that it is easy for two or more readers to synchronise their progress around any double spread together or indeed take different routes and then sporadically converge on something that has caught one reader's eye. All of this can happen at speed over a relatively short space of time. This kind of multi-orchestration of reading of the same text at the same time was indeed what was most commonly observed to happen to these kinds of non-fiction whenever children could make use of them in school (see the Introduction and also Chapter 5).

In *Eyewitness Guides*, the particular relationship between image and writing encoded in the design gives maximum freedom to the readers. Take as an example the double spread 'Water in the desert' from the *Eyewitness Guide, Desert* (Macquitty, 1994, pp. 14–15). Where more conventional non-fiction layout establishes a kind of hierarchical relationship between the main heading, the lead paragraph on the page and the rest of the writing, which any pictures can be expected to supplement, the images here seem to do something different. The largest and most striking images on the page headed 'Water in the desert' are first and foremost a spitting cobra and, to a lesser extent, some tadpole shrimps. These dominate the double spread. Given the salience of these images, particularly the snake which rises bottom to top of the page on the right-hand side and close to the gutter margin, it would be perfectly possible to ignore the stated theme 'Water in the desert' and concentrate instead on the gruesome-looking creatures. (Readers observed in action with this text pretty much did just that, browsing through the text to find the most striking illustrations. See the Introduction.) The page design facilitates this kind of screening out of the written context in which the image appears because of its dramatic salience. In fact, closer analysis of the written text shows that the relationship of the images to the overall topic on this double spread remains implicit. The sub-theme of animals that live near water in the desert which unites the cobra with the tadpole shrimps has to be inferred from the aggregation of the images, and the subheadings, captions and mini paragraphs which accompany them rather than being directly named. (See also Moss, 2002a.)

DK are quite explicit about the role that image takes in their text and the way in which the illustration leads the page design. Their trademark design is an image cropped in such a way that it stands out against the white background of the page and is thereby freed from the clutter of its immediate context. In DK *Eyewitness Guides*, the writing often runs round the shape of the images rather than vice versa. Thus on the double spread in *Desert* labelled 'Birds' the writing is laid up to follow and fit round the shape of the dominant images, notably the picture of a hawk swooping down to land on its prey, wings held apart in broad curves that form an upturned crescent on the page (Macquitty, 1994, pp. 30–31). Such a design solution is in large part dependent on the advent of new technologies to the processes of printing, and in particular to the move from the conventional press to the computer as the vehicle for text design (Moss, 2001b). The technology makes possible new ways of combining image and writing, just as it facilitates much more intense use of colour and close-up. These are the necessary ingredients which feed into the production of picture-led texts.

Picture-led and non-linear non-fiction in and out of school

DK adopted their hallmark design without reference to the school market and its needs. They started as trade packagers, designing texts that could be repackaged in a variety of different languages by keeping the same images but changing the written text. They then largely built their customer base in the UK by appointing local representatives to sell direct to parents. Whilst they remained an independent company, they also stayed outside the Educational Publishers Council and the defining purposes it sets down for its members. For all these reasons the fact that they have bent the rules for information retrieval in their text design has been a selling point that differentiates them from others in the market. In the *Eyewitness Guides*, the fluid relationship between image and writing both stimulates and exploits a kind of playful engagement with the substance of the text, in which the image is used to grab the reader's attention on its own merits, rather than illustrate a point made in the written text. Grabbing the attention of the reader in this way invokes a very different strategy for steering round the contents of a text than leading the reader to the nugget of information they are already seeking.

117

Reviews of Dorling Kindersley within the education community have expressed a certain nervousness over this design style and its value. Has the information content shrunk at the expense of the eye-catching appeal of the pictures? Is there too wide a discrepancy between the attraction of the image and the reading level required to get through the written text (Buckingham and Scanlon, 2003)? But many in the publishing world have also borrowed and imitated their approach. It is hard to treat the design characteristics of MacDonald Young's *Discoveries* as anything other than a homage to Dorling Kindersley. By opting for a combination of photography and drawing rather than photography alone they both imitate and then go beyond the impact of the DK double spread by staging particularly dramatic hand-drawn shots that would be hard to achieve with a camera: a bear plunging its claw into a marmoset's burrow, viewed from inside the burrow looking out (pp. 22–23), or a funnel-web spider poised to strike with head up and fangs bared (p. 33), both illustrations included in *Dangerous Animals* (Seidensticker and Lumpkin, 1995).

There are other ways of exploiting the non-linear design possibilities the double spread affords. Design innovation rests largely with publishers who are less narrowly focused on the school market than the members of the Educational Publishers Council. They are less constrained by fitting the text to contexts predicated on school-based study. The Kingfisher *I Wonder Why* series, for instance, dispenses with the idea of managing the flow of information by carefully differentiating between main heading, lead paragraph and then assorted subheadings or even establishing an overarching theme on each page. Thus in *I Wonder Why: Vultures are bald and other questions about birds* (O'Neill, 1998) these headings can be found on the same page, all in the same font size: 'Who's the best dressed bird?'; 'Do all birds sing?'; 'Which bird looks a fright?' (pp. 18–19). It is quite hard to identify the implied theme which brings these disparate chunks onto the same page together. Both illustrations and headings compete to grab the reader's attention in equal measure whilst the text chunks can be read quite independently of each other, from right to left or top to bottom. Text cohesion above the level of the paragraph weakens. Meanwhile, Aladdin's *I Didn't Know That* series, organised in a similar fashion round a sequence of questions, adds in a picture quiz on each page so that readers hunt for the hidden image, much in the way they would if they were reading a picture book like *Where's Wally?* (Handford, 1989). Increasingly, such design innovations are geared to generating immediate impact. They signal fun rather than methodical study as the most likely motive the reader will bring to the text.

Non-fiction and the pursuit of knowledge or non-fiction for fun?

Whilst some quarters of the publishing industry have been blurring the boundaries between non-fiction for study and non-fiction for fun, this poses something of a dilemma for the topic book market. In many respects, topic books increasingly adopt elements of a non-linear style. Illustrations take the central place on the double spread stretching across the gutter margin to link both halves into a single unit, whilst the writing increasingly shrinks into self-contained paragraphs which tackle a single theme. Cohesion between paragraphs has been weakened. Navigation around the page is increasingly by image as well as writing. But if these new elements are creeping in, topic books destined for the school market still maintain their own distinctive look. By doing so they reassert their own market niche, and through their stylistic difference mark out their claims to providing knowledge appropriate to their projected context of use.

They maintain their distinctiveness in various ways. Partly, the central image remains illustrative of the text which surrounds it. It does not set out to pull in another direction. But perhaps more fundamentally, publishers who directly supply the school market continue to combine elements of non-linear design with an older design logic. This treats the page as a series of columns or rectangles of greater or lesser size that can be aggregated or disaggregated as needs be through the combination of image or blocks of writing placed side by side (Moss, 2001b).

Simon & Schuster's *What do we Know about the Victorians?* (Tames, 1994) shows this use of the page very clearly. Each page is turned into a series of rectangular spaces which are defined by the margins established between image and text-blocks. These rectangles can then be filled and aligned in different ways. So on a double spread headed 'What sort of houses did people live in?' (pp. 18–19) the main heading sits immediately above an image of a row of terraced houses. The two combine into one square placed at the top left of the page. This is then aligned on the right with an oblong text-block of similar height running between the heading and the gutter margin. Immediately beneath and forming a parallel strip across the same page is an oblong illustration aligned with a much narrower text-block of the same height, again running up to the gutter margin. In the final parallel strip this sequence is reversed, with a narrow column of text aligned with a longer oblong image. In effect, the whole page therefore is subdivided into three rectangles. The facing page is subdivided into one landscape strip at the top, with two portrait strips beneath. What unites the two pages is a single frame running round the whole, and the balance achieved through the diagonal sweep of the images as they line up on each separate page.

In many respects this form of layout is a remnant from an earlier print technology, when pages had to be laid up on the press as lines of type assembled into rectangular blocks of print. Room for illustrations could only be created by clearing the type from a segment of the page to leave a rectangular space into which the image could then be inserted (Moss, 2001b). Whilst the print technology has changed, the style persists. Yet now it has become a conscious choice with its own semiotic resonance. The design style associated with the old can be invoked to signify work as against play. Non-fiction books that are still laid up in this way are predominantly produced by those publishers who are most certain that their texts are intended for the school market and contexts where they will form the object of serious study. They play to their prospective buyers.

Even those topic books which on first sight seem to most espouse a non-linear style maintain this general effect by the way in which they align individual items on the page. *How Would you Survive as an Ancient Greek?* (Macdonald, 1995) is a good example of this kind of hybrid design. Aimed at supporting classroom study of the Ancient Greeks as part of the Key Stage 2 curriculum, the images play a prominent part in the text. Often unencumbered by a clear boundary between themselves and the surrounding writing, individual objects seem to jut out into the page defined by their own irregular shapes. But looked at more closely a series of ghost rectangles emerges. The main images and writing on each page are corralled into a central oblong defined by the narrow marginal strip running down each outer edge and across the bottom of the double spread. These margins are themselves created by the strong alignment of a series of little pictures and captions. Within the larger space, writing and images line up to create a series of ghost columns which march across the page. These strongly suggest the sequence in which the writing should be tackled, from left to right and top to bottom. As I commented in an earlier article:

> On the one hand the pages adopt a design style which signals modernity; on the other hand the layout continues to struggle to impose a linear, and vertical sense of order on the potentially chaotic fluidity of the space. It's as if such books can't quite give up the old order, whilst simultaneously trying to adapt to the new.
>
> (Moss, 2001b)

Such texts signal their close association with schoolwork, even as texts that more wholeheartedly employ non-linear design principles signal their association with play. In one sense they can both be read the same way, yet at the same time they also spell out the very different contexts they expect to be associated with. They engineer different kinds of choices.

Conclusion: the function of text design for readers

Reading paths impose both limits and freedoms on what readers can do with texts. At the same time, the ways in which these design solutions are executed take on a semiotic resonance of their own. In part, this seems to depend on how they emerge and percolate across the publishing field from one area to another and the ways in which these design solutions interact with the setting in which they find themselves. These kinds of relationships can be seen at work in the changing design of topic books and how they have been influenced by the kind of design principles that DK represents.

What are the advantages of looking at texts in this way? This analysis links texts to contexts not in terms of the propositions the text content conveys about gender per se but in terms of the use the text suggests for itself and what potential readers are able to make of this in different settings. Some settings close down the possibilities texts offer for being used in different ways; others don't. Observation showed that in contexts where children could most freely choose what they read for themselves, those non-fiction texts which most strongly spelt out their association with schoolwork were most consistently ignored. Instead, children opted for picture-led non-fiction texts with non-linear page layouts which seemed to encourage a playful engagement with the text. I would argue that their design also made these texts easier to share between groups of pupils reading the same text at the same time. Although they may not have had a vocabulary to express the precise reasons for their choices, children themselves seemed to recognise the affordance of one kind of design logic over the other.

Both the contexts for reading which make texts available and the text's design provide readers with different kinds of resources for doing reading and being a reader. The full potential of any one resource may not be realised, for resources can pull against each other as well as with each other. The next chapter will examine in more detail the use children made of picture-led and non-linear non-fiction in informal settings and how this contrasts with the use they made of fiction texts as self-directed reading.

5

READERS IN CONTEXT

Text choice as situated practice

Introduction

The previous chapter took non-fiction texts as its focus and tracked back from the contexts in which non-fiction texts are used in school to the texts themselves, documenting how texts are sorted according to the purposes they are intended to fulfil. The chapter examined some of the salient distinctions in the design of non-fiction texts produced for the school market. This led to analysis of the different possibilities non-fiction texts create for their readers through the adoption of non-linear reading paths, defined by the ways in which images are incorporated into the text, and how any writing is then organised on the page. This chapter will broaden its focus to include a fuller range of both fiction and non-fiction texts which children use in different social settings. The chapter will explore the choices children make about what to read in a variety of settings and the consequences this has for their development as readers.

The book-bag and other interviews

The data drawn on in this chapter come from several sources. Some of the material was collected through classroom observation. It includes transcripts of literacy events which happened during the course of the school day and were audio-taped to complement the field notes. Additional material comes from a sequence of interviews collected over the course of the research in the two school-based studies of literacy in the classroom (see notes 1 and 4 on p. 203). The interviews were structured in a variety of different ways, each designed to get a different purchase on what children thought about reading and their development as readers.

At the first interview children were asked to bring their book-bags along and talk about whatever they contained. In British primary schools, book-bags are the main vehicle through which texts travel to and from school and home. Whilst one might well expect to find the home-reading book inside, children also used them as repositories for a variety of other kinds of materials – pictures they had drawn, or sometimes newspaper clippings they were bringing in to show others, or stickers they were intending to swap. Such texts were live to one degree or another, either in the context of the formal school curriculum, or in the informal contexts children create and have access to beyond that. If a book-bag was not available, children brought their school trays with them. The tray is where primary school children keep their own things in class.

A second interview used in the Fact and Fiction Project focused on out-of-school texts more specifically by asking children to bring in their favourite texts from home. The texts they brought were then supplemented by a variety of texts closely associated with informal contexts rather than the school reading curriculum. These were chosen on the basis of auditing retail outlets in the case-study communities and included football sticker albums, a variety of children's magazines and make-and-do books as well as puzzle books. It was harder to gauge under these circumstances quite which texts might be genuinely live or dead. The full range of materials the interviewer brought to the interview were produced one at a time. Those that the interviewees did not recognise were taken off the table.

A third interview focused on text choices. Interviewees were presented with a range of non-fiction texts selected by the interviewer because they seemed to represent different kinds of design choices. These included non-fiction texts associated with both formal and informal contexts. These were supplemented by a variety of texts with a strong visual component including puzzle and picture books, particularly those where the pictures themselves seemed to require attention in their own right. This selection of texts was refined over the sequence of studies and, in particular, in the light of the follow-up research project which examined the library borrowing records of a Year 6 group during one academic year (see note 3 on p. 203) (Moss and McDonald, 2004). In interview, interviewees were given the opportunity to browse as many of the texts as they wished, in whatever order they liked. The interviewer would follow the conversation that arose from this activity rather than direct it. At the close of the interview, the interviewer would ask interviewees about some of the texts they had ignored.

Almost all of the interviews were conducted with small groups rather than individuals, as this gave the possibility for conversation to arise between readers as it might do in classroom settings, and gave the whole more of the feel of a naturally occurring literacy event, rather than a formal interview. For the purposes of the interviews children were sometimes grouped according to the reading proficiency level they were assigned in school; at other times they were asked to choose one or more friends to come along with them. The groups were generally single sex. This made it possible to explore any differences that might arise in the kinds of choices girls or boys made. Grouping children according to their position in the social hierarchy of readers constructed in class also made it possible to explore more fully the extent to which this designation steered text choice, in line with the observations made about classroom literacy events.

Can and can't – do and don't: what classrooms make visible about children as readers

Reading for proficiency criteria position children in relation to each other, marking out a hierarchy of skill. The project data showed that boys and girls placed at different points in that hierarchy reacted very differently to this state of affairs. This became particularly apparent from watching what children were doing during quiet reading time and the different choices they made at that time.

In the 7–9 age group, to get to the point of fully choosing for themselves what they could read, children have to be assessed by the teacher as being a free or independent reader. For teachers in all of the schools where the research was based, this label operated as a way of signing children off the most intense monitoring regimes for reading in class. Independent readers are those who have reached a skill level which the teacher felt happy with. From the teacher's point of view, their text choices no longer needed as much careful adult monitoring. In practice, being a free reader often meant having different privileges to access a greater range of texts and being able to exercise more choice over which texts would be selected. These children stood in a different relationship to the reading curriculum. Their free access to the widest range of resources made this obvious to their peers.

In fact, beyond the point where the majority of the class might have been released from the close monitoring associated with a reading scheme, primary schools continue to exhort and expect children to choose texts which match their ability as readers, neither operating below nor above what they can do. Thus even in Bluebird School, which of all the schools researched for this book offered its pupils most opportunities to choose texts for themselves and to read for a variety of different purposes, children were expected to choose their library book by applying the 'five-finger test'. If there were five words they couldn't read on the first page, they were supposed to put the book back on the shelf and find another. Proficiency criteria always shadow children's reading choices.

Despite this, within the constraints associated with the particular classroom, children were freest to choose what to read during quiet reading time. As a bare minimum, quiet reading time simply required that children spend some time with a book. (Whether they really read it or not might be up to them.) Often they could also use that time to interact with others, so they did not have to spend it reading alone. They could choose 'wisely' in proficiency terms, by picking something which matched their competence, or they could choose more freely in the knowledge that this book was not destined for a proficiency encounter. They could prioritise reading as enjoyment and play, or they could prioritise reading as work. They could buy into the discourse which sustains 'reading for choice' as a valuable element in the school curriculum or they could use the relative freedom this time gave them to do something else altogether.

Analysing the different choices readers exercised over what and how they read during this time led to the identification of three categories of readers: those who *can and do* read freely; those who *can and don't* read freely; and those who *can't yet and don't* read freely. The distinction between *can* and *can't* was based on the judgements teachers made in proficiency encounters about who was fully competent to read independently and who was not. These judgements were known to both children and adults in class and were a matter of public record. They also laid down the official criteria against which children were expected to choose. *Do* and *don't*, on the other hand, represented the conclusions the researchers came to about how children used their status as competent readers during reading for choice slots.

Some of those children who were deemed to be 'free readers' clearly had a lot invested in their sense of themselves as readers. They were beginning to exercise judgements about what they wanted to read and the kind of reader they were. Observation and interview confirmed they were reading in a self-motivated way, not just for the teachers or as part of schoolwork. These were the 'can and do' group. Others who were deemed competent at reading by the teacher, and accorded the same privileges in terms of what they could read, showed little inclination to read for themselves. They read when they were expected to in class, but seldom went beyond what was asked of them. They showed little commitment to reading as an activity. These constituted the 'can but don't' group. There were more girls in the 'can and do' category and more boys in the 'can but don't' category.

These three categories of readers helped steer the selection of students for interview further, and also for participation in a research activity which provided a few students from each class with cameras to take home so that they could photograph resources for reading in that environment (see Moss, 2001a for an account of this activity). These different orientations to the possibilities afforded readers in school underpin the analysis in this chapter.

Children, text choice and autonomy: some considerations

It is tempting to make what pupils do with texts stand in opposition to what adults make children do with them, as if the purposes of these two groups must inevitably clash, and that adults' intervention leads to the colonisation or distortion of children's pleasures. But this is to over-polarise.

Rather, children move in and out of different social contexts that afford different possibilities for social interaction and incorporation into others' designs and purposes, as well as possibilities for co-opting others into their own plans. The intentions individuals exercise are socially constructed too. In this sense, choices that are made are always socially constrained. Sometimes these social constraints become more fully apparent than at others, sometimes they carry more force, sometimes they may be contested, but they will always be there. Whilst adult control in formal settings may be particularly visible, children can control and constrain each others' actions too. There are also opportunities for collaboration and convergence. Look back at Henrietta Dombey's example of a bedtime story (p. 43) and it becomes harder to see the child's interests and the adult's as working against each other. Choices and constraints mingle rather differently here.

The question to be pursued in this chapter is about who exercises what kind of choice in which context. This means examining the social constraints that operate under the particular conditions in which children come to choose between texts and decide how to read them. The relevant constraints which help shape different choices are of as much interest as the choices themselves. For instance, here is Annie, aged eight, faced with the constraint of having to spend a paired reading session in her class reading with Joe, a child with a designation of special educational needs who rarely interacts with his peers. In the same class as Ella, whom we met in Chapter 3, she has just chosen *Mr and Mrs Pig's Evening Out* from the class library and brought it back to their table. In this instance it is read very much as a picture book and not a reading book.

Transcript 1: Paired reading

ANNIE: Right, *'Mr and Mrs Pig's Evening Out'*// {Reading out the title of the book}

JOE: Is it funny?

ANNIE: It is funny, yeah, you're allowed to laugh./ {She begins reading} '*Once upon a time there lived a family of pigs. There was Father Pig and Mother Pig./ And there were ten piglets./ They were called Sorrell Pig, Baldy Pig, Harold Pig, Sarah Pig, Cindy Pig, Tommy Pig, Unc, Undy Pig, William Pig, Garther Pig, Benjamin Pig*'

JOE: Benjamin Pig?

ANNIE: There's lots of them. Are you going to count them? One two three, four five six, seven eight nine ten! There's ten. {Looking at the picture which accompanies the text.}

JOE: Ten

ANNIE: Wow! '*One evening, Mother Pig called the children to/ her as they were playing all over the house "Now piglets", she said, "your father and I are going out this evening"/ There was a chorus of groans./ "Not far", she said* {first of all in a groaning tone of voice}, *"Not far"* {Annie switches to a cheerful tone of voice} *said Miss Pig, "and I've a very nice lady come to look after you"* And there's all those ten little piggies. {Indicating the picture}

JOE: Mmm

(Bluebird, Year 3. 'Can' and 'Can't yet' readers)

In this school, paired reading is a hybrid literacy event. To some extent it mimics reading for proficiency encounters in so far as readers are expected to read aloud to each other, and can correct each other's performance or help each other out if they encounter any difficulties in making sense of the text. To this end, the teacher had engineered the pairings so that the weaker readers read with the more able. Letting the more competent readers choose who they worked with had led to the most able girls being paired with the weakest boys in almost every case. However, the teacher's expressed intentions about how children were to use the slot mainly revolved around issues of choice and reader enjoyment: 'It's more a promotion of books and working co-operatively together with books ... there has to be some negotiation over the sort of book they choose.' In line with this approach, the children had free rein of the class library at this time and could choose whatever they liked to read from its well-stocked resources. The weakest readers were not expected to stick to their proficiency texts – the reading scheme books they took to proficiency encounters with adults – nor do the bulk of the reading. There was no formal monitoring of how each pair chose to use the time.

In this instance Annie has both chosen the book and is also largely responsible for choosing how to read it. If the book looks like a picture book, then it also contains rather more written text than something like *Rosie the Hen*, and tells the story of how an unsuspecting Mr and Mrs Pig leave their children with Mrs Wolf for a baby-sitter. For most of the time, Annie adopts the voice a mother might use when reading with a much younger child (Annie herself has a younger sister aged five). In her reading she positions Joe as if he too were a younger sibling, treating him as a non-reader, whose interaction with the text needs to be actively directed. Thus she takes time out from the written text to marshal his attention to the pictures:

ANNIE: There's lots of them. Are you going to count them? One two three, four five six, seven eight nine ten! There's ten.
JOE: Ten
ANNIE: Wow!

It is very unclear how far children are helped to help other pupils with their reading in school except by appropriating what they see and hear others do, either in class or at home. Certainly, there was no evidence in this site that pupils were explicitly taught how to work with others deemed less competent than themselves. In this instance, taking on a motherly voice seems to enable Annie to sustain a clear role with a peer in what otherwise might have been a rather difficult situation. The choice she makes on how to handle the situation she is in depends upon the resources she can muster as well as their likely reception. It is quite hard to know from the limited nature of Joe's response what he actually makes of all this, but at any rate in this context he doesn't apparently contest what Annie does. He implicitly concurs with the reader role she casts him in.

The school setting in some senses creates the constraints that these two readers act under on this occasion. But home does not provide Annie with a free space in which to do whatever she wants either. In interview about reading at home Annie made it clear that she is limited in how much money she can spend on things she wants, including books and magazines. She has to share some of her resources with her sister, and she can't put things she acquires anywhere she likes in her room, but must abide by household rules (no posters on the walls, for instance). Talking about her favourite out-of-school texts in the second interview, her choices are crowded round by others' intentions: both what her parents consider worthwhile; and what her peers consider desirable. The favourite texts she brought from home to the interview included two issues of *Girl Talk* containing pictures of the Spice Girls; a scrapbook; a sticker book; a variety of information books, including a tennis book her Dad had bought for himself but which she liked to look at; a picture dictionary; a history book bought to coincide with the History topic at school; and a book about the night sky her parents bought her as a Christmas present. She also brought along a Disney video, *Pocohontas*. The resources available to choose between are those whose entry into this household have already been negotiated in one way or another (see also Moss, 1993a, on the social regulation of video in the home). Many of the non-fiction texts Annie brings along stand for a household investment in an educational pathway to the future. They are about getting on. Her choices reflect the social value others put on what she does.

When asked to choose between a variety of 'out-of-school' resources which the interviewer had assembled on the basis of what was available locally at this time, Annie consistently chose with the social context for reading in mind, both domestically and at school. She reacted to the *Usborne Spotter's Guide Birds Sticker Book* (Holden, 1994) by placing it firmly in the context of reading at home.

Transcript 2: Favourite texts

ANNIE: That's nice, I don't mind that {Talking about a Bird Sticker book.} That's the sort of thing that my mum probably

wouldn't let me get unless we were going on holiday or
something but I wouldn't normally be allowed something
like this. I would like it, but I wouldn't normally be allowed
something like this.

INTERVIEWER: Because?

ANNIE: Because it'd probably be too much money 'cause Mum
really only lets me get comics that are under a pound

She considered the *Merlin's Premier League Sticker Collection* (1996) from the
point of view of both her own leisure interests and in the context of peer
relationships at school:

INTERVIEWER: Last one. Football sticker album

ANNIE: {Turning pages} Well, I'm not really into football at the
moment because I'm into swimming and tennis at the
moment, so I wouldn't get this and it's almost for boys as
well, isn't it? You'd feel a bit silly going round saying 'Oh,
can I join in the swaps?', 'cause I've got a couple of swaps,
you'd feel a bit silly 'cause you're a girl so no.

INTERVIEWER: Why would that make you feel a bit silly, joining in the
swaps?

ANNIE: Well, it's like loads of boys and hardly any girls

INTERVIEWER: If other girls were doing it, would you do it?

ANNIE: Yeah, probably, I might.

Out of the eight texts she was shown, only once did she explain her preferences in terms of the text's formal characteristics:

ANNIE: *The Dandy*, hmm. Well one thing that I don't really like is, I
don't really like reading the bubbles, I'd much rather prefer a story, like, not in the bubbles.

(Bluebird, Year 3. 'Can' reader)

To insist that the most authentic choices children make are those which
pay no heed to the social constraints which govern how texts circulate in
different settings is to divorce children from any meaningful social history.
They inevitably have to negotiate their way through these kinds of encounters. Consequently, this chapter will continue to focus on the interaction
between text, context and reader and how these elements interweave to
steer the choices children make. In the first instance, this chapter will
explore differences in the text choices children made during quiet reading
time, or at those other moments during the school day when they were
most able to choose for themselves amongst the available resources. From
the point of view of this book, such choices are not text preferences made
in the abstract, but rather text preferences which arise in the context of the
affordance and constraints which these school settings represent.

129

Browsing non-fiction: the possibilities of the text

At the time that data were collected for this book, quiet reading time was a standard part of the school day in each of the case-study sites. Although the name suggests that the time was reserved for reading in silence, in fact all of the settings tolerated some pupil talk provided children looked as if they were reading or choosing texts. The easiest way to engineer opportunities for talk was either to meet in the book corner or to look at a book together. Texts that were easiest to share in this context included books of poems; short reading books, if one child was prepared to read aloud to another; multiple copies of plays designed for more than one reader to read together (they were sometimes available as part of reading schemes); or books where there was a strong visual element, including non-linear non-fiction. As we've seen, the latter were disproportionately popular with those boys designated least able at reading.

The non-fiction interview was designed to explore what happened when children had access to these kinds of texts together, and to test out which kinds of non-fiction they would choose, given a wide selection. Various kinds of non-fiction were included. Some were picture-led non-fiction in the *Eyewitness* style. Others were chosen because they looked like fiction books. *Horrible Histories*, for instance, are linear texts that look like chapter books. The bulk of the text is laid up in lines of print with a relatively small type-face. The written text is subdivided into individual sections by headings and subheadings, interspersed with line drawings. The sections vary considerably in size, and include some that amount to no more than a paragraph with heading. Other publishers produce non-fiction in a picture book format. Walker Books have made this approach one of their hallmarks. The *Read and Wonder* series title, *Think of an Eel* (Wallace, 1993); or *How to Look After Your Rabbit* (Hawkins, 1995) are good examples from their list. In addition, non-fiction that looked like it was intended for schoolwork would be present (e.g. *Homes in the Future* (Lambert, 1988); *BBC Fact Finders Roman Britain* (Hall and Jones, 1997)) alongside non-fiction that used stylistic features to make the contents look like fun (*Mapwork 1* (Flint and Suhr, 1992); *Quizmasters: People in the past* (Whitelaw and Whitaker, 1995)). Also on the table would be some fiction books where the illustrations were intended to capture the reader's attention in their own right, such as *Where's Wally?* (Handford, 1989) (included in the school library at Bluebird); Anthony Browne's *The Tunnel* (1997) or a book organised like a comic such as Keith Brumpton's *Rudley Cabot In ... The Quest for the Golden Carrot* (1994). Finally, some fiction books that looked as if they encouraged dipping in and out of were also included. Poetry books were generally used for this category. The selection would be topped up with any books that had been seen shared in class and looked as if they were an object of particular interest (*The Art Book* (1997), observed in use in one site, fell into this category).

Steering a course round picture-led non-linear non-fiction

Picture-led non-linear non-fiction texts seemed to provoke very similar reactions, almost regardless of who was looking at them. First, children would work their way through a specific title, not necessarily from back to front or front to back, but rather by coasting over the pages in any direction until something caught their eye. The navigation through the text was largely image-driven. Once they'd found something they liked, readers would then pause on that particular page for a while, engaging their partner in conversation provoked by a particular item, and then skip on. If children knew the particular text, they might well hunt through to find a familiar page or image. The extent to which this kind of event led to anyone 'reading' the text in the sense of decoding the written text on the page varied, but this seldom seemed the main focus of the activity. Instead, these literacy events are best described as being structured round the talk which takes place as the children look at the text together. The talk can be both on-text – directly shaped by the text contents – or off-text: only loosely related to the particular text's contents.

In the following example, Matt, a 'can't yet' reader from a Year 6 group, picked up a copy of Dorling Kindersley's *Big Book of Cars* (1999) in interview and began the following conversation with the interviewer. (He was being interviewed on his own.)

Transcript 3: Browsing non-fiction

MATT: Why don't I have a look at that car book? It looks quite cool and I'll see if it's got any decent cars in. My grandad has just bought a new car. {He continues to turn over the pages of the book as he talks}

INTERVIEWER: What is it?

MATT: Hyundai.

INTERVIEWER: Yeah, I know what you mean.

MATT: A brand new one. He had to take it into the garage when it had something wrong with it. The back clip was snapped and his windscreen had scratches on it. So he got a new screen ... {Stopping on a particular image} ... It's a horn ...

INTERVIEWER: Oh my goodness, a snake's head. {Commenting on the picture} Is it a snake?

MATT: It's a snake. Has it got a horn?

INTERVIEWER: Yeah. '*Out of my way. The hands of an arrogant motorist ... boa constrictor horns are sold as accessories.*' {Reading out the captions and written text which accompany the image Matt has stopped on} Wow.

MATT: {Continues turning the pages} I want to get some new cars, I think this is mainly old cars {i.e. the text's content}. I got a film the other day and that had all car chases. *The Bourne Identity*. It's not very good but it's got well good chases. Have you seen it?

(Merchant, Year 6. 'Can't yet' reader)

The structure of the conversation is primarily related to the topic 'cars', and covers a variety of information that both of the participants can muster on this subject. Points of interest noticed in the book fit into the overall development of this theme, so the conversation above starts with Matt's grandad's new car, pauses whilst he looks at the picture of a peculiar car horn, then carries on to films which include car chases, and will continue with the subject of computer games that involve cars, before Matt spots the next object in the text worth commenting on several pages further on:

Transcript 3 (continued)

MATT: This looks like a BMX tyre ...

INTERVIEWER: What is it?

MATT: It's a car tyre. That's what I'd look for, a BMX. My mum's got a naff car now. {Turning on through the book} She's got a ... oh, some badges.

INTERVIEWER: *Car badges.*

MATT: I wonder if they've got a Bentley badge? Bugatti, they are well nice.

INTERVIEWER: Yeah, they do bikes don't they?

MATT: They've got to have Porsche one somewhere. Who are ABC? {Referring to picture in the text} Never heard of them.

(Merchant, Year 6. 'Can't yet' reader)

This combination of a loosely themed conversation continuing around the points at which readers pause over the text's contents, and perhaps stop to read parts of the text aloud, is typical of these kinds of literacy events. Children's progress through non-linear non-fiction does not look like the organised hunt for knowledge specified by information retrieval in which the point and purpose of reading non-fiction is to identify what is not yet known and bring any new information into a more clearly defined systematic relationship with the old. Instead, this use of the text looks much more ad hoc, the reader's response to the material less geared to acquiring new knowledge than sharing what they already know in interaction with others participating in the same event.

Which way to go next? Two boys tackle Nature Cross-sections

The priority put on exploring the possibilities for joint conversation between readers as they make their way through these kinds of texts is highlighted in the following extract collected in interview with two boys from a Year 5 class. These pupils were both considered able readers in the context of the reading curriculum. In the interview, they browsed through the texts on the table, picking up anything they were interested in. The boys had already separately and sometimes together considered *The Art Book; Where's Wally?; The Fantastic Journey; The Rotten Romans; Shoot; The Tunnel;* and *The Oxford Second Poetry Book.* Of the two participants, Jacob seemed particularly keen to share his text choices and find ways of getting Sam to look at the same things with him. At this point in the interview he has picked up *Richard Orr's Nature Cross-sections* (Orr and Butterfield, 1995). Unusually for the database as a whole and this interview, the boys begin their progress through this text by perusing the contents page, in response to Jacob's opening question.

Transcript 4: Browsing non-fiction

JACOB: What do we look at, stupid?/ Sam, what do we look at? {In plaintive voice. Turning to the contents page.}

SAM: C-rabs/ rock pools/ {Commenting on visual and written heading on the contents page}

JACOB: That's '*twenty two*' {Reading the page number}

SAM: Oh no, no, what about this/ '*Bee nest*' {Reading heading}

(Farthing, Year 4. 'Can' readers)

Part of the point of this kind of literacy event is to decide which aspects of which texts merit their readers' collective attention. Jacob bids to make this particular book a focus for joint activity, then cedes to Sam the choice of starting point – let's go for bee nest, not rockpools. The event acquires its social dimension through the shared timing of page turning, and the way in which readers then collaboratively or separately move around the page from one part of the text to another. A certain degree of co-ordination and mutual consent is required from the participants if they are to look at the same things on the same page, for the nature of the activity and the text also allows them to make their own separate way round the contents.

In this text, the boys' chosen topic, Bee Nest, consists of a double spread dominated by a large central image showing a beehive in cross-section. The image shows in picture and via the captions the complexity of the hive and the way in which it represents not only a food store for pollen and honey but a bee nursery from which the worker bees will hatch and the centre of worker bee activity. On the top right of the double spread is another smaller cross-section showing how bees develop from egg to larva to adult bee within their cells, whilst beneath this image, again on the right, is another picture showing the hive in its setting inside a tree. Jacob does most of the talking whilst the boys stay on this page, using his invitation to Sam to look as a way of co-ordinating their activity. He initially homes in on the top right image which he takes as evidence that bees eat live prey, an interpretation he voices straightaway. This interpretation seems to stem from the image of a bee entering one of the cells to feed a larva:

Transcript 4 (continued)

SAM: Oh cor
JACOB: Look at all them where they store all their food/ um food
              they kill and then they go in there and eat it// like little
              cupboards {giggles}
INTERVIEWER: Is that what bees eat?/ I thought they just um
JACOB: Yes/ they eat honey as well
SAM: That's the honey
JACOB: They ate the honey
SAM: That's where the honey// oh look, let's a, look at it
JACOB: Oh look they're coming in there to fill the holes up// with
              honey// and they/ and they're gonna kill them// oh
              they're the baby wasps
SAM: That's where they keep the babies
JACOB: Oh look look look/ what's that? (...)/ oh '*pupal/ queen*'/ oh
              no, that's the queen wasp/ right {they turn the page over}
              (Farthing, Year 4. 'Can' readers)

Reading the transcript against the actual page in the book reveals a complex interaction between what these readers already know, what they find out from the images and the written text, and what they find out from each other. Jacob's initial commentary seems designed to grab Sam's attention and involve him in exploring that part of the text that Jacob has identified as having particularly dramatic interest. It is not clear from the transcript if Jacob's interpretation that the image shows bees eating live prey is in part dependent upon what he might already know about wasps. He consistently refers to the bees as wasps on this page. It is only later after he has spent a bit more time looking around the page that he seems to return to the first image and conclude that what he had thought were prey are in fact 'baby wasps'. He would have to have gleaned this information from the written text, though the interviewer's intervention – 'Is that what bees eat?/ I thought they just um' – may have prompted him to look at this in more detail. (The image captions for the smaller cross-section that Jacob initially homed in on use the word larva to describe the changing contents of the cells. The image as a whole is labelled 'Bee development over 21 days'.)

The only caption he seems to directly read out loud during the course of this conversation is the one labelling the pupal queen, a detail included on the bottom right of the larger central drawing.

In fact, this entire transaction happens very fast, involving selected highlights on the page. In effect, the boys edit much of the text out. In less than fifty seconds they have turned over to the preceding page and moved on. Even if Sam had the opportunity to read more of the text than Jacob, given that he spoke less, this still leaves very little time for either reader to get to grips with much of the detailed information the page contains. Indeed, it is not in the least bit clear how far this is really part of the boys' intention in perusing the text together. When they flip back a page to a cross-section of a rock pool, they actually go on to play a version of 'where's Wally?' for a brief moment, a strategy initiated by Sam.

Transcript 4 (continued)

SAM: Try and find the crab
JACOB: {Laughs} Got him
SAM: What does it say?/ There's a crab
JACOB: Razorshell/ There it is/ a different one// {There are three crabs shown in the rock pool on this double spread}

(Farthing, Year 4. 'Can' readers)

They then turn backwards in the book once again to open up a centrefold showing life in the Arctic. Jacob then suggests they play a different kind of guessing game where they will look at the pictures first and then the captions. Perhaps this is a reaction to his initial interpretation and then re-reading of the bee nest cross-section.

Transcript 4 (continued)

JACOB: How about if we say something like 'what is that called?'/ yes/ and it will tell you
SAM: Oh, ooh/ look at that {long sound effect noise} eeeeaaaah
SAM: I know what that's called I think/ I think that's called/ a/ nilwall {looking at a picture of narwhal}
SAM: Oh, here we go/ {Reading the caption} '*A male narwhal's tusks may be used as a weapon in fights with other mates/ males*', I mean./ Ooh, he's after/ he's after a whale// Those (?nails?) are sharp/ that looks like a nail/ yeah {Probably commenting on the image of a polar bear chasing a beluga whale, positioned just above the narwhals}
JACOB: Look at that!/ look,/ he's got his tail out the water/ and his head out the water/ he's only got half his body in the water {Commenting on the cross-section drawing style used for the female narwhal}
SAM: Er look at them,/ er that's not even,/ he's not even in the water

{Commenting on the male narwhal or grey whales on the same part of the page}

JACOB: {Laughs} Ah, bunny rabbits {Moving to another part of the cross-section showing Arctic life on land}

SAM: Ooh er/ Arctic rabbit {Both boys are referring to a picture of an Arctic hare}

JACOB: I know,/ I saw that in a programme./ What are they?

SAM: '*Dall ship/ dall sheep*'/ {Reading the caption} Never heard of that

JACOB: Never heard/ neither have/ look look

SAM: Snowy owl/ tiny owl

JACOB: '*Tundra exposed by*'/ {Reading part of a caption} Is this a tundra?

INTERVIEWER: Probably/ yes

JACOB: Cos um/ when I/ was reading *The Abominable Snowman of Pasadena,*/ this *Goosebumps* book/ well um/ well it had um

SAM: [on *The Simpsons* it had

JACOB: [Abominable snowman and they had a tundra/ but it was er um/ I've forgotten what it was called {they start turning over the page}.

(Farthing, Year 4. 'Can' readers)

The transcript captures the way in which these two follow each other's lead around the images on the page. Their talk encompasses both the actual drawings and some of the captions. Their respective comments are used in different ways, not only to assess what each other knows, and to judge how accurate that knowledge is, but also to take up different positions in relation to this text by, for instance, commenting on the drawing style or linking this text to other texts they know. This phase of activity lasts only whilst they both can find something of interest to prompt the joint conversation. As soon as one or other's interest significantly wanes they move on either to turn the page or to change to another text. In this instance, the conversation stops right here as they swap *Nature Cross-sections* for another text, *Dangerous Animals*.

The reading which takes place in this way is shaped by the social and collaborative nature of the literacy event. In this context, the content of the text becomes a provisional starting point to be fashioned and remade in relation to what others know and can draw on in the talk (Maybin and Moss, 1993). The text doesn't fully determine the selection of material made from it, or how that material will be recontextualised. Other reference points besides the text itself can be incorporated into the conversation. Yet at the same time, it is hard to see how this kind of social exchange could take place in this text's absence. Rather, these kinds of literacy events represent a pattern of social exchange in which readers weave different aspects of the text into a larger conversation (ibid.). The role of the text changes in this process, as they co-opt different aspects of what they can see into their conversation and allow the text more or less room to speak to them.

Finding their way around: two girls tackle Nature Cross-sections

Are there differences in how boys and girls approach this kind of event? The data show that the ways in which either boys or girls jointly negotiate their route through picture-led non-fiction texts are very similar. Here are two girls, one a 'can't yet', the other a 'can/do' reader looking at *Dangerous Animals* followed by the same centrefold on Arctic life in *Nature Cross-sections* that Jacob and Sam had paused over in the extract above. Once again, the talk moves both on and off text.

Transcript 5: Browsing non-fiction

CHARLOTTE: Oooh! {Very loudly, looking at picture of a snake in *Dangerous Animals*.} I held one of these once

LUCY: When?

CHARLOTTE: I was the strongest/ out of me and my sisters

LUCY: What/ so you got to hold it?

CHARLOTTE: I got to hold the middle bit

LUCY: Aargh

CHARLOTTE: It was at a kind of zoo/ and at the show/ and anyone who wanted to hold or stroke a snake/ and we took a picture ... {They begin to look at *Nature Cross-sections*}

CHARLOTTE: Ooh look, you've got white rabbits

LUCY: {Very loud} I like them two/ I like the polar bears

CHARLOTTE: I like the little polar bear

LUCY: Yeah, I like the little one best

CHARLOTTE: Oh yeah I love/ white walls, I like white walls/ I like the white

LUCY: I don't like that picture (...) sharp nose {laughter} {Probably one of the narwhals}

CHARLOTTE: Oh I like them/ what are they called (reading out text slowly) *beluga whales*

LUCY: Oh penguins, I love penguins. {Turning over to the Antarctic life page. More aahs from both girls}

(Farthing, Year 4. 'Can' and 'can't yet' readers)

If the method of navigation is broadly similar as the girls cruise round the page talking about the text, then the subject position they adopt in relation to the Arctic life text is rather different. Where the boys navigated through this page by maintaining a certain distance between themselves and the text, by contrast the girls' exclamations: 'Oh, penguins, I love penguins', is an expression of an altogether different kind of intimate delight in the cute and adorable. The nearest the boys get to this is Jacob's slightly mocking comment: '{laughs}\ Ah, bunny rabbits' which leads directly into an almost self-conscious correction of terms:

JACOB: {Laughs} Ah, bunny rabbits
SAM: Ooh er/ Arctic rabbit {Both boys are referring to a picture of an Arctic hare}
JACOB: I know,/ I saw that in a programme

But this doesn't mean that girls can't be as interested in engaging with the knowledge content of the text. In fact, Lucy and Charlotte turn on to the bee nest double spread which elicits this response as they pause over the main diagram:

Transcript 5 (continued)

LUCY: Look/ look/ it's like a cupboard {laughter}
CHARLOTTE: Yeah cupboard/ look/ if you turn it round like this// it looks like a monster/ that's the face and that's
LUCY: What are these things here? {pointing out pupae in beehive picture}
CHARLOTTE: Oh they're things that they killed and they
LUCY: Maybe they're dead bees/ Are they dead bees?
CHARLOTTE: Maybe they squeeze honey out of them
INTERVIEWER: They might be/ the babies/ they're going to turn into more bees
LUCY: Pupa
CHARLOTTE: Yes/ that's it
LUCY: It's a pupa
CHARLOTTE: Yes/ cos look/ there's a little comb
LUCY: There's a bee there/ bigger/ and then it starts getting hairs on it/ so actually first it's probably that/ then it's that/ then it's that {Working out the sequence in which to make sense of the diagram}
                         (Farthing, Year 4. 'Can' and 'can't yet' readers)

Interestingly, the girls take a quite different approach to self-correction, following the introduction of new information by the interviewer. This leads them on to consider the text much more directly, actively working out what they didn't understand before. For the boys, the social necessity to save face seems to hold greater sway in this context.

Taken to task: gains and losses for 'can't yet' readers

In fact, what is more striking on the database is not so much that boys and girls negotiate their way through these texts differently by pausing over different aspects of the content, as that only one specific subset of boys chose routinely to co-opt these kinds of non-fiction texts into quiet reading time. Classroom observation showed that the overwhelming majority of readers who made use of this kind of non-linear non-fiction in preference to anything else were boys designated weak readers. As I have argued earlier, these literacy events seemed to establish a level playing field between participants, where their relative proficiency as readers, in school terms, no longer counts. Knowledge is not limited to knowledge of the precise contents of the text whilst the claims made by one reader versus another can be tested or resolved in a number of different ways, without necessarily resorting to the text at all. Whatever any participant knows about a particular topic from whatever source can be mobilised for the purposes of discussion, much as Matt mobilises the information he possesses about cars from a number of different sources as he makes his way through a book on the history of motor vehicles. It is possible to assume the role of expert, without being an expert at reading. In terms of their social standing in class this delivers some immediate gains for those deemed 'can't yet' readers. It may also present some difficulties, as Transcript 6 shows.

What's to lose? Two 'can't yet' boy readers navigate In the Beginning

Three boys attended the interview that follows: Mitchel, his friend Terry, and a third boy who went off to look for a particular book on the library shelves whilst the passage below was being taped. Mitchel was considered by his teacher to be a particularly weak reader. His friend Terry was judged to be rather more competent, though he also fell well short of being considered an independent reader. Terry would read a variety of mainly fiction books during quiet reading time and was particularly likely to opt for short picture books which he could work his way through at a single sitting. By contrast, Mitchel was always to be found with a non-fiction book, even though these were not routinely part of the class library stock in his school. For many weeks he had been looking at a copy of *In the Beginning: The nearly complete history of almost everything* (Delf and Platt, 1995) which he seemed to have smuggled out of the main school library into class. (This stock was not technically available for borrowing.) It was not clear where he kept it but he always seemed to be able to put his hand on the book when he wanted to, and in many ways treated it as if it were his personal property.

The book itself is organised as a thematic encyclopedia in which each double spread deals with a different topic. In class, Mitchel would work his way through the pages, pausing only on those which dealt with subjects he was interested in. These mainly included any with pictures of dinosaurs or anything to do with the military. The other book Mitchel kept in school at the time was a lengthy paperback tome covering the history of the SAS which belonged to his father and he liked to keep in his tray. He never looked at it in class, though. For the interview I asked each of the three boys to bring a non-fiction book they liked with them. Terry brought a book about the stars he was reading to gain a Cubs badge on the planets. Mitchel brought *In the Beginning*.

At this point in the interview, the boys had been leafing through Mitchel's book for a while with Mitchel really acting as host and taking both Terry and the interviewer on a tour of his favourite pages. Here the group have paused over the double spread headed 'Weapons' and Mitchel begins to name the objects he is interested in on the page, before Terry interjects with a question:

Transcript 6: Browsing non-fiction texts in informal contexts

MITCHEL:	Yeah, there it is, there's an atom bomb
TERRY:	Where's an atom bomb?
MITCHEL:	There/ atom bomb// That's a V2 rocket
TERRY:	Yeah, I know
MITCHEL:	That's a doodle, that's an AK-47, MP-5, M-16 and there's a doodle bomb
	(Original transcript omitted)
TERRY:	Hang on, what's that then?
MITCHEL:	That?
TERRY:	Yeah
MITCHEL:	That is (...)
TERRY:	No that.
MITCHEL:	Oh that is a spy plane
TERRY:	Oh, oh yeah, a spy plane
INTERVIEWER:	How do you know that, Mitchel?
MITCHEL:	Because spy planes are, haven't got any like big missiles and stuff, they just fly over the base (...)
TERRY:	Do you know, I've got this game called Desert Rat Army

{Terry goes on to discuss the role of spy planes in his computer game. The two continue talking about the computer game and the various kinds of weaponry and planes it includes.}

(Shepherd, Year 4. 'Can't yet' readers)

The image Terry has paused over is accompanied by the following heading and short paragraph which reads:

1943 Flying bomb
Germany launched more than 8,500 flying bombs against London in
1944. Their engines stopped above the city, and the explosives crashed to
the ground.

The captions 'Jet engine' and 'No pilot on board' are placed next to the image itself. Although this may be what Mitchel is referring to when he uses the expression 'doodle' and 'doodle bomb', under scrutiny from Terry and with little time to spare, Mitchel names the object in the illustration as a spy plane. He does not check his answer with the written text.

A little bit later in the interview the boys turned back to this page as the interviewer talked to Mitchel about how he navigated through the text as a whole, and the following exchange occurred:

Transcript 6 (continued)

INTERVIEWER:	When you're looking at something like this {indicating the book} how much of it will you actually read or how much do you look at the pictures do you think?
MITCHEL:	(...) I'd read like, the thing, so, that, like today (...) {Turning through the book}
INTERVIEWER:	Right, so you read like the headings stuff
MITCHEL:	So I'd read like *Dinosaurs*, the heading *Dinosaurs* (...)
MITCHEL:	Then here {Turning on to the double spread on Weapons} I'm reading the information on the names of the guns and everything, that would be easy. *AK-47, MP-5, M-16, Atom Bomb*
TERRY:	Atom Bomb's exploding {Commenting on the illustration}
MITCHEL:	Spy plane/ And/ then ...
TERRY:	It looks like an old gun. See that thing there, that looks like a, wait/ How come it says flying bomb?// I thought you said that was a spy plane?
MITCHEL:	I did
TERRY:	(It's one of those) one of those flying bombs
MITCHEL:	Well I know/ In the Second World War
TERRY:	It's like a flying bomb
MITCHEL:	Yes, they look like planes
TERRY:	But they were bombs
MITCHEL:	Yeah, cos what they done, cos what they wanted to do was fly them into England and then crash them, oh no look, it's a crashing plane. And then, missile is hitting us, pilot crash. {Makes sound of explosion.} Oo, oo, oo {Making sound of a siren} Doctor, Doctor!

(Shepherd, Year 4. 'Can't yet' readers)

On this return visit to the page Terry has noticed the heading and this time round challenges Mitchel's assertion that the image is a spy plane, repeatedly correcting him, even when Mitchel tries to minimise the differences between the two of them. In the end Mitchel resolves the situation by asserting at some length how he thinks such bombs might have worked and adds some dramatic sound effects. By the time he has finished, Terry has gone back to talking about the computer game and the challenge to Mitchel's authority has passed.

The danger for Mitchel here is that what he can say about the Second World War isn't necessarily based on the text he is making his way through. Whilst he does indeed mention 'doodle bombs' in his first verbal tour of the page, he is vulnerable to being challenged about the contents of the text, just as he is on this occasion by Terry. Faced with Terry's question about what the image of the flying bomb represents he resorts to a guess, rather than checking with the written text. This highlights both his weakness as a reader but also his sensitivity to that weakness. Admitting to not knowing will conflict with the role of expert he has adopted in relation to this text. His authority is exposed when Terry returns to the page and takes the time to read the writing. In this instance Mitchel blusters his way through the immediate difficulties over his social standing. These seem to relate both to the claims he can make about what he knows, and also his standing as a reader.

But at the same time he is able to glean some information from this form of social exchange. Next time he makes his way through the text he will be on surer ground when it comes to this same image. In effect, he has networked his way to further knowledge of the text without having to grapple with the writing himself. This kind of collective conversation round the text allows precisely this to happen.

Proficiency reading as play

If weak boy readers are the group who in class most often choose to spend time on picture-led non-fiction when they can, and within this text-type choose texts which help disguise the proficiency level of the reader, then weak girl readers seem to opt for the reverse. As we've seen, the research data showed that they seemed quite happy to choose fiction texts which clearly signalled the expected proficiency level of the reader, often opting for texts which were either at or even substantially below their proficiency level. These might well be proficiency texts, that is to say those texts from reading schemes which are most closely associated with reading as work. The consistency of these preferences became apparent through documenting the choices children made during the course of the school day, as well as in interview. Indeed, in one interview two 'can't yet' girls who were faced with a heap of picture-led non-fiction texts to choose from instead opted for the two texts on the table which most resembled proficiency texts, in this case a Beginner's Bible and an RE topic book, chosen to represent a work-focused style of layout. Ignoring the opportunities to browse the non-linear non-fiction placed in front of them, they wanted to use the time available to them to take it in turns to do 'proficiency reading' from these two books by reading them aloud a page at a time to each other and the interviewer. In fact, the interviewer had to work quite hard to stop them doing this and answer at least some questions about the other possible texts first. The notes below come from the point in the transcript where the interviewer gave in, and let them do what they had in mind.

Transcript 7: Non-fiction interview

INTERVIEWER: That's a lovely one (...) righty ho now you may both take your time reading to me
{Both call out – me first etc ...}

INTERVIEWER: Right, Kerry can start, 'cause then Bridy can find one

Kerry starts reading text about Jesus and the wedding party, then asks Bridy to read. Bridy reads a text about the Hindu religion, and about Muslims, Jews and Christians. Kerry continues the water into wine parable. They continue alternating between the two different texts, a page at a time.

(Shepherd, Year 4. 'Can't yet' readers)

As the notes indicate, in this kind of context weak girl readers may well turn proficiency reading itself into a kind of collaborative play in the company of others. More able girl readers often joined in and indeed sometimes organised this activity. Below are a pair of girls, one a 'can't yet/don't' reader, one a 'can/do' reader, reading the picture book, *You'll Soon Grow Into Them, Titch* (Hutchins, 1983), together during quiet reading time in Bluebird. In one sense, they do this as a proficiency exercise by taking turns to read out the text on each successive page, but at the same time they also amuse themselves by reading their own names into the text in place of those of the characters. By choosing a text which enables them to read below both their respective proficiency levels, as they are here, the question of whether or not either of them can manage this text as readers and pass the proficiency test, as it were, is not an issue.

Transcript 8: Paired reading

HANNAH: Let's read it all over again.

NADIA: This is called '*You'll Soon Grow Into Them, Titch.*' {Reads} *Titch needed new trousers.*

HANNAH: {Reads} *His brother Peter said you can have my old trousers. They're too small for me.*

143

NADIA: {Reads} Then he said, *they're still a bit big for me, said Titch* (...)

HANNAH: And this is (...)

NADIA: You say Hannah (...) Doesn't matter

HANNAH: {Reads} And Hannah *will grow into them, said Peter*

NADIA: {Reads} *And when Titch needed a new sweater*

HANNAH: {Reads} *His sister Mary said, you can have my old sweater. It's too small for me.*

NADIA: {Reads} *It's still a bit big for me said Titch.*

HANNAH: {Reads} *You'll soon grow into it said Mary.* (...)

NADIA: Hannah. Hannah. {Reads} *They both said, you can have our old socks. They're too small for us.*

HANNAH: And Nadia and Hannah said, let's have a new baby {giggles}

NADIA: {Reads} *I think, said mother, that Titch should have some new clothes*

HANNAH: *And so Dad and* Nadia {giggles} (...)

NADIA: {Reads} *They bought a brand new pair of trousers,* don't be silly now

HANNAH: {Reads} *And a brand new*

NADIA: {Reads} *And a brand new pair of socks,* don't be silly now ... {Reads} *There! Said Titch. He um had my old trousers.*

HANNAH: *And my old sweater.*

NADIA: *And my old socks. That's much too small for me.*

HANNAH: (...)

NADIA: *But you'll soon grow into them said Titch.*

HANNAH: Look this is the end of the story.

NADIA: [And that is the end of the story.

HANNAH: [And that is the end of the story.

NADIA: Bye bye. Ning ning.

(Bluebird, Year 3. 'Can' and 'can't yet' readers)

In the research conducted for this book, very few boys opt to collectively play at proficiency reading like this when there are other options available to them. Those boys who freely choose to read proficiency texts when it is also possible to do something else generally undertake this kind of reading as a solitary activity. Boys who struggle at reading find it more difficult or uncomfortable to make their standing as readers public. There is little to be gained by appearing to be on the receiving end of help with their reading in such a setting.

Of course, this may in part depend on how such help arrives. Certainly, it is possible to imagine that the motherly voice which Annie adopts as she reads to Joe in the extract which opened this chapter could pose some problems for peers cast so firmly into the role of a much younger sibling. Yet in the context of girls' play, this is not an impossible role to take up.

Here, for instance, is Katy talking about playing schools with her younger sister, as part of her explanation of why she wants to buy *Coping with Teachers* (Corey, 1993), one of the resources the interviewer has just shown her:

Transcript 9: Favourites interview

KATY:	I'm gonna get *Coping with Teachers*. {Laughing}
INTERVIEWER:	Mmm, you fancy that one, because?
KATY:	Because when we play schools at home Lizzy is the teacher, and I always have to do what she says, so if I get a joke or something um, to make her, persuade her not to be the teacher, it might be a bit better. {Laughing}
INTERVIEWER:	Your younger sister that it is, she's the one who always ...?
KATY:	Yeah, cos she says, 'What's two add two?', and I put my hand up, 'four', and she says, 'No that's wrong!'
INTERVIEWER:	Mmm.
KATY:	And it's right, ha.
INTERVIEWER:	Don't you ever get a turn to be the teacher?
KATY:	No.

(Bluebird, Year 3. 'Can' reader)

This kind of girls' play turns who knows what upside-down. Yet in a way this is precisely part of the point of the game.

Knowing and not knowing

There is a politics to knowing and not knowing which runs through children's social relations both in school and at home. Bente Elkjaer's work suggests that where knowledge is at a premium, boys gain considerable authority from being able to claim to know most, and will prioritise saving face rather than admit to what they don't really know. This creates difficulties for them when confronted with gaps in their knowledge. By contrast, girls seem to find it easier to be on the receiving end of others' help, at less immediate cost to their self-esteem. This can make it easier to find out what they don't already know, though they also run the risk that their general level of skill and/or knowledge may be underestimated by others around them. Elkjaer's hypothesis certainly provides a plausible explanation for why 'can't yet/don't' boy and girl readers make such different uses of the resources available in the same setting. The choices weaker boy and girl readers make during quiet reading time seem in part to reflect a different strategic response to their designation as less proficient readers within the school setting. At the same time, the texts they choose may also allow them to mobilise to best advantage the resources for doing friendship available to them within their respective peer groups.

The affordance and constraint of linear reading paths: fiction texts reconsidered

The previous section considered how some children make use of non-linear non-fiction during quiet reading time by exploiting the possibilities that such texts afford for readers to make their way through the text together, steering their progress according to their several interests. Reading in this context turns into a social exchange which is primarily picture-led. The written text takes second place. The dominant mode here is browsing and dipping in and out. This approach to reading is facilitated by the non-linear text structure. Most fiction texts cannot be shared in this way because they are structured round different kinds of reading paths. They follow the logic of time rather than space (though note how the two girl readers in Transcript 7 read a page at a time from two different texts thus suspending the sense of the text to follow the logic of the time spent reading).

Linear fiction texts are constructed on the expectation that readers will start at the beginning and follow the linear flow of the text right until the end, submitting to the narrative sequence which unfolds in this way. Even picture books, where images play a key role in shaping the meaning of the text and are an integral part of both the text's design and the author's intentions, almost always use linear reading paths that establish a fixed sequence in which the pages should be turned. This creates different conditions for their social use.

In classrooms, staging the reader's progress through the linear structures of fiction texts becomes part of the salient business of the reading curriculum. Indeed, a good deal of the official activities which constitute the reading curriculum in schools are precisely about monitoring and guiding readers' progression from beginning to end of any given text.

Transcript 10: Book-bag Interview

MURRAY: You read a book with the teacher and you read a bit of it each and then like you have to go home and she tells you how many chapters you have to read. You have to read ... pages or chapters ... in the book.

(Farthing, Year 4. 'Can' reader)

At the level of the individual, this may mean keeping a check on how many pages of their reading book they have read – logging the page numbers was a frequent requirement expected of readers in their home reading record – as well as ensuring that they get to the end in a reasonable amount of time. Often getting to the end is a prerequisite for changing from one book to another. When dealing with proficiency texts, getting to the end may also require having read the whole text aloud to an adult listener who can thus verify that the task has been properly completed. Children were very aware of these requirements placed upon them. Indeed, this became part of how they defined their reading as monitored school work:

Transcript 10 (continued)

MURRAY: Like if you don't bring your reading record in and show it to her you have to stay in the whole playtime and if you don't come in playtime you have to stay in the whole lunchtime

(Farthing, Year 4. 'Can' reader)

How far children made meeting these kinds of requirements central to their view of themselves as readers to some extent depended on the strength of the monitoring regime they were subject to, and the sharpness of the definition of reading for proficiency as opposed to reading for choice which the resources available in both home and school enabled (see Chapter 6. See also Moss, 2001a). Certainly, one of the criteria children used when freely choosing between fiction texts was the amount of time you would have to commit to reading it in order to get through. If publishers, libraries, and schools discriminate between children's fiction according to the presumed demands the written language will make on the reader, spelt out in larger print size, bigger headings or conversely a higher density of print to page, then readers reinterpret these characteristics to yield an estimation of the time different texts will take to read, as well as the level of skill required to get through them.

Transcript 11

STEPHEN: They get thicker to read and it takes longer to finish them
INTERVIEWER: Is that better or worse?
STEPHEN: Worse {Laughs}

(Kingfisher, Year 3. 'Can' reader)

The general assumption in much of the literature on reading preferences is that children choose texts with only the content in mind: because they want to find out more about this particular topic, or have a stronger feeling for this kind of genre rather than that. But from watching children during quiet reading time in class it becomes apparent that their choices often seem to be driven by the possible social relationships which ensue from sharing different kinds of text in this particular context. In fact, one of the key features about both the non-linear forms of non-fiction and the forms of fiction which children choose to read together at these times is that they are possible to share in this context in ways in which longer chapter books, for instance, are not.

147

Finding the time to read

Linear fiction makes different demands on readers' time. One of the advantages of reading non-linear non-fiction in school in the ways described above is that it is relatively easy to do so in the varied conditions schools provide. It maximises the opportunities to read with others, and requires relatively little time. Indeed, this kind of activity can fit relatively easily into more or less any time slot. Dipping in and out can be done equally well in quite short bursts or longer chunks of time. Once the text has been put aside, the activity can be restarted simply enough from a new place.

Linear fiction texts are rather different. If the reading is interrupted, the reader has to pick up the plot at the point they left off, reorientate to the story world, and their place in its evolving sequence, and then muster the sustained concentration to get back into the text and move on to the next bit. The need to develop this kind of commitment increases as fiction texts lengthen. In school, the conditions children have at their disposal may or may not facilitate this move back into a story world. There are the distractions of the noise and movement of other children in the classroom, the likelihood of only a short time to read and a lack of control over when that time will come to an end. It is not possible for individual readers to decide that they have come to a satisfactory stopping-off point in the text and then halt with the intention of picking up the story again later on. On the contrary, reading starts and stops largely at the teacher's direction and in accordance with the flow of other activities in the classroom. As a consequence, although all children are expected to bring reading books and/or library books into school with a view to reading them at some time during the day when the occasion allows, not all of those who are entitled to do so choose to use this time to tackle lengthy chapter books. Many prefer instead to settle down to read at length in the conditions they can find at home. Here are two boys talking about the difference between reading at home and in school:

Transcript 12

INTERVIEWER: So what's best, reading at home or reading in school?
TREVOR: Reading at home, because you can read for as long as you like at home
MURRAY: At school we get half an hour

(Farthing, Year 4. 'Can' readers)

Elsewhere in this interview, Trevor comments on the reading he does in class:

TREVOR: But I don't like reading, when I'm in a mood like, when I don't like to read chapter books, I just read baby books

INTERVIEWER: What would you read if you weren't in the mood for a chapter book then, Trevor?
TREVOR: *Pathways*, [Collins *Pathways* reading scheme] easy books
INTERVIEWER: Why would you read that?
TREVOR: Because if it's like a really hard book and it was a really long book, what I don't like doing is like halfway through a book, when you've got interested in it, and then having to stop

(Farthing, Year 4. 'Can' reader)

In a similar way, Georgia, an avid reader of lengthy fiction at home, uses quiet reading time in class to read her way through what she recognises as less demanding books:

Transcript 13

GEORGIA: In our kinder box there's mainly, there's not as many books, like ones for free [readers] ... like things like, there's more like, easier ones and, whereas these are a bit harder {indicating her library book} ... easy ones take about five minutes for me to read, cos once I remember I read about 11 or 12 and they were easy. {Referring to the number of books she got through in one quiet reading session.}

(Bluebird, Year 3. 'Can' reader)

That the 'easy books' she chooses are well within her competence becomes clear from the emphasis Georgia puts on the number she has read within a short time period. She does not consider her choices a mark of her proficiency as a reader. (The researcher plotted the books she got through in that particular quiet reading session's field notes. Georgia and one other able boy reader in the class seemed to vie to see who could notch up the highest number of books read at a single sitting, perhaps in response to the researcher's activity.)

The loneliness of the long-distance reader

As Georgia and Trevor's comments indicate, children develop different ways of choosing between linear fiction texts in school time. Choosing shorter texts which are easier to get through within a limited time period is one way of matching the resource to the context of use. Children can also choose linear texts which are themselves subdivided into free-standing sections. Each section may require commitment to the writing's linear reading path, but the sections themselves don't have to be read in any particular sequence. Poetry books come into this category, as do joke books, or indeed non-fiction texts such as the *Horrible Histories* series, which provide snippets of information of varying length loosely aggregated into a larger whole. These kinds of texts become more manageable precisely because it is easier to dip in and out of them. If the mini-texts from which they are constituted are short enough, then they are also amenable to being shared in something like the same kinds of ways as the non-linear non-fiction described above. That is to say, by looking at such a text together, individuals can direct each other's attention to some amongst the range of mini-texts on offer, as the mini-texts themselves don't have to be read in a fixed sequence. Snippets can then be shared by reading them aloud to others in the group.

By contrast, lengthy linear fiction texts which are structured as a continuous narrative can really only be turned into this kind of simultaneous experience if a group are reading the text aloud together. Whilst proficiency texts are sufficiently short that a group could anticipate reading the whole text in this way in a single setting, anything more substantial makes achieving this level of close co-ordination difficult. In school, of course, this kind of co-ordinated real time experience of a single linear text happens when teachers read the class-reader aloud to children, carefully staging their collective progression from beginning to end. When they establish reading groups they often expect children to behave in the same way, reading aloud to each other and turning over each page at the same time so that their progress through the book remains in step (see Murray's comments in Transcript 10).

Yet the bulk of the chapter-book reading children undertake happens rather differently. Most of these texts will be chosen individually and read by children on their own and at their own pace. Such texts become available for sharing retrospectively, as, for instance, when one or more reader has read the same text and can pool what they know about it. This process poses its own challenges. Here are David and Peter, two able boy readers, who have both identified an interest in Roald Dahl books, attempting to do just that in interview as they jointly recall some favourite moments from *Matilda* (Dahl, 1991).

Transcript 14

INTERVIEWER:	And which is your best one of all the Dahls?
PETER:	... it would have to be *Matilda*
INTERVIEWER:	Mhm, because, what do you like about that one?
PETER:	It's got like, it's got
DAVID:	Exciting, I'd say
PETER:	Yeah, exciting and it's, I like the
DAVID:	It's his best one as well
PETER:	Yeah, and I like the
DAVID:	And it's scarey because Miss Trunchbull, she's this really [really nasty teacher and she picks up these girls by the
PETER:	[and and and
DAVID:	[pony tail and she

PETER:	[it's really funny and because Matilda just puts lizards every-where
INTERVIEWER:	She does what?
PETER:	She has lizards and she put one in the teacher's drink
DAVID:	No that was the boy, another girl, not Matilda
PETER:	I thought it was Matilda
DAVID:	No, it was Matilda's best little friend. He scooped it up, she scooped it up from her pond and then put it in her pencil case and brought it to school, and she tips it into Miss Trunchbull's (...)
INTERVIEWER:	What happens in the end to Miss Trunchbull?
DAVID:	Miss Trunchbull, does she get killed or does she get sent to jail?
PETER:	Sent to jail

(Bluebird, Year 5. 'Can' readers)

Sharing the text in this way means focusing in on selected moments. In this instance these two agree over their enthusiasm for the text although they recall the actual details slightly differently. Of course, in any given group certain texts have a high chance of being mutually recognisable. Some will have become familiar through their inclusion in the class library, being read aloud in class, or because they had attained a particular salience within a year group at a particular period of time: Roald Dahl, Jacqueline Wilson, *Goosebumps, Horrible Histories,* and later *Harry Potter* have all enjoyed this kind of social prominence. But often the likelihood of children recognising or being equally familiar with something others had read is quite small. Here is David in the same interview searching for some common reference points which might help establish quite what kind of a story his current reading book, *Treasure Island,* is:

Transcript 14 (continued)

DAVID:	Ah this is from my home. I got it for, I think it was two years ago or something and I haven't read it
INTERVIEWER:	Mhm, *Treasure Island*
DAVID:	Yes, *Treasure Island,* I've heard the story of *Treasure Island* quite a few times, and I've seen the Muppets' *Treasure Island* and films, and it's from home, and it's, I guess you know what it's about, you know *Treasure Island.* And I've got a few more of these {i.e. children's classics}.
INTERVIEWER:	When you said you'd heard it, you'd heard the story, what do you mean, you'd heard it where?
DAVID:	Well {David explains at some length how he knows about the story from a film called *Pagemaster,* and includes some details about Long John Silver.}

151

(Original transcript omitted)

INTERVIEWER:	Do you know the story of *Treasure Island*, Paul?
PETER:	No, I've never heard it. I haven't heard any people say anything about *Treasure Island*
DAVID:	Well I know Treasure Island, everyone knows Treasure Island in, not the Treasure Island in this book, but there's lots of things about treasure, loads of them
PETER:	Yeah Treasure Island, I've read a book which, it's um, *Charlie and the Treasure Island*. I like it 'cause it's got like loads of adventures about ten adventures in one day
DAVID:	Lots of people I know who've heard Treasure Island, but they haven't seen *Treasure Island* the classic
PETER:	I've seen that in a library, but I haven't read it

(Bluebird, Year 5. 'Can' readers)

The very different routes by which children come to know about and then read particular titles create different conditions in which to share knowledge of the texts' contents and establish a view of themselves as readers.

Deciding what kind of reader to be

Both recognising and then logging the pragmatic choices children make about what to read in which context produces a different kind of account of readers and their relationship to what they read. This is choice as situated action, rather than as a pure expression of an inner self or of a personal commitment to particular kinds of themes, topics or narrative structures. It is also about choice as compromise. In other words children's choices often steer by what fits here and now, and how the affordance and constraints embedded in the structure of the text can be linked to the affordance and constraints of the context. Here, once again, are David and Peter, who had described themselves to the researcher as chapter-book readers ('I think Peter and me mostly like to read the chapter books, don't we?') explaining their reading choices in school:

Transcript 14 (continued)

INTERVIEWER:	So like for that {i.e. chapter-book reading} you need to be somewhere quiet/
DAVID:	Yes
INTERVIEWER:	And at home? Could you do that kind of reading at school?
DAVID:	No not really. When you've got books like this one at school {Indicating a non-linear non-fiction text, *The X-Ray Picture Book of Incredible Creatures* (Legg and Scrace, 1995)} or something, you only get to read books like this and you never

152

	read, actually get to read in detail, you always have to like flick through it and look at the pictures and get all snippets of bits. You never get to successfully read like a whole page
PETER:	I normally read a whole page, I don't go, just
DAVID:	Most people just open up the book and flick through it and go 'Miss I've finished reading this book' and put it back and get out another book
PETER:	I just, I just start reading
INTERVIEWER:	You would actually take a page and then you would read the page
PETER:	[When I'm reading
DAVID:	[I try and read the whole page but it's a bit annoying 'cause Oscar and Adrian and the rest of them in our class, they're a bit, like, friends, they like me and they're friends with me but they always want to talk about the book [when you're trying to read it
INTERVIEWER:	[Yes they do actually, yeah, that's very true! They like/ What do they talk about when they're?
PETER:	They talk about
DAVID:	Games and silly things they've done to their sister 'cause Adrian really hates his sister
INTERVIEWER:	So even when they've got their *Goosebumps* books out, even [though they like their *Goosebumps*
DAVID:	[They're a bit unmature they're quite unmature
PETER:	[They, like, read, like, these sort of books with, like, bugs and they go 'That bug's like'
DAVID:	'That looks like my sister' {Mimicking Adrian's voice}

(Bluebird, Year 5. 'Can' readers)

What David is simultaneously describing and distancing himself from here is the style of roaming round picture-led non-fiction which was documented in the first half of the chapter. David represents the social character of this kind of interaction as an annoying distraction which prevents him from paying concentrated attention to the 'whole page'. Unable to escape from others' chatter and bound to follow their collective pace through non-linear non-fiction texts, he ends up having to 'like flick through it and look at the pictures and get all snippets of bits'. He adapts what he does to the conditions under which reading takes place in school. For him this means that his chapter-book reading mainly takes place at home, whilst at school he ends up joining in browsing with the group. Yet in representing the choices he makes in this way, he also passes value judgements on what kinds of reading are best, and positions himself and others in relation to these judgements.

Chapter books and the value judgement of reading more

David and Peter's use of the expression 'chapter books' to identify their own distinct preferences as readers in this interview is interesting. The researchers first encountered this phrase in the course of undertaking the research, initially in teachers' talk about their book stock. In one sense the phrase 'chapter books' is purely self-explanatory. It designates those fiction books which are long enough to be subdivided into chapters. But as used in classrooms it also carries within it a value judgement about what kinds of books are best, and what kinds of commitment to reading children should be making. For teachers, the phrase 'chapter books' signals the kind of horizon to reading for choice which they are pushing children towards. In bringing this phrase into the interview (the boys, not the interviewer, introduced it), the boys use the expression to establish their credentials as readers who are capable of tackling the more demanding kinds of fiction books and, indeed, take their own reading seriously.

Transcript 14 (continued)

DAVID: I think Peter and me mostly like to read the chapter books don't we?

INTERVIEWER: That's your favourites?

PETER: Yes, chapter books definitely

INTERVIEWER: Do you think that's the same with other people in the class or are you quite different from them?

PETER: I don't think everyone does

DAVID: Everyone likes chapter books, but most people, some people in my class don't like to read at all really, they'll pick up a comic and start chatting to the person next to them

PETER: They'll talk about the person next to them's book so it gets

DAVID: And then that other person talks to another person and it [goes on round

PETER: [It goes on like a big circle

                                (Bluebird, Year 5. 'Can' readers)

In fact, they make clear in the subsequent conversation that the other 'people' they are describing are all boys. In the context of this conversation these two use the identification of their preference for reading chapter books to draw a line between themselves and many of their peers in the class. They represent this other group as less committed to reading and generally less mature in their approach to the classroom (see the previous extract from this same interview quoted above). Proficiency and choice criteria elide so that the chapter-book reader becomes at once more proficient, but also more dedicated to the act of reading. Readers who choose this kind of text have the stamina and the serious commitment to the activity which others lack.

There is a sense of the politics of being a reader in this conversation, a recognition of the kinds of choices people make, and how those choices mark people out, one from another. Yet quite who stands which side of the line changes in different contexts. These two begin the interview by making clear that their preference for chapter-book reading marks them out. But they also can't quite pin down who else might or might not read like them or how many might really fall into which group. Indeed, the large group of boys whom they mainly identify as the non-readers, or casual readers of comics or non-fiction, in fact often sit with chapter books in front of them, as the researcher remarks:

INTERVIEWER: So even when they've got their *Goosebumps* books out, even [though they like their *Goosebumps*

DAVID: [They're a bit unmature they're quite unmature
(Bluebird, Year 5. 'Can' reader)

Moreover, these two also adapt their own behaviour in class in a context where it is hard not to join in with your friends. They too browse non-fiction. In fact they also do this in this interview, for they briefly browse through the two non-fiction books Peter has brought from his tray in exactly the manner described in the opening section of this chapter. Whilst they may recognise the prestige associated with chapter-book reading they pragmatically adapt what they do to both the occasion and the resources which it makes available.

Telling the 'can/do's' from the 'can/don'ts'

The terms 'can/do' and 'can/don't' distinguish between different patterns of reading behaviour that the researchers observed during quiet reading time, and at other moments during the school day when children could steer their reading activity for themselves. As far as teachers were concerned these children had passed the main proficiency hurdles in reading. Their designation as free readers implied that whilst their competence at reading might still need to expand and grow over time, they were deemed to have sufficient levels of skill to be able to choose their own reading material and read largely independently of intensive teacher monitoring. But at the same time the researchers observed that whilst some of these children made good use of these freedoms, others did not. In class, for instance, 'can/don't' readers were most likely to spend the majority of their time clustered around the area where books could be chosen, talking with their friends, or if they settled with one book would be most likely to flick through it, to use David's expression, and then pop up to change it again very rapidly. (The use of reading for choice time in Farthing School, included in Chapter 3 as captured in the researcher's field notes, reveals this pattern of behaviour quite clearly.)

Whilst the category of 'can't yet/don't' readers stood up across the range of data, and was reflected in consistencies in what and how children spoke about their reading and how they described the range of resources they interacted with, the boundary line between 'can/do's' and 'can/don'ts' can be more difficult to draw. Children who looked quite clearly as if they fitted into one category in one context might show themselves in a different light in another setting. This could work both ways. David and Peter, for instance, had been identified as 'can/do' readers from classroom observation. In class they settled down to read one way or another whenever they could. In interview, however, Peter's view of himself as a reader comes across quite differently from David's.

Like David, Peter was keen to stress his interest in tackling 'chapter books'. Here he is in an early part of the interview commenting on books he has borrowed from the school library. (It was school policy to take out one fiction and one non-fiction book.)

PETER: Yeah I have quite a few fiction books, actually I've got um a fiction book, I can't remember what it's called but it's an adventure one with, it's got chapters as well and the non-fiction book was *How Would You Survive as a Gruesome Greek* [probably *How Would You Survive as an Ancient Greek?*]

(Bluebird, Year 5. 'Can' reader)

But taken as a whole in this conversation his contributions generally follow in David's wake. David seems to make most of the running in terms of establishing the salient themes and expressing judgements about himself and others as readers, judgements with which Peter then seems to go along. At this point in the interview the interviewer probes them on when they get time to read their home-reading books:

Transcript 14 (continued)

INTERVIEWER: When do you actually get to read them?
PETER: I actually get to read them at home, but I haven't read it since, I haven't read *BFG* {his home-reading book} since {sound of flipping pages}
INTERVIEWER: He's looking in his book {i.e. his home-reading record book}
PETER: The fifth of the second '97. [The interview took place on 17/3/97]
INTERVIEWER: ... So have you been reading anything in between whiles?
PETER: Um no
INTERVIEWER: What do you prefer to do at home, when you've got some time to yourself?

PETER:	Well I play on my computer, or I start reading other books, 'cause I like reading, it's one of my hobbies, or I go round my friend's house
INTERVIEWER:	And what kind of things do you read at those times?
PETER:	I read like, same as Daniel, I read fat books, 'cause I like reading them. I've got about fifty in my book-case 'cause I like reading them
DAVID:	I've got hundreds of them. My favourite book in my whole collection has to be Enid Blyton's *The Famous Five and The Fantastic Four* (sic)
PETER:	I like *Famous Five*, I like reading them. The books I've got, I've got quite a few of them, but I've got so much I can't count them all, 'cause I've got a stack that big.

(Bluebird, Year 5. 'Can' readers)

There are a number of contradictions in the account Peter gives of himself as a reader. On the one hand, he signs up to David's definition of the two of them as chapter-book readers; on the other hand, the books he was actually making use of in quiet reading time and brought to the interview were both picture-led non-fiction books: *The X-Ray Picture Book of Incredible Creatures*, and *Mythical Monsters, Legendary Creatures*. These lend themselves to being shared in group settings of the kind David bemoans in the extract above. Meanwhile, his reading record book showed he hadn't been reading his home-reading book for some time. Although he nominated reading as his hobby, he also referred to spending time on his computer or going round to his friend's house as things he preferred to do with his time at home. Asked to describe the other books he read, he used the expression 'fat books', as a generic category rather than referring to specific titles, and in this part of the conversation seems mainly concerned to match or exceed the size of David's book collection overall. (He borrowed this expression 'fat books' from David's talk earlier in the interview.)

By contrast, David sprinkles the interview with references to specific titles or series he likes: *Dinotopia; Famous Five; Goosebumps;* various Roald Dahl books; and *Treasure Island*. He often goes into extensive detail about the plots of the books he has read and what he likes about them, which are his best (*Dinotopia*), and which are not so good (*Goosebumps* and *Horrible Histories*). Likewise, David's use of the expression 'fat books' works into the conversation about *Treasure Island* in quite a different way:

Transcript 14 (continued)

DAVID:	Lots of people I know who've heard Treasure Island, but they haven't seen *Treasure Island* the classic
PETER:	I've seen that in a library, but I haven't read it

INTERVIEWER: What made you decide now to pick it off your shelf, David, 'cause you were saying it's been there for quite a while?

DAVID: Well, it was actually my mum who chose it, 'cause I'd totally forgotten about it, and my mum brought it down and said, do you want to read this? And I thought, yeah, that looks good, 'cause I like reading big fat books

INTERVIEWER: Did she know that you were stuck for something to read?

DAVID: Yes, she knew that there wasn't very many good books actually and I brought in *Goosebumps* book to read and then I lost it. That was on a Monday, ages ago, {and he continues with a detailed account of how his *Goosebumps* book went missing in school}.

(Bluebird, Year 5. 'Can' readers)

This interchange is really about how he and his mum negotiate over what he might like to read next, in which she presents him with some choices which he can either say yes to, because they fit what he likes, or turn down. The fact that she recognises his preferences seems as important as the actual choice he makes. The anecdote is about choosing, not about his proficiency as a reader.

If it is reasonably easy to work out what David's tastes are from the account he gives, Peter remains more of an enigma, unable to muster such a compelling account of himself as a reader. Indeed, at times he seems to suggest he doesn't really read any more. Here he is discussing how long he has been reading Roald Dahl books, which he had described as his favourites:

PETER: I have been reading them when I was really young. My mum and dad's been reading them and I've enjoyed them when I was little

INTERVIEWER: Were your mum and dad reading them to you before you could read to yourself?

PETER: When I started getting older, I started reading Roald Dahls with my mum until I could read by myself. *Now I can read all by myself so, I don't read that much any more so//* [my emphasis]

(Bluebird, Year 5. 'Can' reader)

The difficult transition from being read to, to being a solitary reader is something he returns to elsewhere in the interview.

The point of these observations is not to try and catch Peter out, as it were, or depict him as a less credible witness than David. Rather, it is to try and highlight a number of difficulties in attempting to work out who is really doing what round reading, and what reading means to them. It may be that David's easy assumption that chapter books are the only kind of books worth reading works better for him than it does for Peter. For

David the term 'chapter books' defines where his own core interests currently lie: in sampling a range of fiction which works at this length. But for Peter the label seems more problematic. He understands its status implications, and tries to match what David can lay claim to. By contrast, when he takes back the space to express his interests in reading in his own terms, he has this to say:

Transcript 14 (continued)

PETER: I like reading books with other people 'cause I read quite a lot of books with my brother and he enjoys it a lot

INTERVIEWER: And what kind of books do you read with him Peter?

PETER: I read like little books 'cause he's only about six. I read him like books about you know these stage books that are about that thick and I read his books to him 'cause he doesn't know how to read properly yet. He is quite good and I help him.

(Bluebird, Year 5. 'Can' reader)

He is much clearer on what are the pleasures to be had from sharing reading in this context. Perhaps he is simply less sure what to do elsewhere now that reading has become so much more his own business both at home and at school. Given that he can and does tackle a range of books in different settings, does it really matter that he has a more hazy view of himself as a reader than David? It may be that despite the uncertainties posed by the account he gives of himself, that Peter is just reading differently from David.

The kinds of difficulties presented by Peter's case can be found working the other way round in relation to 'can/don't' readers. Leo, identified as a 'can/don't' reader in the same class as David and Peter, was seldom observed reading but rather took advantage of the time put aside for this purpose in class to pursue other activities. Indeed, the single sex reading group he belonged to was recognised by the teacher as the group most likely to abandon the books they were meant to be tackling, which they did with monotonous regularity. When asked about his reading in interview he was quite direct about how little store he set by school-sponsored reading, and indeed in some respects quite clearly casts himself as a non-reader. Asked about how he'd chosen his library book, he commented as follows:

Transcript 15

LEO: Well, I wasn't very interested in many books, but Mrs M said this one would probably be good, 'cause it's won two awards so I read it and it's OK.

When the interviewer asks if he's finished it he says:

LEO: No, not all of it

INTERVIEWER: How much have you read?
LEO: Just started it, up to, I'm not sure, about Chapter Two
INTERVIEWER: Do you think you're going to stick with it or will you take it back?
LEO: I'll probably take it back

(Bluebird, Year 5. 'Can' reader)

In the course of the interview he twice quite firmly declares: 'I never read my reading books or my library books.'

This seems to be his general rule. Despite the teacher's efforts, it is quite clear he is not going to change that habit now. Yet this public and ostentatious refusal to take part in school reading hides the fact that he does actually read at home. He has two current passions: *Goosebumps* books and information books on animals.

Transcript 15 (continued)

LEO: Oh books, at the weekend I'd read information, but through the week before I go to bed, I'd read the collection that I was talking about, *Goosebumps*
INTERVIEWER: So before you go to sleep, every night do you read *Goosebumps* or just sometimes?
LEO: Most nights, most nights

(Bluebird, Year 5. 'Can' reader)

It's as if the public stance he takes towards the reading curriculum is a way of detaching himself from the cultural environment of the school and keeping it at a distance. The kind of reading he does at home is for his own purposes and to please no-one except himself. He is refusing to make what or how he reads a matter of public validation:

INTERVIEWER: Would you say you're collecting the *Goosebumps?*
LEO: Yeah, definitely
INTERVIEWER: And when you collect them do you actually read them?
LEO: Yeah, I'll collect one and then when I've read that my mum will get me another one so
INTERVIEWER: What does she think to the *Goosebumps?*
LEO: She doesn't even read them 'cause I read them like when I'm up in my bedroom and meant to be going to sleep

(Bluebird, Year 5. 'Can' reader)

The pattern to his reading is no-one's business except his own.

Conclusion

Many of the arguments made about boys as readers depend upon assessing who is really reading what, where. Yet it is all too possible to use the available data to over-generalise from one context to another in the rush to judgement about what readers do, or indeed come to slightly skewed conclusions precisely because of the status given to some kinds of reading over others. Elaine Millard provides a cautionary overview of much of the available questionnaire data on children's reading habits from precisely this point of view, highlighting the ways in which the kinds of questions asked may have the effect of distorting the conclusions that can really be drawn from this kind of data. She used this insight to design rather different research tools which generated a more interesting and subtle picture. Thus instead of asking children to name the books they had most recently read, she asked her sample to tell their own story of their development as readers, and then used the different positions children adopted in the accounts they provided to discriminate between their sense of themselves as readers (Millard, 1997). Her analysis showed that more girls than boys presented themselves as committed readers, though very few boys expressed much interest in non-fiction. This last point gets slightly hidden in her account. This may be because she uses the data she has collected to draw attention to the limited ways in which the secondary English curriculum helps sustain children's interests in reading. She sees this as a failure to connect with children's real interests. She concludes that non-fiction may well be a neglected resource as far as boys are concerned. That is not the case which is being argued in this book.

As I've argued above, a return to the quantitative data on children's reading preferences in the light of the kind of ethnographic data on children's reading preferences presented here shows how little evidence there really is to support the assertion that boys prefer non-fiction. Only a minority of children express a preference for non-fiction over fiction reading material in any of the large-scale surveys (Children's Literature Research Centre, 1996; Gorman *et al.*, 1984; Hall and Coles, 1999; Whitehead *et al.*, 1977). Even fewer report only reading non-fiction. (In Hall and Coles' sample this rests at 2.8 per cent (Hall and Coles, 1999).) By far and away the majority of those who read non-fiction are reading fiction as well. Where the analysis seems to have gone awry is in dealing with the fact that the majority of that minority (those who express a preference for non-fiction, or say they read it only or often) are boys. This leads to an unwarranted extrapolation from the data, and the conclusion that boys in general prefer non-fiction or that non-fiction better matches their interests.

The range of data collected for this book establishes a different picture. In classroom settings where they could most freely choose the texts that they wanted to read, there were more boys than girls amongst those who chose non-fiction. But these boys were also most likely to be those at the bottom of the ability spectrum. Moreover, the predominantly non-linear forms of non-fiction they chose lent themselves to being shared in this setting in the terms identified above, broadly speaking as a focus for talk which might well be prompted by some aspects of the text, but which wouldn't require detailed reading of its contents. There was very little evidence in the project data of these same boys dedicating much time to this kind of non-fiction at home. What they may well therefore be choosing is not so much the specific content of the text, as the social possibilities such texts foster in shared settings where a group of children can gather, exchange and compare what they know using the text as a prompt.

Testing the analysis against library-borrowing data

The follow-up to the original research project, called Mixed Methods, tested these understandings of children's book choices by examining the school library borrowing records of ninety Year 6 children at Bluebird, roughly a third of whom had participated in the earlier detailed ethnography when they were in Year 3. By chance, this cohort contained two-thirds boys so the database provided a substantial window onto boys' reading habits. The library records were for the whole year. There was no significant difference in the number of titles that boys and girls took out over the course of the year. Analysis of the books borrowed showed that only 10 per cent of the titles that children took home were non-fiction. Forty-three per cent of the sample borrowed no non-fiction, of whom 55 per cent were boys. Only 4 per cent of the sample borrowed more non-fiction than fiction titles over the course of the year, all of them boys with a designation of Special Educational Needs. This small number of individuals also borrowed comparatively few texts (see Moss and McDonald, 2004, for a more detailed account of this research). Comparatively few of the non-fiction texts borrowed were picture-led non-linear non-fiction. This reinforces the argument made above that these kinds of texts are chosen in quiet reading time because of the social opportunities they provide in that setting.

The assumption in much of the commentary on children's reading preferences is that the school English curriculum overemphasises narrative fiction at the expense of non-fiction. As such, it does not adequately represent boys' interests. For some, boys' relative underperformance in English derives from this point. But almost all of those boys (and girls) who in interview reported reading non-fiction at home also reported reading fiction, just as Leo does above. Those boys who were most passionate about reading, in talk, in observation, in questionnaire returns and in interview, were most passionate about reading fiction. By contrast, those boys who spent least time reading at home, and had the least to say about their reading, either at home or school, were most likely to spend time on non-fiction in class. Taken together, these points indicate that those readers in this age group who establish a firm view of themselves as readers do so overwhelmingly in relation to fiction texts. This is as true of boys as it is of girls. The fact that many commentators substantially overlook boys' interest in fiction, or find ways to disregard it, deserves attention in its own right.

6

GENDER, LITERACY AND ATTAINMENT IN THE CONTEXT OF EDUCATIONAL REFORM

Introduction

The previous three chapters have focused on how children become aware of what counts as reading through participating in the range of literacy events that make up the school day. The texts, the contexts and the roles available to readers in any event, all play a part in shaping what goes on. Both the continuities and discontinuities between one event and another help form girls' and boys' developing sense of what it means to read and to be a reader. This is not a uniform process.

Taken together, the data demonstrate that reading in schools does not encapsulate a single point of view about what reading is, nor how it should be done. There are at least three different logics at work in school settings – reading for choice, proficiency reading and procedural reading – which pull against each other and at times compete to take centre stage in the classroom. Each one positions pupils differently. Children navigate their way through these differences, adopting a variety of roles both within and outside particular literacy events and the configurations of text, context and reader that they contain. They may undercut as well as accept the positions they are offered by drawing on the conflicting range of resources that schooling makes available to them.

By concentrating on why the same reading curriculum provokes very different kinds of responses amongst different groups of pupils, this book has shifted the grounds of the argument about why boys do less well at reading and writing. In particular, it has moved the focus away from boys in general to the formation of specific groups of readers within the same classroom who gain access to texts under different conditions. These different groups of readers face different dilemmas, depending in large part on how they perceive their own social standing in relation to the reading curriculum. The social regulation of the reading curriculum produces points of conflict and tension that children have to resolve.

This view of school literacy as multifaceted rather than uniform within a single site opens up new questions for literacy research: about how gender and the social regulation of literacy interact; about the relationship between the social regulation of literacy at school and at home; and about the politics of choosing, for, as children themselves recognise, the choices they make about their own reading are seldom unfettered or unconstrained by the wishes and intentions of others. This chapter will begin to draw the threads of the argument together by considering where debate on gender and attainment now stands both in light of the arguments made in this book and in the context of the kind of reform of the literacy curriculum now taking place in England.

The data for this chapter include field notes collected during classroom observation, library-borrowing records from one of the case-study schools, and interviews held with teachers, parents and pupils as part of the original research and for the follow-up ethnography.

Literacy, gender and attainment: exploring tension points in the reading curriculum

This book has consistently put forward a social explanation of differences in boys' and girls' literacy attainment that rests not so much on factors outside of school but instead on the different kinds of literacy events that happen within it. The analysis has shown how the diversity of social interactions that take place round reading in school classrooms, both within and outside the official reading curriculum, provide the means to construct, maintain and intensify variation in outcomes in literacy attainment. In classrooms the prominence given to teachers' judgements of individuals' competence at reading inevitably spells out children's place in relation to their peers. Such judgements interact with children's view of their gendered sense of self and the claims they seek to make about their own social standing, with different consequences for boys and girls according to their place in the reading hierarchy. Within the reading curriculum, gender is always intersected by the designation of ability. This analysis is very different from assuming that the problem boys face with the literacy curriculum is that its content or style panders to girls' interests, not theirs, and should be redressed accordingly.

The research reported in earlier chapters identified three groups of readers made visible in classrooms: the 'can't yet/don't' group; the 'can/do' group and the 'can/don't' group. The terminology attempts to capture the extent to which these groups form through, on the one hand, teachers' judgements about individuals' competence at reading and the access to resources that flow from that and, on the other, pupils' response to these conditions. For even as classrooms create dilemmas for pupils through the tension between different aspects of the reading curriculum, they also provide resources and opportunities for pupils to appropriate literacy in other ways. This produces different profiles of underachievement as boys and girls positioned at similar points in the hierarchy of readers negotiate their way through the reading culture of the classroom in disparate ways. Gender emerges at this level.

Those who do least well within this system are those for whom the conflict between their own estimation of their social standing and the school's is most intense. Boys identified as slow readers are particularly likely to fall into this category precisely because of the emphasis they put on the public display of successful competence in their relations with their peers. The way in which boys who have been designated as low-attaining readers gravitate towards non-linear non-fiction both demonstrates their need to escape from the role of the poor reader into the role of the expert and also helps explain why in the longer term this kind of response may be self-defeating. For the strategies they adopt in order to claim high status for what they already know makes it harder to find a space in which to grapple with those aspects of reading that they find most difficult. (See Terry and Mitchel's exchange in Transcript 6 of the previous chapter for an example of the dilemmas posed and how they were in this instance resolved.)

Girls designated low-attainers at literacy react differently from boys to being grouped in this way. Classroom observation suggested that girls in this group experienced less conflict over being seen to do less well, in part because there seemed to be less at stake for them in adapting to the role of being on the receiving end of others' help. They were willing to spend time on reading materials chosen to match their level of attainment, and were happy to share such texts with others considered more able than themselves. The strategies they adopted ensured that this group continued to make slow if unremarkable progress. Yet by accepting the position of 'slow reader', these girls also ran the risk of adapting to others' low expectations of their capabilities. Observation showed that they rarely challenged others' expectations about what they could do. If they seldom pushed themselves, then others rarely did this for them. In some cases the kinds of texts they were assigned to read were well within or even substantially below their competence. Because they seldom made a fuss, they could be easily overlooked.

Boys who were designated 'poor readers' were much less likely to accept that assessment. Yet in reacting against the label they also placed themselves in a position where it became far harder for them to receive help. They would cover up or avoid what they couldn't do and developed little stamina for tackling tasks they could not immediately master. These tactics meant they were more likely to fall further behind, thus in turn necessitating further avoidance of the task at hand as the gulf between this group and their peers widened still further. Whilst they attracted attention in class this often fell on managing their poor behaviour. These different profiles of underachievement require different kinds of redress.

Why underachievement in literacy is not just a matter of basic skills

Discussion of underachievement in the literacy curriculum often rests at this level, with the acquisition of basic skills. But the research documented here shows that children at the opposite end of the proficiency ladder faced different but equally powerful dilemmas as they emerged from the close regulation of their reading, enacted in carefully staged proficiency encounters. At this point they moved into a looser form of social regulation as 'free readers' where they were increasingly expected to 'choose wisely' what to read for themselves. In effect, this meant both deciding how to spend their time and knowing what to spend it on. The terms 'can/do' and 'can/don't' readers are a means of discriminating between the patterns of response to these freedoms which the research documented (see Chapter 5). The 'can/do' group made the most of the opportunities they had to read and undertook this as a largely self-directed activity. They seemed to possess a clear sense of themselves as readers and used this to steer what they did quite purposefully. More girls than boys operated as 'can/do' readers.

'Can/don't' readers did not make the same use of the freedoms they had. There were more boys than girls in the 'can/don't' category. Despite having passed the relevant proficiency threshold, boys in this group were more likely to use quiet reading time to cluster in the book corner or socialise quietly with a few friends with or without a text to hand. They seldom used this time to settle down with a chapter book. When they had made a choice of what to read at home they were also more likely to abandon that choice after a few pages, or alternatively stick with something they didn't really like, spinning out reading it over many months thus obeying the requirement to be reading something with little care for what it was. In part, this demonstrates the difficulties children face in knowing how to choose what will repay the kind of investment in time and sustained attention that longer reading materials require.

But evidence collected on the full range of research instruments – from classroom observation, questionnaire and interview – also suggested that girls' friendship networks seemed to cue them differently from boys' to the dilemma of what texts to choose. For girls, being friends seemed to encompass sharing information about the kinds of things they liked to read on their own. If they found something they liked they would let others in their circle know. By contrast, 'can/do' boys networked far less around linear texts. If they were committed to reading at this length, this was often pursued as a solitary activity without reference to their friends. Often parents seemed to play the most crucial role in sustaining these boys' interests. This meant that from the perspective of their friendship networks their choices did indeed look idiosyncratic. There were exceptions: titles or series that gained a particular prominence across a wider group for a period of time such as the *Goosebumps* series, the *Horrible Histories* series and later the *Harry Potter* books. Yet the prominence of these kinds of texts did not necessarily translate into their readership. In the first phase of the research, exploration through interview of the craze for *Goosebumps* titles in the Year 5 class in Bluebird revealed that whilst many boys in this class collected the titles, and indeed brought their collections into class to show to their friends, very few actually read the ones they owned. Possession seemed to matter more than time spent reading them.

Does it matter if a significant number of boys designated 'free readers' invest less time in reading than girls and share their interests less freely? That depends. There is a strong case to be made that those who read most are most consistently exposed to a greater variety of written language which they can then appropriate more completely for use in their own writing (Barrs and Cork, 2001). The act of reading feeds the act of writing. This argument fits the pattern of pupil performance demonstrated in the Key Stage statutory attainment tests at the end of primary school where the greatest discrepancy between boys' and girls' attainment is in writing, and clearly demonstrated towards the top as well as at the bottom of the ability spectrum. If fewer boys spend time reading for themselves, this may well be one of the main factors that contributes to this pattern (Ofsted, 2003).

Some boys and girls make their way through the literacy curriculum successfully. Others do not. The gender-differentiated patterns of response to the social organisation of literacy in the classroom and the tension points it creates raise further questions for pedagogy. Two key issues stand out. On the one hand, how should classrooms provide support for reading for choice as children make the transition into operating as free readers? Indeed, what kinds of support encourage autonomous reading? And on the other, how can teachers create an inclusive classroom culture from the perspective of those at the bottom of the proficiency ladder, which enables all children to pay the attention that is required to the aspects of written language that will take them forward as readers and writers? These concerns will lace their way through the rest of the chapter. But the chapter will also raise more general questions about how schools manage the contradictions between teaching reading for proficiency and teaching reading for choice, and the difficulties of doing so in the context of government-sponsored educational reform.

Pedagogic discourse: making sense of reading pedagogy

The research data collected for this book has focused on how children both see and understand the social organisation of literacy in the classroom. It has not sought to enter the debate over the respective merits of different reading pedagogies. Such debates pit one method of reading instruction against another with claim and counter-claim as to their relative efficacy. 'Reading for choice' and 'reading for proficiency' as used in this book do not line up with particular instructional methods. They are orientations to the business of reading which are embedded in the social structure of particular kinds of literacy events. Evidence for both can always be found in school. (And I would argue at home, too. See Moss, 2001a and Street and Street, 1991.) No matter how fully a particular school may espouse a self-contained and internally consistent approach to phonics teaching, allied with the most robust expression of 'reading for proficiency', this will not be the only version of 'what counts as reading' to be found on the curriculum. Equally, those schools or classrooms most committed to teaching reading through a 'real books' approach will organise events which exemplify reading for proficiency as well as reading for choice.

Bernstein's theory of pedagogic discourse is a useful reference point at this stage in the argument (Bernstein, 1996). Bernstein argues that pedagogic discourse is always composed of two elements: an instructional discourse which 'creates specialized skills and their relationship to each other' and a regulative discourse which is a 'moral discourse which creates order, relations and identity'. If the instructional discourse specifies *what* the content of the pedagogic discourse will be, then the regulative discourse specifies *how* that content will be acquired under specific conditions. The two always travel hand in hand because the specification of the 'what' of pedagogic discourse always implies a sequence, a mode and a manner in which that discourse will be acquired; in other words, it already helps constitute its regulative aspect.

For Bernstein the regulative always takes precedence over the instructional in pedagogic discourse. He argues that relations of power are embedded in the way in which the instructional discourse is itself delineated and organised; become evident in the ways in which access to that knowledge base is paced and managed through the regulative discourse; and finally find their expression in the social relations that ensue between teachers and taught. This will be true whatever the precise object of the pedagogy and the particular knowledge content it sets out to deliver.

Bernstein identifies two forms of pedagogic discourse which establish different social relations between teachers and taught: visible and invisible pedagogies. Visible pedagogies create strong boundaries to the knowledge base they encompass and embed that knowledge base in an overtly regulative regime. By contrast, invisible pedagogies blur the boundaries to the knowledge base and embed the regulative discourse within the instructional discourse in different ways. In so doing they mask the regulative relations which the pedagogic discourse then implies rather than pronounces. Neither is intrinsically 'better' than the other (Bernstein, 1990). Rather, each produces different pedagogic relations, with different social consequences (Moss, 2000b).

169

Different methods of teaching reading vary in the comparative visibility of the regulative discourse they employ (Moss, 2002b). Most programmes of instruction that are based on phonics adopt a visible pedagogy, whilst programmes of instruction that are based on real books adopt an invisible pedagogy. They can be assigned to Bernstein's categories by examining the ways in which they organise their knowledge content and by the social relations that ensue for teachers and taught. Phonics programmes generally take the form of a visible pedagogy by virtue of the fact that they exemplify a well-boundaried knowledge base, clearly delineated from other forms of knowledge, and which sets out strong hierarchical relations both in the forms of knowledge it encompasses and in the ordering of the pace and sequence in which that knowledge must be acquired. By contrast, approaches to reading instruction based on the selection of 'real' books have traditionally espoused a form of invisible pedagogy which blurs the boundaries to the forms of knowledge deemed relevant to learning to read, making less absolute the distinction between what might be considered relevant to this task and what might not, as well as weakening any necessary sequence in which the relevant skills must be acquired. In this context, relations between teacher and taught flatten out. Experts and novices operate on a less sharply differentiated basis.

For Bernstein, different social consequences will flow from the precise ways in which instructional and regulative discourses are embedded in any particular pedagogic discourse. The choices made are crucial. Yet it is also always possible to disentangle and recombine the instructional and regulative in new ways. The object of the pedagogic discourse, considered in the abstract, does not dictate the regulative order. In other words, it is possible to produce knowledge of the same object – say the graphic correspondence for particular phonemes – as part of a particular pedagogic discourse which is either more or less strongly classified or more or less weakly framed. If phonics-based pedagogy has traditionally presented itself as a highly visible discourse, strongly classified and framed, there is no inevitability about this. It is perfectly possible to imagine a pedagogic discourse which takes 'phonics' as its object, but which weakens both the instructional and regulative discourse. (I would argue that *Playing with Sounds*, a course of instruction in phonics produced by the Primary National Strategy for use in the early years, attempts to do precisely this (DfES, 2004).) Equally, aspects of the reading curriculum traditionally associated with whole-language approaches can be transformed from invisible to visible pedagogies. (See Moss, 2002a for an example of this kind of translation, explored in relation to the non-fiction writing curriculum and using picture-led non-fiction as the starting point.)

Visible or invisible pedagogies and the question of attainment

The ethnographic data collected for this book show that in many ways pupils in classrooms orientate to the regulative over and above the instructional aspects of the pedagogic discourses that they encounter. The regulative is what they see first and foremost, and they read the instructional through that. Given that reading for proficiency was almost always conducted as a more visible pedagogic discourse than reading for choice, it is not surprising that the forms of social regulation associated with proficiency so strongly feed into children's views of themselves as readers. What are the consequences of this kind of orientation to the regulative for pupils' attainment?

If we take the concept of visible and invisible pedagogy and apply it to the data presented in this book, then the four case-study schools fall into two pairs, one adopting highly visible pedagogies (Kingfisher and Bluebird), and one adopting relatively invisible pedagogies (Shepherd and Farthing). Each of these pairings contains one school working in areas with high levels of poverty and social disadvantage (Kingfisher and Shepherd) and one working in areas with a much more affluent and socially advantaged population (Bluebird and Farthing). Despite their different catchments, the two schools with the most clearly visible pedagogies consistently demonstrated far higher attainment grades for reading amongst their pupils, and stood out in the performance league tables on those grounds, so much so that during the period of research both were named by Ofsted, the government school inspection agency, as particularly high-achieving schools in the national context. Yet the kinds of visible pedagogy they constructed operated on very different terms.

As we've seen in Chapter 3, in Kingfisher reading for proficiency took pride of place on the curriculum. Across the database, these kinds of literacy events were most strongly classified, and also most strongly framed (see pp. 79–81). The school extended explicit regulation of these kinds of events from the children to the parents. Field notes recorded that the Head could be expected to approach parents who were not keeping up with the home-reading record in the playground in the morning to find out why not. Given everything this book has said about the difficulties created for (some) children by the high visibility that seems to accrue to the judgements made about their proficiency as readers, why should this regime produce such outstanding results? It seems to me that there are two likely explanations. First, the visible pedagogy ensured that school and home converged on the same clear set of procedures to demonstrate to children what reading was for and how it should be accomplished. Consistently exercised and always given priority in both contexts, nobody could be in any doubt about what was being expected of them. Second, everyone within these classrooms was equally subject to exactly the same kind of regulation. There was no distinction to be made between those who were pinned down within this regulatory environment and those who were not. One might almost describe it as a kind of equality of submission. No one could escape, therefore all were on a level playing field, regardless of one's precise place on the proficiency ladder.

Bluebird was different. In this school every aspect of the curriculum was made visible. This applied equally to reading for choice as well as reading for proficiency or procedural reading. Children were expected to know and articulate the precise ground rules for action in any given context, and also discriminate between them. In the classroom observed, groups would form and reform, depending on the curriculum content, and would be sent to different places within the classroom space accordingly. Sometimes groupings were mixed ability, sometimes not, but changing the curriculum content almost always had the effect of changing the group and its social organisation. As with the other schools, the regulative led, but at the same time the way the regulative was enacted seemed to leave most space for the instructional itself to peep through. More attention focused on what was to be learnt as well as how. As I argued in earlier chapters, what reading for choice might mean and the kinds of texts it could encompass had most definition in this setting. This also meant that of all the classrooms observed, children got most direct support for dealing with increasingly complex areas of the curriculum.

Paradoxically, in the two schools which adopted relatively invisible pedagogies, the children seemed no less aware of the patterns of regulation they were expected to submit to, but the forms of regulation themselves did not point so clearly to a distinct body of knowledge nor help specify how it might be acquired. It is perhaps no accident that in both these two settings procedural reading dominated the curriculum.

Whichever way they balanced the mix of literacy events which made up their respective curricula, the two schools with more visible pedagogies made it easier for children to know what they were setting out to learn and, in effect, kept more of them on board for more of that process. Their results can be read in this light. But this success was not without its costs either to individuals or communities. It could be argued that the gains in reading attainment within Kingfisher were bought at the expense of offering children a broader view of reading for choice. There was little room left in this approach to foster reader autonomy or take children outside a relatively narrow range of texts. Whilst in Bluebird, the sheer pressure of dealing with the constantly changing demands for attentive participation seemed too much for some. This school's Year 3 classroom saw most open rebellion on the part of 'low attaining' boys over their place at the bottom of the proficiency ladder. Different consequences do indeed flow from the way in which instructional and regulative discourses combine.

The next section extends this discussion by examining a programme of government-sponsored education reform intended to improve literacy attainment in England: the National Literacy Strategy. In common with literacy policy elsewhere, this can be characterised as a turn towards a more visible form of pedagogy (Bernstein, 1996; Moss, 2002b). Yet whilst such reforms may indeed reshape literacy curricula or pedagogy, the kinds of questions this book has raised about how both boys and girls react to the social regulation of literacy in school persist. Such changes simply produce new conditions under which those same questions need to be pursued.

Literacy attainment and educational reform: the National Literacy Strategy in England as a telling case

Since the research undertaken for this book began, a good deal has changed in the structure and formation of the literacy curriculum in English primary schools through the advent of the National Literacy Strategy (NLS) and its subsequent evolution. The NLS has been at the heart of a government-sponsored attempt to improve pupils' performance in the literacy curriculum, a policy initiative which was largely founded on disparities in children's attainment in areas of socio-economic disadvantage (Ofsted, 1996). The National Literacy Strategy has significantly reshaped the configuration of literacy events which instantiate the reading curriculum in primary schools in England (see Moss, 2000a and Moss, 2004 for earlier analysis of these changes). It has also altered the context in which the difference between girls' and boys' performance in reading and writing is both tracked and addressed (Ofsted, 2003).

Whilst the methodological background to the programme of reform has been variously described (Barber, 1996; Beard, 1999; Fisher *et al.*, 2002), in essence it has involved a concerted attempt to standardise delivery of the literacy curriculum and produce a much more transparent and explicit pedagogy covering the full range of literacy skills. To this end it has also introduced a complex range of policy levers (Earl *et al.*, 2000), with the main focus resting on the introduction of a Literacy Hour in which to deliver a given literacy curriculum as set out in the National Literacy Framework (DfEE, 1998).

When first introduced, the Literacy Hour prescribed a clear sequence of teaching activities for all age groups, encompassing the full range of literacy skills including phoneme-grapheme knowledge and reading for meaning. The recursive sequence of the Hour was designed to commit teachers to covering each aspect of literacy in equal depth whilst simultaneously enabling teachers to spend a larger proportion of their teaching time working with groups rather than individuals. By standardising the format of the Hour and laying down a term-by-term and year-by-year outline of the curriculum topics that should be covered in the accompanying Framework document, the NLS aimed to ensure maximum continuity in practice between individual teachers, between schools and over time, and thus ensure that all children had full access to the same range of literacy skills. Advocates of NLS refer to this combined emphasis on standards, accountability and support as a defining characteristic of the reform package.

Examining NLS with visible pedagogies in mind

In Bernsteinian terms, the NLS is clearly a visible pedagogy. The Framework document divides the knowledge content of the literacy curriculum into three distinct strands organised under the headings: word, sentence and text. Each strand includes a term-by-term, year-by-year specification of what should be taught when. Coverage of the curriculum as specified is tied to the choreography of the Literacy Hour, which itself moves from whole-class teacher input to small group work with the teacher, or independent work undertaken at the same time by the rest of the class, back to whole-class plenary. The distinct pattern of activity that the Literacy Hour encompasses stands in sharp isolation from other curriculum spaces and times where reading and writing might go on.

The approach was designed to build a more inclusive curriculum by ensuring equal access to it across the ability range, coupled with clear forms of support targeted at the level of need. As part of this process, those elements of reading for proficiency which had previously been conducted as individual encounters between teacher and students moved into whole-class or group settings, whilst elements of reading for choice became more clearly subject to teacher direction. Teaching reading in the Literacy Hour was expected to include far more direct input from the teacher, and be geared to building pupil competence in whole-class and small group settings using the age-specific objectives specified in the Framework document rather than simply monitoring or assessing what individual children could already do. In effect, aspects of literacy teaching which had previously been delivered separately were merged into the same space and time, with the intention of ensuring much more uniformity in teacher practice and in pupils' experience of the literacy curriculum than was the case immediately prior to the introduction of NLS.

Changing the social structure of key literacy events creates new conditions for literacy learning. In an early assessment of the Literacy Strategy, I argued that the structure of the Literacy Hour was likely to benefit those designated 'low attainers' (Moss, 2000a) by switching the emphasis in reading proficiency from the individual to the group. I anticipated that reading aloud within a group rather than in an individual context would offer a new kind of collective cover to all those involved. Those struggling with the text would be able to 'blend in' with their neighbours' voices. At the same time, others' voices would provide positive support for the activity itself and help keep the focus on the text, thus sharpening attention to what needs to be learnt.

Making word level work as well as sentence and text level work an explicit focus of the literacy curriculum throughout the primary school promised similar benefits. Such a move grants equal status to word level work, regardless of who is undertaking it, and does so right the way up the school rather than increasingly restricting teaching on this aspect of literacy to 'low attainers', with the knock-on effects for the social standing of those so designated. Changing the pattern of literacy events in these ways offered to improve the self-esteem of those at the bottom of the literacy hierarchy whilst maintaining a sharp focus on the stuff of literacy.

The NLS was quite explicit about its intentions in restructuring the social geography of the classroom in this way. The expectation was that such practice would in itself raise standards by creating a context for learning that would minimise rather than accentuate differences in performance between individual pupils. But a lot depends on how far those charged with carrying out such a programme of reform understand the underlying rationale and can deliver on the programme's intentions. It is also possible to use such a programme to sharpen the emphasis on literacy as work and make more visible the distinctions between learners. (See also Bourne, 2000 for an early assessment of the potential benefits of the NLS as well as some dangers.) How has it worked out in practice?

What happens to the NLS in action? Reregulating literacy from the pupils' perspective

The follow-up study to the original research reviewed the translation of the NLS into classroom practice during 2002 to 2003 using the same range of ethnographic tools (see note 4 on p. 203). They record a particular moment in the roll-out of the reform programme and are not intended as an evaluation of the reform programme as a whole. (The kind of practice observed at that time has since moved on and adjusted in the light of the policy's close monitoring and review.) Nevertheless, this snapshot does provide evidence of the enduring tensions within the literacy curriculum, and highlights some of the difficulties in trying to rebalance the relations between parts.

At the time the data were collected, the classrooms observed had fully adopted the structure of the Literacy Hour with its fixed time sequence of whole-class to individual or small group work back to plenary. Each Hour encompassed word, text and sentence level work, with such work often given different emphasis in separate segments. The exception to this approach to closely following the structure of the Hour was in one Year 6 class, where the sequence had been adapted to make a longer time for pupils to write each day, in line with preparation for the examinations they would take that year. In this school, Year 6 children were ability grouped for the duration of the Hour, went to separate classrooms with different teachers and followed a separate programme of activities. In the analysis that follows I will focus on those classrooms that were most closely following the structure of the Literacy Hour.

Moving literacy events to the front of the class

Any reform programme has both intended and unintended consequences. In many respects the changed patterns of curriculum delivery in these classrooms looked pretty much in line with the Strategy's original intentions. Yet the study also showed that this reorganisation of the classroom space created new dilemmas (Moss, 2004). If one set of problems had been successfully addressed, then others emerged.

The introduction of the Literacy Hour had certainly ensured far greater consistency in the range of work covered. Compared to data collected on the original research project, classroom observation showed that post NLS there was indeed a much greater emphasis on teaching a similar range of literacy skills on a regular basis and in a similar way across the week, across year groups and across schools. Prior to the introduction of the NLS, moving to a different class or a different school would often have meant learning a whole new way of doing literacy (see the differences in approach to literacy teaching outlined in the Fact and Fiction Project schools in Chapter 3). Post NLS, comparing schools in two different local education authorities (LEAs) showed a close convergence on more or less exactly the same model of practice. Whilst the precise activities devised in each classroom might still vary, the time committed to word, sentence or text level objectives did not. Common patterns to the management of 'interactive whole-class teaching' strengthened this sense of shared routines within the Hour which teachers and children now both expected and understood. Because teachers planned with reference to the Literacy Framework's term-by-term specification of the appropriate curriculum content for a given year group, curriculum coverage was broadly similar. By and large this new mode of teaching provided pupils with a much clearer definition of what was expected to be learnt at any particular time. The disposition of resources in the classroom reinforced this.

A far greater proportion of time committed to the literacy curriculum was now spent in direct teaching, orchestrated from the front of the class. This was reflected in the way classrooms were arranged. In each of the classrooms visited, more of the wall space was taken up by materials which were directly relevant to the literacy curriculum, and which children could call on in that context. Thus in one classroom, cards with the words 'When', 'What', 'Who', 'Why', 'Where' printed on them were prominently displayed at the front of the class to support story-planning. Also on the wall up near the board were the written objectives for that day's Literacy Hour ('Our literacy learning objectives: To recognise and spell common prefixes and what they mean').

Cards showing both prefixes and word roots were positioned beside the board as a reminder of work already undertaken, and awaiting further classroom use. (Children would be called up to the front of the class to combine them into appropriate pairings.) A Year 3 classroom in a separate school had an exactly similar range of resources on show. In all the classrooms visited, displays associated with topic work had either shrunk or disappeared.

The physical geography of the rooms had changed too. Room layouts ensured that pupils' attention was more closely focused on the central space at the front of the class. The board itself was in constant use as a reference point for the sequence of texts which would appear upon it during the Hour, as the teacher moved from one task to another. Children's attention was directly marshalled towards this surface in a number of ways: by creating more opportunities for any shared text to be read aloud from the body of the classroom; and by creating more opportunities for individuals to come to the front and manipulate the text whilst others watched (e.g. by annotating, underlining or moving parts of the text on display).

Under these circumstances, reading had become much more publicly orchestrated and visible work for a larger part of the available time. In effect, the act of reading had migrated from the individual book in the child's lap or on their desk to the public space of the board. Under the teacher's direction, children joined in reading this shared text aloud or fell silent as required. Judgements made on how well that reading had been done were often passed in this shared context. At least at the level of collective routines, the mode of instruction seemed to have sharpened attention to the stuff of literacy in its written and spoken aspects and the relationship between these two, as again and again children were invited to read aloud from a text all could see.

Navigating through the Hour meant remembering the resources and routines which belonged in each of its particular segments and paying attention to the task the teacher had defined. Continuity was built up in this way, as the routines were repeated from one day to the next and week to week, even as the texts varied. In interview, and through classroom observation, children seemed well attuned to what would be expected of them, when.

INTERVIEWER: So what do you use the [handheld] whiteboards in your lesson for?
RICHARD: For literacy, sometimes she tells us to get them out and if there is something with the answers you can write them down and hold them up.

(Merchant, Year 3. 'Can' reader)

In this sense pupils could keep up with what was being asked of them. When asked, they could remember the work in terms of the objectives that had been specified:

177

INTERVIEWER: Can you tell me briefly what you were doing this morning?

RICHARD: We were doing prefixes. Prefixes like helping us to understand words and things.

INTERVIEWER: ... And what other kinds of things do you do in literacy?

RICHARD: Um, we are doing, in the beginning of our first term ... we were doing like verbs, nouns, things ... And this term we are doing like connectives and things

(Merchant, Year 3. 'Can' reader)

The surface orchestration of the curriculum, its familiar routines, its named content are all recalled here. But there is a difference between learning how to participate in the event and applying the knowledge gleaned there to other settings. What the teacher teaches and what the child learns in this sense are not necessarily the same thing. A sense of this difference really surfaces in independent time, the twenty minutes of the Hour set aside for children to work on their own. If the strong choreography of the shared spaces in the Hour brings what children do closely under teachers' control, then this is the time available for children to take over the task for themselves.

Independent work and the handover from teachers to taught

The initial advice given to teachers in the Framework document, which set out the structure of the Hour and the content that should be covered within it, identified the purposes of independent work in the teacher's terms. First, it would enable the teacher to provide more tailored input on reading or writing to groups differentiated by ability, as they worked with them in rotation through the week. Second, it would enable the rest of the class to work independently 'without recourse to the teacher' (DfEE, 1998, p. 12). Both the Framework document and the initial training for the NLS emphasised the need for the rest of the class not to interrupt the teacher with requests for help during this time. This provided a clear break with previous practice in which children who got stuck on a particular procedural task would form a queue at the teacher's desk, waiting for the teacher's advice on how to proceed. There was much less guidance on the positive function that independent work could have in shaping pupils' learning in this different context as they worked under their own steam, or indeed clear expectations for what autonomous and self-directed learning might look like. Instead, the potential contents of this segment of the Hour were described in terms of the range of teaching objectives that could be covered from the full curriculum list. There was little reference to how such a sequence of tasks might make sense from the pupils' point of view or cohere into sustainable activity over the course of the week. In this respect, the emphasis in the official documentation fell on the regulative discourse.

In fact, the planning regime seemed to make it quite difficult for teachers to build connections between the range of activities that needed to take place in each separate segment of the Hour, including independent time. Initial advice, compounded by the structure of the weekly planning sheet issued with the Framework document, suggested teachers plan a minimum of five tasks tailored to different ability groups to be undertaken in independent time over each week. Like the five sessions of guided small group work, these tasks might or might not be connected to or sustained by the additional input planned for whole-class and plenaries. In effect, this guidance enshrined ability groups as the focus for both teaching and self-directed learning during independent time.

Under pressure from the range of objectives at word, sentence and text level that teachers were required to cover, the Literacy Hour seemed to fragment into separate sections, each filled with a particular activity to be completed within that time frame. It was very rare, for instance, to see a writing task in independent time which flowed on from one day to the next. Over the course of the Hour, students might well have to stop one kind of task and start another, as they moved from whole class to small group or independent work. As the Strategy evolved, the advice to teachers was not to worry about making connections where none were to be found but to deliver on the spread of objectives all the same.

TEACHER:	I did the word level work ... on the whiteboard
INTERVIEWER:	That's right, yes
TEACHER:	Yes, I did that first deliberately. Did that, got it out of the way ... And then went on ... Because there was no link at all.

(Merchant School, Year 3 teacher)

Whilst teachers continued to strive to make sense of the array of tasks that they needed to deliver, at word, sentence and text level, highlighting connections between them when they could, children reacted more closely to the conditions under which they were expected to complete each task. In the whole-class setting this meant joining in with the group under the teacher's watchful eye. In independent work it was much more up to individuals how much they got involved and the level of effort they committed to the task. Some knew that if they didn't do very much, the task itself would soon be over. Richard, for instance, would often spend an inordinate amount of time during independent work looking for a pencil, finding a ruler and slowly writing his name whilst the minutes ticked by. Using these strategies he could escape having to write very much before the class were pulled back together. In this context he acted very much as a 'can/don't' writer.

Inclusion versus differentiation in the Literacy Hour: support for those at the bottom of the reading ladder

The data collected at the time suggested that the impact of this reregulation of the literacy curriculum involved both gains and losses. For students placed at the bottom of the reading ability ladder, gains were clearest during the whole-class time as teachers tailored the whole-class work to the day's learning objectives. What happened during independent time was more varied. In one of the schools observed, the children placed in the lowest attainment grouping in a Year 4 class regularly spent their independent work time outside class with the teaching assistant. This was against the then official advice on how to deploy teaching assistants. But it meant that this group enjoyed freedoms that others in the class did not. They were able to talk with each other about the task and swap ideas. With the help of the teaching assistant they often produced a joint product which could be brought back to class for the plenary where it compared very favourably with anything the children left in class had done. School tradition adapted to the requirements of the NLS meant that those children left in class were restricted to silently working their way through a worksheet, unless they were working on the small group task with the teacher. As those inside could hear the interaction of those outside and then got to see the product, many wanted to be part of the group that left, on the grounds that 'they have more fun'. Being in the lowest attaining group looked more like a reward than a punishment. This pattern of support to the lowest achievers, tied to the work of the class as a whole, represented a new departure for this school and had arisen post the introduction of the NLS.

By contrast, in a Year 3 class in a different school, where independent work consisted of quite sharply differentiated tasks which were distributed to each ability group to work on on their own, the group of boys consigned to the lowest attainment band consistently complained about the work they were given and seemed increasingly unable to fully access the curriculum content that was notionally open to all. The gulf between the work this group were asked to undertake and the curriculum objective set for the class as a whole seemed if anything to become more visible under these conditions. The same structure to the Literacy Hour, managed slightly differently, had generated different responses.

In practice, covering the literacy curriculum via the Framework document and its sequence of objectives laid out term by term and year by year represents a paradoxical double move. On the one hand, the Literacy Hour stands for a more inclusive curriculum which is predicated on the whole class continuing to follow the same objectives, rather than peeling off at their current level of performance. To this end in whole-class settings there was much more explicit support for word, sentence and text level tasks. This seemed to help children home in more closely on what they were being asked to do. But on the other hand, it seemed more difficult to link the differentiated work that children were asked to undertake elsewhere within the Hour back to the central task. Differentiation of the tasks set in independent time often looked like a matter of routine rather than support tailored to the particular set of hurdles children might face in completing a given objective. Compliance with the regulative aspect of the task took precedence over its instructional content.

From the perspective of the original research, much of the reading within independent time now looked like procedural reading. Yet during this time, children undertaking procedural reading tasks were increasingly expected to operate on their own, without recourse to the kinds of help from classmates and the teacher that used to be available. Expectations could be lowered all round, as children in the lower ability groups were simply given easier tasks, rather than tasks that would enable them to learn more. Whilst the number of tasks set had certainly proliferated, the quality of pupils' engagement with that activity on their own terms was uncertain.

The study showed that by insisting on the combination of word, sentence and text level objectives as the focus for literacy teaching within the Literacy Hour, and by reordering those aspects of the curriculum which fell under teacher or pupil control, the NLS had indeed brought reading for choice, reading for proficiency and procedural reading into a new relationship in the same time and space. Yet the contradictions and tensions within the literacy curriculum shifted their shape in this new context, rather than disappeared.

Seeking ways forward in a high stakes, high accountability culture

There are different ways of reacting to this kind of analysis. Some commentators object to the way in which visible pedagogies make explicit distinctions about reading competence and see this as the main obstacle to greater equality of outcomes. Why make reading the central ground upon which social hierarchies are built in school anyway? Why not grant fuller recognition to the many different kinds of knowledge that children can bring to bear on classroom activity from outside school and so establish a more equitable playing field for all children (Marsh and Millard, 2006)?

This kind of distaste for the social hierarchies that visible pedagogies build amongst learners, particularly in their role as readers, finds its reflection in arguments over reading pedagogy too. Those who champion teaching reading via 'real' books rather than the carefully staged language found in structured reading schemes, for instance, are in part arguing against a process which so obviously controls access to the written word by casting teachers in the role of gatekeepers, whilst placing pupils in the position where they can only submit to the judgements made about them and the restrictions which flow from this. Although on the surface such a debate can be characterised as a disagreement over methods and their relative efficacy (whole word versus synthetic or analytic phonics) or about the content of the reading curriculum which each method leads to ('real' books versus reading schemes; or interesting stories versus the appropriate combinations of phonemes and graphemes), what is also at stake is a more covert concern for the different forms of social regulation that such opposing pedagogies invoke.

If the argument put forward in this book is construed in these terms, then at first sight all of the problems seem to lie with the literacy events which draw attention to proficiency judgements and the stratification of competence they construct. Proficiency becomes the enemy of choice. Debate about the nature of the reading curriculum post the introduction of the NLS has certainly been fuelled by exactly these kinds of oppositions. For at least some of its critics, the emphasis the NLS places on attainment outcomes expressed in measurable scores misses the point about the true value of the literacy curriculum whilst significantly reducing any pleasure children can gain from reading to the empty practice of drill and skill routines (Powling *et al.*, 2003). Whilst on the other side of the argument, others complain that not enough is being done to make more children proficient faster (Stuart, 2003). Some argue that the NLS has compromised any principled attempts to teach the basic skills of reading in a systematic way, anyway, precisely by introducing the distraction of text level objectives too soon. Once again, the reading curriculum becomes a battleground in which it is only possible to take sides, lining up with one method against another.

By contrast, this book argues that there is an inevitable tension between reading for choice and reading for proficiency. The question is not whether one should give way to the other, but rather how they can be combined and sustained to best effect as part of the reading curriculum as a whole. In many respects this means equipping children with better means to navigate their way through those tensions, rather than seeking to disguise them, or wish them away.

Pupil autonomy versus teacher control: the place for reading for choice

Prior to the introduction of the NLS, those literacy events exemplifying reading proficiency, reading for choice and procedural reading varied in the extent to which they fell under teacher direction or pupil control, and according to whether they were undertaken as individual or group activities. Under these conditions, reading for choice organised as quiet reading time gave children considerable opportunity to control what they did and read in different ways. After the introduction of the NLS, the study showed that reading for choice no longer really operated in the same way.

Within the Literacy Hour this aspect of the curriculum has been primarily defined in terms of the choices teachers make from the range of genres specified in the Framework document. Reading a range of genres is now linked to accomplishing other kinds of curriculum tasks, most often writing. Delivery of the reading and writing curricula accordingly converge into a series of procedural tasks:

TEACHER: Usually I do a two-week block on a genre. Stories with familiar settings, two weeks on that I did. Then I did a couple of weeks on chronological reports.

(Merchant, Year 3 teacher)

This convergence has had an impact on the kinds of texts that are used. If a high priority is put on meeting word, sentence and text level objectives in a brisk sequence within each Hour, then the logic of efficient planning drives teachers to draw on materials that match these timings. In many cases this has meant shrinking the texts. Teachers either choose a text which is short enough in its entirety to fit the available time; or present an extract from a longer text which can meet the required objectives; or present a text written with the objectives in mind, in effect a textbook, with the text divided into chunks which fit the available slots. Reading is increasingly defined as teacher-directed work, its outcomes judged in terms of the product pupils generate either through their immediate participation in spoken exchanges or through the written texts which they are expected to subsequently produce.

Outside the Hour, opportunities for self-directed reading time have diminished too. This is exemplified in the general reorganisation of the classroom space. The 'soft corners' associated with quiet reading time have largely disappeared from classrooms, along with the opportunity for children to make use of them once they have finished their work. In a curriculum driven by the firm boundaries of the Literacy and Numeracy Hours, work fills the slots available. There is no time for some to finish at a different pace from others. Quiet reading time has shrunk under pressure from the need to audit time spent on the curriculum elsewhere. It no longer counts as part of the official literacy curriculum. One of the main occasions for children to choose what and how they would read has lost its place in the classroom.

Of course, given the uneven use made of quiet reading time as demonstrated in Chapter 3, this might be a justifiable loss. But it also means that this kind of curriculum reform leaves unresolved how children move from understanding reading as school-directed work tied to the tight choreography of the teacher to reading as autonomous action that can adapt to their own purposes, enabling them to fully exploit the potential of many different sorts of texts. If these kinds of dilemmas matter in relation to the reading curriculum, then they may well matter more in relation to writing where it is harder to fully develop commitment to the task in circumstances when so little space is allowed for individual intentions and purposes to thrive (Moss, 2004).

Yet there is nothing in the structure of the Literacy Hour which makes this inevitably so. Quiet reading time could easily migrate into the twenty-minute period of independent work and in a number of ways. If children were set an extended writing task to work on in that space over the course of the week, they could migrate to self-directed reading after its completion. If independent work was conceived of horizontally across the week in this way then the tasks pupils attempted, whether focused on word, sentence or text, could take the time they needed over the course of that week rather than having to fill a space which is already so tightly defined.

It is not surprising that the introduction of the NLS has thrown up new dilemmas as it has changed the material base to literacy, the resources that can be mustered to make it happen, and the structure of the events in which it takes place. In many respects the NLS remains an admirable attempt to 'level up' pupil performance and offer all children a richer experience from the literacy curriculum. But close observation of the new kinds of literacy events that it has spawned show continuing tensions within the literacy curriculum. The structure of the Hour has not in and of itself built a more inclusive curriculum, able to resolve the dilemmas faced by those at the bottom of the reading hierarchy. Nor has it fully supported children's transition into directing reading and writing for their own purposes.

Supporting children's choice of text or offering opportunities to choose

The fact that reading for choice as pupil-directed activity has fallen so easily out of the official literacy curriculum reflects the ambivalent place this kind of pursuit has in school. It is not, after all, direct teaching. Its potential value can seem hard to justify precisely because this is the case. Although the point of turning children into committed readers is fully accepted, finding the means to help children achieve this end is less straightforward. Giving children responsibility for choosing what to read next produces uncertain results. Some resist being lured in this way despite the best efforts of parents and teachers, as this parent's comments on her son's reading make clear:

> I don't think he really knew how to choose a book ... he'd bring a book home in his book-bag and have no interest in it and I'd say to him 'well, why have you chosen it? ... If you're not interested in a book, then there's no point in bringing it home', (... and I'd say it) should be really interesting, and you can't put it down and how lovely that is, and no recognition in his face at all for what I was

talking about. So I'd say to him, 'well try and take a bit more time when you are choosing a book', so, I think it was just that he couldn't, sometimes, he would pick up a book with a nice cover, open the page and just be completely bored.

(Farthing, parent of Year 4 'Can' reader)

This 'can/don't' reader fulfils the school's requirement to take a book home to read. But he doesn't spend time with the book he has chosen. His mother accounts for this in two ways: by suggesting that he is insufficiently clear about what reading could offer him; and by highlighting the difficulties of knowing which text to choose. Yet this reader's reaction to the task he has been set – find a book to read at home – precisely highlights the difficulties in moving from reading as teacher-directed work to reading as self-directed choice. As things stand, how do adults support this transition?

How adults account for children's reading choices

Adults react to children's text choices in different ways. In part, this depends on whether what children choose matches adult expectations about what and how they should read (see Moss, 2001a). When children's choices are out of sync with adult expectations the children themselves become subject to further exhortation and direction. Choice over what and how to read looks increasingly restricted for readers on the receiving end of this kind of attention, no matter how well intentioned or well-managed.

By and large, teachers pay most attention to how children exercise choice when the choices they make are seen to conflict with their proficiency at reading, or when their choice is most obviously not to read at all. Here is a teacher describing the support given to the 'can't yet/don't' reader glimpsed in Chapter 3, clutching a book that was beyond his competence to read during quiet reading time:

> For Morris, we've actually put into play quite a few different strategies for him because his case is that he's really turned off reading, really quite a negative attitude towards it and has refused to read ... so what we've done, we've used some books from the special needs department, ... space, space adventures and what have you. They're all adventure based books, and ... we've tried giving him word cards so that he can go and learn the words before school, before he can get into the gist of the text, because he can cope with the basics if he's well motivated and concentrated and trying really hard, but if there are a lot of words he struggles with, then he gets, you know, very negative and he starts to feel dejected really. It's a sort of downward spiral.

> (Bluebird, Year 3 teacher. 'Can't yet' reader)

The teacher's intention is to find texts Morris might be interested in, but which also match his level of proficiency. Collected prior to the introduction of the NLS, this extract makes clear some of the difficulties involved in trying to deliver on the aims associated with reading for proficiency in a context which is also geared towards reading for choice. Teachers are very aware of the potential contradictions between these two imperatives. Indeed, part of their responsibility is to try to manage the tensions they create.

In the following extract, a Year 5 teacher voices precisely this point as she reflects on a struggling reader in her class:

TEACHER: He doesn't always choose appropriate books, he chooses quite difficult books sometimes, or right at the beginning of the year he was choosing books that were beyond his ability to read fluently and accurately, just too many mistakes

INTERVIEWER: What kind of thing would he pick that were beyond him?

TEACHER: ... They were very densely written, very challenging books, with vocabulary that he just couldn't even begin to decode

INTERVIEWER: Do you know why he had them?

TEACHER: He was picking them from the library and despite discussing them with him he still wanted those books and I think part of it was image

INTERVIEWER: Yes

TEACHER: ... He didn't want to be seen reading a very childish book and he didn't want to be heard making mistakes so he would babble so that we couldn't correct him or he thought that was the way he was getting round that.

(Bluebird, Year 5 teacher. 'Can't yet' reader)

In this kind of case, the most obvious response is to re-balance choice so that it acts in the interests of proficiency:

INTERVIEWER: How do you account for the progress that he made during that time?

TEACHER: Because I've slowed him down and I've sometimes asked him to read other texts to me that were slightly more to his level and also he started realising that if he read books that were more suitable to his level, he could actually read and understand them and he's getting more satisfaction out of that, so he, so that has got better ... (Otherwise) I think he'd still be babbling.

(Bluebird, Year 5 teacher. 'Can't yet' reader)

In this instance the solution proffered brings choice and proficiency successfully back into line. In most of the classrooms observed such active management of what children choose was more likely to be focused on readers deemed to be struggling than on those who had successfully passed the relevant proficiency threshold.

The logic of moving readers on

Teachers shoulder responsibility for supporting children's text choices as part of their role. They recognise that this may mean steering children towards texts which match their proficiency level but that it also means finding texts that they might enjoy, that will keep them reading or that will take them in new directions. The assumption is that the right text will significantly expand what children can do, whereas the wrong text risks turning children off reading. Brokering a good match between text and reader may take place as part of the routine monitoring of children's reading in class. Post the introduction of NLS it survives as part of guided reading. It can also happen relatively informally.

In this kind of discussion, knowing which text might work for which reader is seen as crucial. Alongside proficiency, the criteria teachers use in arriving at this judgement depend upon their perception of the quality of the text, its usefulness in developing children's reading habits and the strength of interest they think it will garner. These are not treated as synonymous, and may also appear to be actively in conflict. Thus texts that are popular with children may be considered poor quality from the teacher's point of view, whilst what the teacher considers quality texts may find no takers amongst the class. If the former is the case, teachers are then left with the conundrum of whether to allow or even actively support access to this material, or instead try and move children on. During the earliest period of data collection, the *Goosebumps* series raised this dilemma for at least some of the teachers interviewed. In Kingfisher, the teacher librarian was ambivalent about their value. She was dismissive of the quality of the texts but balanced that against their usefulness to particular kinds of readers:

> I've bought them for the school and I think they've got a place. What I really like about them is that they have such, they're totally boring, and I fall asleep when children read them to me, but they have such a restricted vocabulary that children can actually make progress with them and they can build up stamina, and I think children who are sort of in between, there's a place for them getting hold of these and getting confidence from them, but I really think they have to be stopped from reading too many
>
> (Kingfisher, teacher/librarian)

By contrast, in Bluebird, the librarian was much clearer that whilst children might choose to read *Goosebumps* for themselves, the library should offer them something better:

INTERVIEWER: What about the sort of stuff like *Goosebumps* which you were saying they are reading, would you put those in here?

LIBRARIAN: No I wouldn't because, they do like them, and I've read them at home with my son and he wants to read them because they're supposed to be *the* thing to read and everybody else is reading them, but he didn't enjoy it ... There's no story to them, they're like shallow, hollow

INTERVIEWER: ... If a Year 5 child is, that's what they're into, you know, they're into *Goosebumps*, would you try, would you see, in your librarian role ...

LIBRARIAN: If they're reading it and they're interested in it and they're reading, I wouldn't put them off it, because that's great they're reading and they're really like enjoying it, but if they like that sort of book, well I'd say if you like that type of book, you'll really like this. And give them something that's got the same sort of kill factor in it or scare factor, but it's something that they're going to learn far more from

(Bluebird, teacher/librarian)

In both cases, these teachers produce arguments for and against these particular texts even as they arrive at opposite conclusions about whether their institutions should stock them or not. There are also different regulatory relationships embedded in these accounts as these teachers anticipate steering children's text choices in one way or another on beyond where they already are. The terms in which they do so are closely allied with the broader regulatory environments in each of these schools. Thus in looking ahead, the teacher in Kingfisher argues that children 'have to be stopped from reading too many [*Goosebumps*]', a straightforward prohibition; whilst the teacher in Bluebird concentrates on persuading children to choose something else: 'if you like that type of book, you'll really like this'. The monitoring of children's choices in Kingfisher was more geared to building proficiency, whilst in Bluebird choice was more clearly tied to sustaining readers' interest in and commitment to the act of reading.

The logic of leaving readers where they are

Teachers weigh their support for children's current choices against their sense of where children's reading should go next. Yet looking across the interviews as a whole, teachers were often more tolerant of sustaining boys' existing interests in materials which in other circumstances they might regard as being less than ideal:

> Things like *Shoot*, football magazines, I do actually keep a stock of over there ... because I do think that, with boys particularly, you have to meet them a bit more than half-way and if you want them to read you have to provide them with things that they want to read, so I would, I think you should keep a selection of magazines.
>
> (Farthing, Year 4 teacher)

This willingness to follow boys' lead in part derives from an acceptance that boys are more reluctant to read than girls:

> I find the girls will pick up a novel, a story and stick with it and really enjoy it and give good reasons why they've chosen it and why they like that author and other books they've read in that series and that sort of thing, whereas the boys become quickly bored. I mean they'll enjoy the short stories and the picture books and that sort of thing for the fiction, they will read that, but you present them ... with anything that's text and lacking in pictures or even has got just black and white line drawings, they're not that interested.
>
> (Shepherd, Year 4 teacher)

The logic of sustaining boys' existing interests stems from the assumption that reading something is better than reading nothing at all. The interests that teachers then set out to meet and invoke on boys' behalf are not necessarily interests in particular kinds of texts, but in a larger topic, such as football or cars, which a variety of different texts can then be mapped onto.

Girl readers were not treated in the same way. The actual topics they might be interested in, as opposed to particular texts, were less visible in classrooms. Topics that might be traditionally associated with girls on similar terms (gymnastics, horse-riding, dance, popular music) were seldom used as an enticement to read. Indeed, in the teacher interviews the kinds of material most closely associated with girls' interests, either by virtue of their content (Spice Girls was an obvious example during the first phase of the research) or the way in which they signalled their target audience through text design (the inclusion of close-ups of cuddly animals, or extensive use of pastel colours), were most likely to meet with teachers' active disapproval:

> That's diabolical, *Looking After Your Dog*. It's revolting, I would exclude that on taste grounds, Puppy Tips! {Exclaiming over heading} ... No I couldn't possibly let that one in.
>
> (Kingfisher, teacher/librarian)

The consequence is less that girls are denied free rein to follow their interests – they did this anyway – but that the kinds of support they are offered focus more clearly on reading as an end in itself rather than as an adjunct to something else. In effect, this reinforces the kinds of reading they already do. By contrast, the support offered to boys regarded as reluctant readers pushes them towards topics which may well have a social currency, but where their attention is only weakly focused on the substance of the text itself. Meanwhile, some of the linear texts that boys do often pick up – poetry, or other kinds of linear texts divided into small chunks that readers can dip in and out of – are largely overlooked because they fall outside of any narrative that explains this choice. The apparent conflict between interest and quality works out differently for boys and girls.

The teachers' comments included above demonstrate the terms in which boys who are reluctant to read, whatever their level of proficiency, become visible in classrooms. But the social conditions that produce and make sense of what these boys do are masked by the current discourse. Following boys' perceived interests does not in itself remedy the difficulties they face, nor is it a reliable guide to where to go next.

The kind of support teachers offer readers depends on how they balance proficiency, interest and their assessment of the quality of the text in any particular case. Which one will take precedence also depends on the teacher's view of the readers concerned. As things stand, guiding children's choice implies handing over responsibility for applying these same principles to children so that they can put them to work for themselves. But in a crowded curriculum, all of these principles can also easily move back into the teacher's hands to be delivered from the front of the class.

Reading paths and text choice reconsidered

This book has argued that children's text choices cannot be understood in the abstract without reference to the contexts in which children come to read. Children recognise that different kinds of text design lend themselves to different kinds of use in different settings and steer their choices accordingly. In this light it is possible to see that one of the reasons that poetry was a popular choice in quiet reading time is that these kinds of linear texts lend themselves to being shared under these circumstances. Readers can sample short stretches of text from the book as a whole, finding passages to read aloud to others. Choosing what to read during quiet reading time is therefore rather different from choosing what to take home, where reading will be undertaken under solitary conditions. Choosing lengthy fiction texts poses children most problems as it is harder to see from the cover, the blurb or even the opening lines, which ones will really repay the kind of commitment of time that such texts require. How do children grapple with this dilemma?

The study of library borrowing in Bluebird was intended to explore this issue further. Undertaken using the library records obtained when the original cohort observed in Year 3 had moved into Year 6 (see note 4 on p. 203), the study examined the choices the year group made over the course of a full year's library use. For administrative purposes, the library-borrowing records logged the name of the child, their form group, the date of their visit to the library, the title borrowed and the first part of the author's surname or, if non-fiction, the first part of the Dewey number under which it was classified. This provided valuable information about what had been borrowed when and for how long. In addition, the study retrieved and coded the features of each text borrowed according to the reading paths they contained before analysing the coded library-borrowing records alongside other information collected from this cohort in their final year at school. The additional information included standardised reading test scores gathered in school over the preceding three years and a questionnaire collected from the cohort when they were in Year 6 which asked about their friendship networks (who they preferred to socialise with); their reading networks (who they either lent books to, borrowed books from or shared recommendations of what to read with); and their reading habits. (A full account of the statistical methods employed can be found in the Final Report from the project on the ESRC Society Today website (url: http://www.esrcsocietytoday.ac.uk) and in Moss and McDonald, 2004.)

Coding for text design

The text codes employed focused on aspects of text design that the ethnography had suggested guided children's text choices. These included the physical size of the page; the dimensions and frequency of any illustrations; the ways in which illustrations and writing were co-ordinated on the page including the dominant reading path (linear or non-linear); the style of layout; the use of colour; the size of typeface; and the number of pages in the book as a whole. Ninety-four per cent of the 720 titles borrowed by this group over the course of the year were identified and coded in this way. Cluster analysis of the data revealed several identical text profiles that shared exactly the same combination of individual text features (see Moss and McDonald, 2004). Indeed, the dozen most common text profiles were employed by 67 per cent of the fiction titles. This suggests that this combination of features has an empirical basis in the ways in which publishers design for the book market. Thus the smallest size of fiction texts, with the smallest size of print, were least likely to include illustrations and were most likely to be amongst the longest.

Looking at these text features in the round, it became possible to identify two interlocking aspects of text design which seemed to work together to produce different kinds of reading experience. These were the reading

191

path the text employed, and the role either pictures or writing played in the organisation of the text as a whole. Three different reading paths were identified. The first are non-linear reading paths which organise round the space of the page, juxtaposing image and writing without imposing any particular order in which individual items must be read. Dorling Kindersley's *Eyewitness Guides* exemplify this approach. The second are linear reading paths which sustain a fixed sequence to the order in which the text must be read over some length. *Harry Potter* is a good example. Whilst the third are linear-dip reading paths which organise the text sequentially but in shorter chunks so that the reader can dip in and out rather than reading in a fixed order from beginning to end. Books like *Horrible Histories* and most poetry books fall into this category.

At the same time, texts vary in the extent to which either pictures or writing lead the design. Picture-led texts give the illustrations pride of place; text-led texts make the writing central; whilst text-picture composites balance the two so neither one dominates the design. These two categories work together to produce different kinds of text organisation. Dorling Kindersley's *Eyewitness Guides*, for instance, are picture-led, non-linear texts, whilst a picture book such as *Where the Wild Things Are* (1992) is a picture-led linear book. A 'read alone' book designed for beginning readers and containing one continuous story but no chapters, such as Rose Impey's *Precious Potter* (1994), is a linear text–picture composite. Each mode of text organisation lends itself to being shared in different ways and requires a different kind of commitment from its readers (see Chapter 5).

The formation of reading communities

Analysing children's text choices in this light produced some interesting results. In the context of this book I want to concentrate on just one finding from the analysis: that the most significant influence on borrowing patterns in this year group was neither gender nor reading attainment as expressed in standardised reading tests, but the child's class in school, in other words, the social group with whom they borrowed books.

Differences in the patterns of library borrowing associated with each class initially showed in the number of books borrowed. Pupils in one of the three classes borrowed significantly more books, whilst pupils in one of the other two borrowed significantly fewer. Yet each class had visited the library the same number of times, and contained a similar profile of children in terms of educational attainment, gender and social class background. What explained the difference in borrowing patterns?

Explored via the text-coding categories, it soon became apparent that the class that borrowed fewer books were also borrowing much higher numbers of longer texts. Forty-seven per cent of this group borrowed books of 187 pages or more compared with 22 per cent in the other two classes. These books not only contained more pages, they also had the smallest typeface and the fewest illustrations. In other words, they were taking out books that committed them to spending longer getting through the text. This preference was particularly strong amongst the boys in this class and also seemed to have an impact on the choices of those designated with special educational needs. By contrast, the class that borrowed the greatest number of books borrowed the greatest variety of text types, including more non-fiction and more text–picture composites. In effect, these two classes were choosing very different kinds of reading experience through the use they made of the library.

At the time of the analysis the children had moved on from primary to secondary school and were no longer available for interview. But the three class teachers were still in place, as was the school librarian whose son had been in the class that consistently borrowed lengthier linear texts. Talking to the librarian led her to recall the individuals in that class and what she knew about the social networks they participated in as well as the efforts she herself had made to sustain her son's reading over that year. She described him as a leader rather than a follower amongst his peers, and as a member of the football crowd. She also regarded him as not a particularly keen reader and mainly remembered trying to sustain his reading over that year by offering him a range of longer titles that she thought he ought to be reading, including *Harry Potter*. She remembered that he hadn't been so keen on *Harry Potter*, but had kept it out for several months as he ploughed his way through it. The library records certainly confirmed this.

The teacher whose class he was in remembered the group rather differently. Presented with a selection of the texts the children had actually borrowed, chosen to represent the main text types used in the analysis, she spontaneously picked up a copy of *The Hobbit* (1992) from the table before the interview began. She remembered that one of the weakest readers in the class that year had insisted on borrowing it and had somehow made his way through it from beginning to end – to his great satisfaction. She had been uncertain whether she ought to allow him to keep it. She remembered a lot of the boys in this group as avid readers, but expressed some puzzlement over why this should be so, and claimed no credit for having made it happen. She did not represent herself as exercising a decisive influence on the choices they made, and seemed slightly baffled by the array of text types brought to the interview. It was as if she had handed over to this class the freedom to choose what they borrowed for themselves. In return, this class seemed to have converged on lengthy linear texts under their own steam.

By contrast, the teacher whose class had borrowed the most titles did not so much remember individual readers from the year group as home in on the merits of the various kinds of text on display. Faced with a choice of texts which stretched across all text profiles, from picture-led fiction with relatively large print, to non-linear non-fiction, or 'linear-dip' texts which were organised into a succession of bite-sized chunks, as well as lengthy chapter books, he found something positive to say about them all. He expressed a clear view of the importance of the school library in encouraging children to read and explore a wide variety of texts. He also said that he expected his classes to borrow and return their books on a regular basis and kept a close eye on his groups to make sure that they did so.

These two classes built active reading communities in different ways. In the class that borrowed the highest number of books, their teacher's sense that any text might have a value, coupled with his insistence that whatever they borrowed should be returned within two weeks, seemed to push children to pick books which in one way or another lent themselves to being read faster. By way of illustration, one of the girls in this class was a proficient reader, whose library-borrowing record showed that she shared a good number of the books she read with her two closest friends, either directly passing titles from one to another, or sometimes borrowing the same title at the same time. Yet she regularly supplemented the longer chapter books she borrowed with text–picture composites that she could expect to get through in a single sitting. These had far fewer pages, and on each page a good proportion of the available space was taken up with illustrations. In design terms these were 'read alones', books designed to guide children into reading for themselves, as a first step on the road to becoming a free reader. In borrowing these titles she was certainly not steering by proficiency criteria.

By contrast, the class that borrowed the least books seemed to have used the absence of any strong steer from the teacher to influence each other about what was worth reading. Interestingly, of all the teaching groups, this class were most likely to have responded positively to questions in the questionnaire about reading networks. Their answers indicated that there were two gender-based reading networks in this class, one of five girls and another of five boys. It is tempting to imagine that this group had converged on lengthy texts via the school librarian's son. Perhaps this is how this kind of text had become so prominent in this class, as other children followed his lead and then made use of the space left open to them to use the library as they wished, unconstrained by judgements about which texts really matched their proficiency. Retrospectively, it is not possible to be sure. Looking at the range of lengthy linear texts they borrowed the group do not converge on a single author or single genre (*White Fang* (1991) was borrowed as well as books by Brian Jacques). The length of the text looks more salient than the specific content.

Presented with these accounts it becomes hard not to choose between them, preferring one kind of library-borrowing regime over another. It is possible to applaud the teacher who so strongly encourages readers to borrow a wide range of texts, or the librarian whose persistence in offering her son lengthy linear fiction finally seems to pay off in producing a class prepared to tackle substantial reads. But this is really to miss the point. What matters more than the specific strategy these teachers adopt is the strength of the group response. In each case, children in the same class had converged on a similar pattern of borrowing via the reading networks their classes represented. There are social dimensions to the choices children make. They do not happen in a vacuum as an expression of purely individual taste. Interests are shaped through social interactions with significant others as well as in relation to the available resources and their fit with the social opportunities to use them. Analysis of the school-based library-borrowing records showed evidence of this kind of social exchange. Where there were sufficient copies available, children might borrow the same titles together; or they would pass a single copy from one to another at successive visits; or they might subsequently read something one of their friends had had out. Such reading networks extend as well as confirm existing preferences.

Children follow each other's lead in deciding what to read. What they do depends upon what becomes visible and of interest within specific settings. The real objective for teachers in supporting children's reading therefore rests not so much in closely monitoring the choices individuals make but in supporting conditions in which children themselves can both network round texts and also significantly expand each others' choices. Teachers have a role in creating the social context in which a wide variety of text-types becomes visible to children whilst devolving to them the responsibility for choosing between them.

Sustaining reading networks as a curriculum goal

The routes children take to a sustained interest in reading are varied. There is not a single means of achieving this end. They may variously rely on friends, family or school to provide both the resources and the opportunities to read which shape the choices they make. Sometimes the particular circumstances which support committed reading stem from deliberate adult intervention. They can also arise almost fortuitously. For instance, in one school visited in the follow-up study after the introduction of the NLS, a Year 4 class were encouraged to have their library books with them at the beginning of each day and read them in a short period of time still set aside for quiet reading. There was some movement around the class allowed at this time, from desk to drawers, or over to a class display of poetry books, so that one way or another children became aware of what each other were reading. The library books had to be returned once a week. As it so happened, the school librarian did not trust the children to accurately use the computer system for checking books in and out of the library. Her answer to the problem of how to manage books coming back in and going out was to collect all the returns in the morning, and herself put them through the system. Then when the children came to the library later in the day she would only have to issue their new choices. But this left no time to re-shelve the returned books which would be left on a central table in the library until later. As a direct consequence, children visiting the library in the afternoon would find the books they'd seen friends with earlier in the week apparently waiting for them to take out. Without any deliberate intention in this respect, this class were building a reading culture in which it became possible to both share and extend existing patterns of text choice. The circumstances were right to encourage recommendations from one reader to another as well as knowing how to avoid texts which weren't considered worth the investment.

Of course this does not amount to a tip which should be implemented everywhere. Indeed, a Year 3 class observed in the same school, and subject to the same conditions for the return of library books, did not enjoy the same effect because most of this class were still required to read their 'reading book' during quiet reading time. The library books they borrowed mainly went unread, and certainly weren't to be seen in class time. Heaping them on a table in the library under these conditions had no equivalent impact. Making sustaining reading networks an explicit curriculum aim would enable teachers to reflect on how far their own practice delivers on this, in what ways, and what else they might add to what they already do.

Whilst at the moment a good deal of effort goes into extolling the virtues of tackling ever longer texts, it is far less clear whether or how schools really create opportunities for children to network round texts, exchanging ideas about what repays attention in the time and according to the occasions that they have for reading. The absence of this kind of support may have particular impact when reading networks at home cannot supplement for what schools themselves do not do (Moss, 2001a).

Making a difference: is it possible to generalise from the specific case?

This chapter has asked whether the curriculum reform ushered in by the National Literacy Strategy has substantially changed the conditions under which gender differences in attainment play out. Of course, a lot will depend upon which aspects of literacy teaching this new reform programme has been standardised around and how it connects to or substantially reshapes patterns in the social organisation of the curriculum that have gone before.

The current policy environment puts a premium on identifying and fixing problems which have become visible through discrepancies in outcomes in pupil attainment tests. Preferred solutions are expected to be capable of being carried from one site to many with consistent results. If one way of fixing the problem doesn't quite have the desired effect, then another must be found. Yet paradoxically from a policy-making perspective, the close monitoring of performance conducted according to the same prescription increasingly robs the system of much variety of practice to choose from.

By contrast, this book has consistently demonstrated that the same principles often lead to different outcomes in different local settings. In terms of gender differentiation, a lot depends on how the inevitable tension-points between different aspects of the literacy curriculum are managed in local settings and the impacts this then has on what children perceive literacy to be, both for themselves and for others. This only becomes available for analysis by reviewing the shape and structure of the range of literacy events which make up the literacy curriculum in particular settings from the perspective of the pupils, paying particular attention to the resources those events encompass and the roles they make available to readers.

This kind of scrutiny of social interaction requires more than a checklist of ideal features whose presence or absence can be swiftly spotted and then used as an absolute measure of quality. Yet in many ways the current round of curriculum reform has introduced precisely this kind of monitoring of teacher practice. With its readily identifiable choreography, immediately visible to the observer's eye, the Literacy Hour promises instant assessment of the value of what is observed in practice by virtue of what is made visible: through the way in which the teacher moves children from one activity to another, over a sequence of clearly specified objectives, laid out on the board for all to see. The choreography of time is reinforced by the choreography of space. Together they clearly focus attention on the central area at the front of the classroom where what children need to pay attention to for the duration of the encounter appears and disappears, as one text follows another on the whiteboard, blackboard or flip chart. The success of each event seems to rest with surface compliance with the requirements for content coverage, and whether the rules for delivery are seen to be followed, rather than what those rules mean in play for whom (Moss, 2004). The dream is of a standardised product producing similar results.

The alternative is to start the other way up by looking for local solutions to particular problems, identified by reviewing the curriculum in action from the pupils' perspective. In this light, understanding the impact of what currently takes place is as important as knowing how to change it. This book outlines a strong set of shared principles which make such a review possible. If explicit support for 'reading for choice' as autonomous action becomes a curriculum aim, then it becomes possible to consider how and where that aim is supported in practice under current conditions, with what effect. The same is true for 'reading for proficiency'. This is not a question of reviewing official policies, but of looking at the material basis for reading as a social activity as it unfolds on the ground.

Conclusion

The links between the social organisation of the classroom and outcomes from the literacy curriculum demonstrated through this research suggests a number of features which may be crucial in flattening out performance differences between boys and girls. First, schools need to provide an inclusive classroom culture which enables all children to pay sufficient attention to those aspects of written language that will take them forward as readers and writers. Blurring the social distinctions between those placed at different points on the reading ladder does not in itself achieve these aims. Neither does subjecting children to a firmer regulative order unless it creates a more visible learning – as well as teaching – culture. Schools have to create a context where all children are both able and willing to receive the help they need in developing their skills, regardless of where they are placed on the literacy ladder. This may well mean tackling the social hierarchies children build for themselves along gender lines as well as sharpening the pedagogic focus on the mechanics of literacy.

Second, schools need to pay more attention to how they manage the transition from literacy as teacher-directed work to literacy as self-directed activity. In the past, one key arena where this happened was through the classroom management of reading for choice as quiet reading time. Reading for choice needs to be materially underwritten both by giving readers the opportunities to choose for themselves from a wide range of resources, and also by enabling children to find out more about what they might choose between. Teachers are used to promoting reading by including a range of text types on the literacy curriculum. They are less used to actively supporting reading networks which sustain themselves. Yet such networks demonstrate to other readers why the commitment to reading might be worthwhile. Making such networks visible in class, and encouraging children to share what they have found worth reading, and what they have not, provides more explicit support for reading itself and a mechanism for tackling gender differences in the number of readers who can and do read in a self-motivated way (Moss, 2000a).

But finally and perhaps most importantly, this book has also outlined a set of principles for reviewing the curriculum in action and what it makes visible to pupils about 'what counts as reading'. It has highlighted the tensions between reading for proficiency and reading for choice as they are instantiated on the curriculum and the difficulties children face in navigating their way through this territory. From this perspective, fixing gendered outcomes from the literacy curriculum is not about teaching to the interests of one specific group over another. Rather it is about reviewing the distinctions that the curriculum itself makes about what literacy is for whom, and finding new ways of helping children themselves reconcile and resolve the dilemmas the literacy curriculum sets them.

APPENDIX 1

Fact and fiction analytic matrix

	Procedural	Procedural	Proficiency	Choice	Choice
Context					
Curriculum slot	History topic – Ancient Greece	History topic – Ancient Greece	Science. Reading to helper	Finishing work	English
Location	Seated at the tables	Freedom to move around the classroom	Two chairs at a table in the quiet reading area	Bean bags and comfy chairs in the 'soft' area containing the class library	Tables
Activity, official/ unofficial	With the textbook page open, children listen as the teacher reads from the text, then pauses to explain and add to the passage before going on.	Using the topic books in class to compile information about the Greek gods, for writing up as a Fact File/Get the best books quick before they go, and find the good bits.	Child opens her reading book and reads aloud whilst the adult helper corrects any mistakes. The child stops when asked.	Finding a book to read/browsing and chatting with friends whilst choosing books from the kinder box	Finding a passage to read out loud/ browsing and chatting
Discursive orientation	'Today we're going to find out about Alexander the Great.'	'Some of you know lots about this already, more than I do. Find out as much as you can.'	'Can I have your home reading book to just write in it, darling? Well done, E. Next? Um, N.'	'If you've finished your work, you can go to the kinder box.'	'The reason I've asked you to do this is that we're going to put our favourite jokes into a book.'
Readers					
Formation	The teacher is the main reader; the children listen together, sharing one book between two.	The pupils are the main readers, working in friendship groups, mainly single sex.	Parent helper and child	Children who have finished their work	Whole class, sharing text with partners on their tables, mixed-sex

Access	Equal access to the same text	Unequal access to a range of texts some of which the children themselves have brought in	Regulated access to texts. The child must bring their reading book and their home-reading record book. If the reading book is too hard they may be asked to change it	Unequal access	Unequal access to the selection of texts given to each group by the teacher. (More girls than boys ended up with the photocopied texts.)
Subject identity	Children as novices	Children as experts	Child as novice, subject to scrutiny	Subject identity regulated by peers, not teacher	Positioned by the teacher in between 'being good pupils and working well', and 'having fun'
Text					
Textual characteristics	Historical narrative; verbal text, with subheadings and some images	Various, most non-fiction, with relatively high ratio of image to verbal text, using double spread	Picture book, narrative fiction and handwritten record	Wide range: fiction, non-fiction, picture books	Joke books
Text as material object	Paperback, stapled folio	Most hardback, bound folio	Large quarto hardback and school exercise book	Mix of paperbacks and hardbacks in different sizes and shapes according to text type	Some photocopies of double spreads; some paperbacks including stapled folios
Text's use category	Textbook	Topic books	Reading book and reading record book	Class library	Class library, Year 5s
Text location/ source	Teacher's desk	Display table, pupils' trays and topic shelf	Kinder box via book bag and book-bag	Kinder box	Basket, labelled 'Joke Books'
Source	Shepherd, Year 4	Bluebird, Year 5	Bluebird, Year 3	Bluebird, Year 3	Kingfisher, Year 3

APPENDIX 2

Transcription conventions

This book includes a number of passages of spoken discourse which have been variously transcribed by the authors in whose publications they first appeared, or by the research team who worked on the Fact and Fiction Project. Transcription conventions may differ according to user. Below is a list of the conventions mainly used in this book.

[	*a square bracket* indicates overlapping utterances
=	*equal marks at the end and beginning of the line* indicate that there is no gap between the utterances of two speakers
/	*forward slash* indicates pause of less than two seconds
//	*double forward slash* indicates pause of more than two seconds
(2.0)	*number within parentheses* indicates the approximate length of pause in seconds
ye:s	*colon mid word* indicates stretching of sound that follows
(word)	*words in brackets* indicate transcriber's uncertainty about whether they have correctly heard the sound
(…)	*ellipses in brackets* indicate indecipherable speech
:	*colon in the margin* indicates discourse that has been omitted as irrelevant in the context in which the discourse is being discussed
{turns page}	*brace brackets* indicate contextual detail of actions relevant to, but outside of, the discourse
italics	*italics* indicate when the speaker is reading aloud from a written text
normal punctuation symbols	(e.g. full stops, commas, question marks) indicate intonation. A full stop indicates a falling pitch or intonation. A comma indicates a continuing intonation with slight upward or downward contour. A question mark indicates a rising vocal pitch or intonation.[1]

1 Adapted from system developed by Gail Jefferson, printed in J.M. Atkinson and J. Heritage (eds) (1984) *Structures of social action: Studies in conversation analysis.* Cambridge University Press, pp.ix–xvi.

NOTES

1 The Fact and Fiction Project, funded by the ESRC, was based at the University of Southampton. Project research staff were Gemma Moss and Dena Attar. The project ran for two years between 1996 and 1998.

2 This sequence of projects culminated in the Negotiated Literacies Project, which was funded by the ESRC and ran at the Institute of Education, University of London, 1993–1995. Gemma Moss acted as project director and researcher. This project followed a cohort of students who had been interviewed about the range of media texts, which they circulated amongst themselves in informal contexts over a period of four years. The children were aged between 7 and 11 at the start of the period of data collection.

3 Mixed Methods in the Study of Pattern and Variation in Children's Reading Habits was funded by the ESRC in 2000 and based at the Institute of Education, University of London, and the University of Southampton. The project research staff were Gemma Moss and J.W. McDonald.

4 Building a New Literacy Practice through the Adoption of the National Literacy Strategy was funded by the ESRC and ran at the Institute of Education between 2001 and 2003. Gemma Moss acted as project director and researcher.

REFERENCES

Ang, I. (1985) *Watching Dallas: Soap opera and the melodramatic imagination.* London: Methuen

Arnot, M., Gray, J., James, M. and Ruddock, J. (1998) *Recent Research on Gender and Educational Performance.* London: Ofsted

Arnot, M., David, M. and Weiner, G. (1999) *Closing the Gender Gap.* London: Polity Press

Attar, D. (1990) *Wasting Girls' Time.* London: Virago

Attar, D. (1996) 'Quantitative Review: Summary of sources and data on texts for children, production and distribution at 27 November 1996'. Unpublished paper prepared for the Fact and Fiction Project

Baker, C. (1991) 'Literacy practices and social relations in classroom reading events' in C. Baker and A. Luke (eds) *Towards a Critical Sociology of Reading Pedagogy: Papers of the XII World Congress on Reading.* Amsterdam: John Benjamins

Barber, M. (1996) *The Learning Game.* London: Gollancz

Barrs, M. (1993) 'Introduction: Reading the difference' in M. Barrs and S. Pidgeon (eds) *Reading the Difference.* London: CLPE

Barrs, M. (1994) 'Genre Theory: What's it all about?' in B. Stierer and J. Maybin (eds) *Language, Literacy and Learning in Educational Practice.* Clevedon: Multilingual Matters with the Open University

Barrs, M. and Cork, V. (2001) *The Reader in the Writer.* London: CLPE

Barrs, M. and Pidgeon, S. (eds) (1993) *Reading the Difference.* London: CLPE

Barrs, M. and Pidgeon, S. (eds) (1998) *Boys and Reading.* London: CLPE

Barton, D. (1994) *Literacy: An introduction to the ecology of written language.* Oxford: Blackwell

Barton, D. and Hamilton, M. (1998) *Local Literacies: Reading and writing in one community.* London: Routledge

Baynham, M. (1995) *Literacy Practice: Investigating literacy in social contexts.* London: Longman

Beard, R. (1999) *National Literacy Strategy: Review of research and other related evidence.* London: DfEE

Bernstein, B. (1990) *Class, Codes and Control: The structuring of pedagogic discourse.* Vol. 4. London: Routledge

Bernstein, B. (1996) *Pedagogy, Symbolic Control and Identity.* London: Taylor & Francis

Bloome, D. (1992) 'Reading as a social process in a middle school classroom' in D. Bloome (ed.) *Literacy and Schooling.* Norwood, NJ: Ablex

Bloome, D., Carter, S., Christian, B., Otto, S. and Stuart-Faris, N. (2005) *Discourse Analysis and the Study of Classroom Language and Literacy Events: A microethnographic perspective.* New York: Lawrence Erlbaum

Bourne, J. (2000) 'New imaginings of reading for a new moral order: A review of the production, transmission and acquisition of a new pedagogic culture in the UK' in *Linguistics and Education,* Vol. 11(1), pp. 31–45

Bourne, J. and Jewitt, C. (2003) 'Orchestrating Debate: A multimodal analysis of classroom interaction' in *Reading, Literacy and Language,* 37(2), pp. 64–72

Buckingham, D. and Scanlon, M. (2003) *Education, Entertainment and Learning in the Home.* Buckingham: Open University Press

Butler, J. (1990) *Gender Trouble: Feminism and the subversion of identity.* London: Routledge

Cameron, D. (1985) *Feminism and Linguistic Theory.* London: Macmillan

Cazden, C. (1988) 'Social context of learning to read' in N. Mercer, (ed.) *Language and Literacy from an Educational Perspective.* Milton Keynes: Open University Press

Cherland, M. (1994) *Private Practices: Girls reading fiction and constructing identity.* London: Taylor & Francis

Children's Literature Research Centre (1996) *Young People's Reading at the End of the Century.* London: Roehampton Institute

Clarricoates, K. (1987) 'Dinosaurs in the classroom – the "hidden" curriculum in primary schools' in M. Arnot and G. Weiner (eds) *Gender and the Politics of Schooling.* London: Hutchinson for Open University Press

Cohen, S. (1973) *Folk Devils and Moral Panics.* London: Palladin

Davies, B. (1993) 'Beyond dualism and towards multiple subjectivities' in L. K. Christian-Smith *Texts of Desire: Essays on Fiction, Femininity and Schooling.* London: Falmer Press

Davis, K. (1994) 'What's in a voice? Methods and metaphors' in *Feminism and Psychology,* 4(3): pp. 353–361

DfEE (1995) *English in the National Curriculum.* London: HMSO

DfEE (1998) *The National Literacy Strategy: Framework for teaching.* London: DfEE

DfES (2004) *Playing with Sounds: A supplement to Progression in Phonics.* London: DfES

DfES (2005) *Improving Boys' Writing.* E-publication

Dombey, H. (1988) 'Partners in the telling' in M. Meek and C. Mills (eds) *Language and Literacy in the Primary School.* London: Falmer Press

Dombey, H. (1992) 'Lessons learnt at bedtime' in K. Kimberley, M. Meek and J. Miller (eds) *New Readings.* London: A & C Black

Dyson, A. H. (2003) *The Brothers and Sisters Learn to Write: Popular literacies in childhood and school cultures.* New York: Teachers College Press

Earl, L., Watson, N., Levin, B., Leithwood, K., Fullan, M. and Torrance, N. with Jantzi, D., Mascall, B. and Volante, L. (2000) *Watching and Learning: OISE/UT evaluation of the implementation of the National Literacy and Numeracy Strategies.* London: DfEE

Elkjaer, B. (1992) 'Girls and information technology in Denmark – an account of a socially constructed problem' in *Gender and Education,* Vol. 4:1/2, pp. 25–40

Epstein, D., Elwood, J., Hey, V. and Maw, J. (eds) (1998) *Failing Boys? Issues in gender and achievement.* Buckingham: Open University Press

Fisher, R., Brooks, G. and Lewis, M. (2002) *Raising Standards in Literacy.* London: RoutledgeFalmer

Fokias, F. (1998) 'Changing Practice through Reflection' in M. Barrs and S. Pidgeon (eds) *Boys and Reading*. London: CLPE

Freebody, P. (2001) 'Theorising new literacies in and out of school' in *Language and Education*, Vol. 15: 2 and 3 pp. 105–116

Gilbert, P. (1993) *Gender, Stories and the Language Classroom*. Geelong: Deakin University Press

Gilbert, P. and Taylor, S. (1991) *Fashioning the Feminine*. Sydney: Allen & Unwin

Gilbert, R. and Gilbert, P. (1998) *Masculinity Goes to School*. London: Routledge

Goodwin, P. and Routh, C. (2000) 'A brief history of timing: The impact of the National Literacy Strategy on the marketing and publishing of resources to support literacy teaching' in *Reading*, Vol. 34:3, pp. 119–123

Gorman, T. P. and Kispal, A. (1984) *Language Performance in Schools. 1982 secondary survey report*. London: DES

Green, J. and Bloome, D. (1997) 'Ethnography and ethnographers of and in education: A situated perspective' in J. Flood, S. Heath and D. Lapp (eds) *Handbook of Research on Teaching Literacy Through the Communicative and Visual Arts*. New York: Simon & Schuster Macmillan, pp. 181–202

Gregory, E. (1996) *Making Sense of a New World: Learning to read in a second language*. London: Paul Chapman

Hall, C. and Coles, M. (1999) *Children's Reading Choices*. London: Routledge

Heap, J. (1991) 'A situated perspective on what counts as reading' in A. Luke and C. Baker (eds) *Towards a Critical Sociology of Reading: Papers of the XII World Congress on Reading*. Amsterdam: John Benjamins

Heath, S. B. (1982) 'What no bedtime story means: Narrative skills at home and school' in *Language and Society* 11, pp. 49–76

Heath, S. B. (1983) *Ways with Words*. Cambridge: Cambridge University Press

Hey, V. (1997) *The Company She Keeps: An ethnography of girls' friendship*. Buckingham: Open University Press

Hodgeon, J. (1993) 'Talking to parents' in M. Barrs and S. Pidgeon (eds) *Reading the Difference*. London: CLPE

Horsman, J. (1991) 'The problem of illiteracy and the promise of literacy' in M. Hamilton, D. Barton and R. Ivanic (eds) *Worlds of Literacy*. Clevedon: Multilingual Matters

Kelly, A. (1987) *Science for Girls*. Milton Keynes: Open University Press

Kress, G. (1994) *Learning to Write*. London: Routledge

Kress, G. (2003) *Literacy in the New Media Age*. London: Routledge

Kress, G. and van Leeuwen, T. (1996) *Reading Images: The grammar of visual design*. London: Routledge

Lee, A. (1996) *Gender, Literacy Curriculum: Rewriting school geography*. London: Falmer Press

Leggett, J. and Hemming, J. (1984) 'Teaching magazines' in *The English Magazine*, Vol. 12, Spring 1984, pp. 8–14

Mac an Ghail, M. (1994) *The Making of Men: Masculinities, Sexualities and Schooling*. Buckingham: Open University Press

Mace, J. (1998) *Playing with Time: Mothers and the meaning of literacy*. London: UCL Press

Marsh, J. and Millard, E. (eds) (2006) *Popular Literacies, Childhood and Schooling*. London: Routledge

Martin, J. R. (1985) *Factual Writing: Exploring and challenging social reality.* Geelong: Deakins University Press

Martin, J. R., Christie, F. and Rothery, J. (1994) 'Social processes in education: A reply to Sawyer and Watson (and others)' in B. Stierer and J. Maybin (eds) *Language, Literacy and Learning in Educational Practice.* Clevedon: Multilingual Matters with the Open University

Maybin, J. (1994) 'Children's Voices: Talk, knowledge and identity' in D. Graddol, J. Maybin and B. Stierer (eds) *Researching Language and Literacy in Social Context.* Clevedon: Multilingual Matters with the Open University

Maybin, J. (2006) *Children's Voices: Talk, knowledge and identity.* Basingstoke: Palgrave

Maybin, J. and Moss, G. (1993) 'Talk about text: Reading as a social event' in *The Journal of Research in Reading*, 16:2, pp. 138–147

Meek, M. (1996) *Information and Book Learning.* Stroud: Thimble Press

Michaels, S. (1986) 'Narrative presentations: An oral preparation for literacy with first graders' in J. Cook-Gumperz (ed.) *The Social Construction of Literacy.* Cambridge: Cambridge University Press

Millard, E. (1997) *Differently Literate.* London: Falmer Press

Miller, J. (1996) *School for Women.* London: Virago

Mills, C. (1988) 'Making sense of reading: Key words or Grandma Swagg' in M. Meek and C. Mills (eds) *Language and Literacy in the Primary School.* London: Falmer Press

Mitchell, J. C. (1983) 'Case and situation analysis' in *Sociological Review*, 31:2, pp. 187–211

Morley, L. and Rassool, N. (1999) *School Effectiveness: Fracturing the discourse.* London: Falmer Press

Moss, G. (1989a) *Un/Popular Fictions.* London: Virago

Moss, G. (1989b) 'Powerful texts. Feminism and English teaching' in *The English Magazine*, Vol. 22, pp. 14–20

Moss, G. (1993a) 'Children talk horror videos: Reading as a social performance' in *Australian Journal of Education*, 37:2, pp. 169–181

Moss, G. (1993b) 'Girls tell the teen romance: Four reading histories' in D. Buckingham (ed.) *Reading Audiences: Young people and the media.* Manchester: Manchester University Press

Moss, G. (1996) 'Negotiated Literacies: How children enact what counts as reading in different social settings'. Unpublished PhD thesis

Moss, G. (1999) 'Texts in context: Mapping out the gender differentiation of the reading curriculum' in *Pedagogy, Culture and Society*, Vol. 7:3, pp. 507–522

Moss, G. (2000a) 'Raising attainment: Boys, reading and the National Literacy Hour' in *Reading*, Vol. 34:3, pp. 101–106

Moss, G. (2000b) 'Informal literacies and pedagogic discourse' in *Linguistics and Education*, Vol. 11:1 pp. 47–64

Moss, G. (2001a) 'Seeing with the camera: Analysing children's photographs of literacy in the home' in *Journal of Research in Reading*, Vol. 24:3, pp. 279–292

Moss, G. (2001b) 'To work or play? Junior age non-fiction as objects of design' in *Reading: literacy and language*, Vol. 35:3, pp. 106–110

Moss, G. (2001c) 'Literacy and the social organisation of knowledge inside and outside school' in *Language and Education*, Vol. 15:2 and 3, pp. 146–161

Moss, G. (2002a) 'Explicit pedagogy' in M. Barrs and S. Pidgeon (eds) *Boys and Writing.* London: CLPE

Moss, G. (2002b) 'Literacy and pedagogy in flux: Constructing the object of study from a Bernsteinian perspective' in *British Journal of Sociology of Education*, Vol. 23: 4, pp. 549–558

Moss, G. (2003a) 'Analysing literacy events: Mapping gendered configurations of readers, texts and contexts' in S. Goodman, T. Lillis, J. Maybin and N. Mercer (eds) *Language, Literacy and Education: A reader*. London: Trentham Books. pp. 123–137

Moss, G. (2003b) 'Putting the text back into practice: Junior age non-fiction as objects of design' in G. Kress and C. Jewitt (eds) *Multimodal Literacy*. New York: Peter Lang. pp. 73–87

Moss, G. (2004) 'Changing practice: The National Literacy Strategy and the politics of literacy policy' in *Literacy*, 38 (3), pp. 126–133

Moss, G. and Attar, D. (1999) 'Boys and literacy: Gendering the reading curriculum' in J. Prosser (ed.) *School Cultures*. London: Chapman. pp. 133–144

Moss, G. and McDonald, J. W. (2004) 'The borrowers: Library records as unobtrusive measures of children's reading preferences' in *Journal of Research in Reading*, Vol. 27:4, pp. 401–413

NATE, Language and Gender Committee (1985) *Alice in Genderland: Reflections on language, power and control*. Exeter: Nate

Neate, B. (1992) *Finding Out about Finding Out: A practical guide to children's information books*. Sevenoaks: Hodder & Stoughton in association with UKRA

OECD (2004) *Learning for Tomorrow's World: First results from PISA 2003*. Paris: OECD

Ofsted (1993) *Boys and English*. London: DfE

Ofsted (1996) *The Teaching of Reading in 45 Inner London Schools*. London: Ofsted

Ofsted (2003) *Yes He Can: Schools where boys write well*. London: Ofsted

Powling, C., Ashley, B., Pullman, P., Fine, A. and Gavin, J. (2003) *Meetings with the Minister: Five children's authors on the National Literacy Strategy*. Reading: National Centre for Language and Literacy, University of Reading

QCA (1998) *Can Do Better: Raising boys' achievement in English*. London: HMSO

Radway, J. (1984) *Reading the Romance*. Chapel Hill, North Carolina: University of North Carolina Press

Rockhill, K. (1993) 'Gender, language and the politics of literacy' in B. Street (ed.) *Cross-cultural Approaches to Literacy*. Cambridge: Cambridge University Press

Rosen, H. (1988) 'The voices of communities and language in classrooms: A review of *Ways with Words*' in N. Mercer (ed.) *Language and Literacy from an Educational Perspective*. Milton Keynes: Open University Press

Rowan, L., Knobel, M., Bigum, C. and Lankshear, C. (2002) *Boys, Literacies and Schooling*. Buckingham: Open University Press

Shuman, A. (1993) 'Collaborative writing: Appropriating power or reproducing authority' in B. Street (ed.) *Cross-cultural Approaches to Literacy*. Cambridge: Cambridge University Press

Sola, M. and Bennet, A. (1994) 'The struggle for voice: Narrative, literacy and consciousness in an East Harlem school' in J. Maybin (ed.) *Language and Literacy in Social Practice*. Clevedon: Multilingual Matters with the Open University

Solsken, J. (1993) *Literacy, Gender and Work in Families and in School*. Norwood, NJ: Ablex

Spender, D. (1982) *Invisible Women: The schooling scandal.* London: Writers & Readers Publishing Cooperative

Stanworth, M. (1981) *Gender and Schooling: A study of sexual divisions in the classroom.* Pamphlet No. 7. London: WRRC

Stone, R. (1983) *Pour out the Cocoa, Janet.* London: Longmans

Street, B. (1984) *Literacy in Theory and Practice.* Cambridge: Cambridge University Press

Street, B. (ed.) (1993) *Cross-cultural Approaches to Literacy.* Cambridge: Cambridge University Press

Street, B. (2003) 'What's "new" in New Literacy Studies? Critical approaches to literacy in theory and practice' in *Current Issues in Comparative Education,* 5(2)

Street, J. and Street, B. (1991) 'The schooling of literacy' in D. Barton and R. Ivanic (eds) *Writing in the Community.* London: Sage

Stuart, M. (2003) 'Fine tuning the National Literacy Strategy to ensure continuing progress in improving standards of reading in the UK: Some suggestions for change'. At: http://www.standards.dfes.gov.uk/primary/publications/literacy/686807/nls_phonics0303mstuart.pdf

Teale, W. H. and Sulzby, E. (eds) (1986) *Emergent Literacy: Writing and reading.* Norwood, NJ: Ablex

Vygotsky, L. S. (1962) *Thought and Language.* Boston: MIT Press

Walden, R. and Walkerdine, V. (1985) *Girls and Mathematics.* London: Bedford Way Papers

Walkerdine, V. (1981) 'Sex, power and pedagogy' in *Screen Education,* 38, pp. 14–25

Walkerdine, V. (1990) *Schoolgirl Fictions.* London: Verso

White, J. (1990) 'On literacy and gender' in R. Carter (ed.) *Knowledge about Language and the Curriculum: The LINC reader.* London: Hodder & Stoughton

Whitehead F., Capey, A. C., Moddren, W. and Wellings, A. (1977) *Children and Their Books.* London: Macmillan

Whyte, J. (1986) *Girls into Science and Technology.* London: Routledge & Kegan Paul

Williams, A. and Gregory, E. (1999) 'Home and school reading practices in two East End communities' in A. Tosi and C. Leung (eds) *Rethinking Language Education from a Multilingual to a Multicultural Perspective.* London: Centre for Information on Language Teaching and Research

Williamson, J. (1981/2) 'How does girl number twenty understand ideology?' in *Screen Education,* 40, pp. 80–87

Willis, P. (1977) *Learning to Labour: How working class kids get working class jobs.* London: Gower

Wray, D. and Lewis, M. (1997) *Extending Literacy: Children reading and writing non-fiction.* London: Routledge

Younger, M. and Warrington, M. with Gray, J., Ruddock, J., McLellan, R., Kershner, R., Bearne, E. and Bricheno, P. (2005) *Raising Boys' Achievement. Final Report.* London: DfES

Children's books referred to
in the text and/or used in interview

Aiken, J. (1975) *A Necklace of Raindrops: and other stories*. London: Puffin

Bailey, D. (1988) *Planes*. London: Macmillan

Baker, J. (1991) *Window*. London: Julia MacRae

Beaton, C. (1996) *Fun to do: Masks*. London: Merehurst Ltd

Browne, A. (1997) *The Tunnel*. London: Walker Books

Brumpton, K. (1994) *Rudley Cabot In ... The Quest for the Golden Carrot*. London: Orion Children's Books

Bryant-Mole, K. (1995) *Does It Bounce?* London: A & C Black

Christopher, M. (1979) *Dirt Bike Racer*. London: Little Brown and Co

Corey, P. (1993) *Coping with Teachers*. London: Hippo, Scholastic

Dahl, R. (1991) *Matilda*. London: Heinemann New Windmill

Deary, T. (1994) *The Rotten Romans*. London: Scholastic

Delf, B. and Platt, R. (1995) *In the Beginning: The nearly complete history of almost everything*. London: Dorling Kindersley

Dineen, J. (1991) *Young Researcher: The Greeks*. London: Heinemann

DK (1999) *Big Book of Cars*. London: Dorling Kindersley

Dr Seuss (1979) *I can read with my eyes shut!* London: Collins

Flint, D. and Suhr, M. (1992) *Mapwork 1*. Hove: Wayland

Forrest, M. (1992) *Ancient Greece*. Aylesbury: Ginn

Foster, J. (1988) *The Oxford Second Poetry Book*. Oxford: Oxford University Press

Fox-Davies, S. (1996) *Little Caribou*. London: Walker Books

Grandreams Ltd (1995) *My First World Atlas*. London: Grandreams

Greaves, M. (1990) *Tattercoats*. London: Frances Lincoln.

Greenaway, T. (1996) *The Really Fearsome Blood-loving Vampire Bat and other Creatures with Strange Eating Habits*. London: Dorling Kindersley

Hall, J. and Jones, C. (1997) *BBC Fact Finders Roman Britain*. London: BBC Educational Publishing

Handford, M. (1989) *Where's Wally? The Fantastic Journey*. London: Walker Books

Hawkins, C. and Hawkins, J. (1995) *How to Look After Your Rabbit*. London: Walker Books

Holden, P. (1994) *Usborne Spotter's Guide Birds Sticker Book*. London: Usborne

Hutchins, P. (1970) *Rosie's Walk*. London: Bodley Head

Hutchins, P. (1983) *You'll Soon Grow Into Them, Titch*. London: Bodley Head

Impey, R. (1994) *Precious Potter*. London: Orchard

Jordan, M. and Jordan, T. (1996) *Amazon Alphabet*. London: Kingfisher

Kearey, I. (ed.) (1997) *Looking After Your Dog*. Bristol: Parragon

Lambert, M. (1988) *Homes in the Future*. Hove: Wayland

Legg, G. and Scrace, C. (1995) *The X-Ray Picture Book of Incredible Creatures*. London: Franklin Watts

London, J. (1991) *White Fang*. London: Constable

Loverance, R. and Wood, T. (1998) *See Through History: Ancient Greece*. Oxford: Heinemann

Macdonald, F. (1995) *How would you Survive as an Ancient Greek?* London: Watts Books

Macquitty, M. (1994) *Eyewitness Guides: Desert*. London: Dorling Kindersley

Marchand, P. (1994) *The Living Forest*. London: Kingfisher

Merlin (1996) *Merlin's Premier League Sticker Collection 96*. Milton Keynes: Merlin

O'Neill, A. (1998) *I Wonder Why: Vultures are bald and other questions about birds*. London: Kingfisher

Orr, R. and Butterfield, M. (1995) *Richard Orr's Nature Cross-sections*. London: Dorling Kindersley

Phaidon Press (1997) *The Art Book*. London: Phaidon Press

Powling, C. (1997) *Roald Dahl (Tell me about)*. London: Evans Brothers Ltd

Rayner, M. (1976) *Mr and Mrs Pig's Evening Out*. London: Athenium Books

Reading for Information Red Set (1994) Leamington Spa: Scholastic

Reeves, M. and Hodgson, P. (1962) *Elizabethan Citizen*. London: Longmans

Rollin, G. (ed.) (1996) *Playfair Football Annual 1996–97*. London: Headline

Royston, A. (1991) *Small Animals*. London: Dorling Kindersley

Royston, A. (1992) *Minibeasts*. London: Dorling Kindersley

Royston, A. (1992) *See How They Grow: Lamb*. London: Dorling Kindersley. pp. 10–11

Seidensticker, J. and Lumpkin, S. (1995) *Dangerous Animals*. Hemel Hempstead: Macdonald Young

Sendak, M. (1992) *Where the Wild Things Are*. London: Picture Lions

Silver, D. (1998) *Tropical Rain Forest*. New York: McGraw-Hill

Tames, R. (1994) *What do we know about the Victorians?* Hemel Hempstead: Simon & Schuster

Thompson, C. (1993) *Looking for Atlantis*. London: Red Fox

Tolkein, J.R. (1992) *The Hobbit*. London: Grafton

Unstead, R. J. (1956) *People in History 3: Great Tudors and Stuarts*. London: A & C Black

Wallace, K. (1993) *Think of an Eel*. London: Walker Books

Whitelaw, I. and Whitaker, J. (1995) *Quizmasters: People in the past*. London: Dorling Kindersley

INDEX

eBooks – at www.eBookstore.tandf.co.uk

A library at your fingertips!

eBooks are electronic versions of printed books. You can store them on your PC/laptop or browse them online.

They have advantages for anyone needing rapid access to a wide variety of published, copyright information.

eBooks can help your research by enabling you to bookmark chapters, annotate text and use instant searches to find specific words or phrases. Several eBook files would fit on even a small laptop or PDA.

NEW: Save money by eSubscribing: cheap, online access to any eBook for as long as you need it.

Annual subscription packages

We now offer special low-cost bulk subscriptions to packages of eBooks in certain subject areas. These are available to libraries or to individuals.

For more information please contact webmaster.ebooks@tandf.co.uk

We're continually developing the eBook concept, so keep up to date by visiting the website.

www.eBookstore.tandf.co.uk

4932 070